PRODUCTIVITY, GROWTH AND DISPERSAL OF INDUSTRIES

PRODUCTIVITY, GROWTH AND DISPERSAL OF INDUSTRIES

By

Debasis Patnaik

Department of Economics
School of Sciences
University of Hyderabad
HYDERABAD – 500 046

DISCOVERY PUBLISHING HOUSE PVT. LTD.
NEW DELHI-110 002

Published by:
Tilak Wasan
DISCOVERY PUBLISHING HOUSE PVT. LTD.
4831/24, Ansari Road, Prahlad Street
Darya Ganj, New Delhi-110002 (India)
Phone: +91-11-23279245, 43764432
Fax: +91-11-23253475
E-mail: parul.wasan@gmail.com
info@discoverypublishinggroup.com
web: www.discoverypublishinggroup.com

***First Edition:* 2011**
ISBN: 978-81-8356-818-0

Productivity, Growth and Dispersal of Industries

Printed at:
Shree Balaji Art Press
Delhi

Dedicated to

The Fond Memory of

My Dearest Grandmother Srimati Hari Priya Patnaik
Who Passed Away in the Month of October 1997

and

My Revered Father Late Professor Srish Chandra Patnaik
Who Passed Away in the Month of December 1989

PREFACE

Scholars for long have been working in the independent fields of industrial growth, productivity and dispersal across many countries including India. However, a possible view to provide further avenues for research has been lacking. This book attempts to bridge this research gap by bringing growth, productivity and dispersal together in a linkage approach across these well established diverse and independent areas of economic and industrial analysis. This has resulted in providing a possible method of assessing equity-efficiency relationships to provide insights into problem of growth and productivity dispersal across decentralized regions.

Testable variables like factory numbers, employment figures, output-measures utilized 2-digit Indian industry level data from CSO Factory Sector based on National Industrial Classification (NIC)-1987. But to mitigate problems arising out of change in product composition and terminological differences, a comprehensive assessment and classification was undertaken considering Census of Manufacturing (CMI) data from 1946-1957, Sample Survey of Manufacturing Industries (SSMI) for 1958,NIC-1970 and NIC-1998 and Concordance Tables prepared.

A wide-ranging literature review on a theme specific method helped in understanding the difficulties of linking the diverse fields of industrial knowledge to provide for an integrated view of industrial development. Therefore, each of the above independent areas were explored independently in separate chapters to see potentials of further analysis therein. While individual industry growth and productivity assessment provided scope for policy analysis, gaps of possible interpretations showed need to bring alternative development parameters of dispersal and measures into view. Likewise an independent assessment of regional industrial dispersal showed scope for classifying industries into use specific sectors as in Chapter-6 to undertake trend analysis and also test Williamson and Self Perpetuation Hypothesis in each of the industries.

Chapter-6 undertook a diagrammatic representation of results if dispersal of all variables of the industries over the long term period of 40 years. This had the advantage of revealing the nature of industrial dispersal and interpretation via Williamson vs Self Perpetuation theories. Further sub region specific research n these industries could have revealed the nature of industrial enterprise, skill, training and finances that could be necessary to develop a technologically rational society in a time specific incremental manner. However this was beyond the scope of this research.

Finally, in Chapter-7 an Impact Analysis of contributions of Total Factor Productivity, partial Factor Productivity, Capital Intensity of Regional Dispersal of Industries for decadal time periods and for a long term 40 year period was undertaken. These time periods covered successive five year plans including Plan holidays, industrial recession and retrogression, recovery and growth periods. It traced the nature and extent of causal relationships (b estimate) in the estimate of simple linear regressions of regional dispersal on each of the explanatory variables. This was undertaken after assessing for multiple regressions estimations that provided low R^2, F and t, R-bar sq with high SE. The dependent variable was distinguished in four specifications considering HH of Net value added and of employment and Coefficient of Variation of both Net value added and employment. Then industry specific recommendations were suggested as possible. Other combinations were not undertaken due to time constrains and can easily be extended by suitable researchers.

A few possible recommendations undertaken were: Wood (IN27)was seen as needing attention for purposes of employment planning to provide boost to rural entrepreneurship ad rural employment and being Labor Intensive was seen as aiding poverty alleviation programme. Thus such a Linkage analysis contained the potential for strong policy planning in industry and economy was justified.

Similarly, in 1966-75, the decadal period of recession, Non-Metallic Mineral Products (IN32) showed higher $(b/r)^2$ implying even in capital goods industry with high capital intensive-ness, recession was a cause for low total factor productivity growth (TFPG) and low employment dispersal. Food Industry (IN21-22) was more concentrated and so high K.L influence could not bring out NVA dispersal in Food Industry. K/L growth did not influence NVA dispersal in textiles (IN25) and Machinery other than Transport(IN36) but it did influence employment dispersal in these industries despite recession.

Another implication that came out was that economic reforms of 1991 had not undertaken Intermediated Planning which could have brought regional equity and growth in Indian economy.

Few samples of results as mentioned above showed that this linkage approach had a comprehensive quality accommodating industry specific and period specific inferential results and possible recommendations.

This book will be helpful to earnest scholars and researchers from fields of Industrial Management, Industrial Economics, Regional Economics, Productivity Economics, Microeconomics, Economics of Growth and Plan, Research Methodology, Economics of Technological Progress, Dispersal economics, and also Economic Ethics, Management and Social Science to attempt to undertake scientific methodology for research into socio-economic-political and methodological issues. Data, results and interpretations can be used by various categories of planners (national and regional), decision makers, think tanks for intra national and international comparative academic and knowledge oriented scientific understanding for integrating diverse strands of knowledge to make sense of the world in a more integrated manner for generating domain specific insights.

The author has been deeply indebted to his mentor and supervisor Professor V V N Somayajulu without whose help and guidance this work would have failed to receive the required form. Dr Soe Win, a scholar from Myanmar, was patient enough to teach the nuances of computers and one is deeply obliged to him as well. Finally, a mother's patience, sacrifice and blessings have been deeply instrumental in sustaining the author through all the tribulations of research. There have been many contributions from many earnest helpers but lack of space constrains one from brining their names into print.

ACKNOWLEDGEMENTS

I am deeply indebted to my Research Guide, Professor V. V. N. Somayajulu for enabling me to complete the *Ph. D.* Dissertation under his Supervision and Direction. He not only gave me a long rope to pursue the research work involving huge databases and large study material but was also available at various stages of my work as and when I needed him. Apart from my Ph.D. Research work, his immense and long winding discussions on various topics of Economics, whenever the opportunity presented itself, will hold me in good stead in the years to come.

The Head of the Department of Economics, Prof. B. Kamaih, has been extremely helpful with his useful suggestions in the moments of crisis that such a large work entailed. I am personally obliged to Prof. K.N. Murty for facilitating my academic moorings in the Department auspices. Prof. Achchi Reddy was also kind enough to provide valuable suggestions when I joined this Department. Dr. B. Nagarjuna was always there whenever I needed him. Dr. Uma Shankar Patnaik also lend a helping hand. Other Faulty of the Department were also kind and helpful with words of encouragement to expedite my work. Mention must be made about the Staff of the department, especially, Mrs. Jayashree, Mr. Venkateshwara and others, who made my life devoid of strain that helped me focus on my research work. The Dean's Office was also helpful, wherever it was needed. The Chief Warden's Office, Administrative Office, Hostel Office, etc. all were helpful. One cannot forget the help of Prof. Appa Rao, Chief Warden, and Prof. Shiv Kumar, Warden, of Hostel – E (NRSH) where I stayed for the period of my work.

The Staff of the Indira Gandhi Library of the University of Hyderabad have provided much needed help whenever I approached them. Mention must also be made of Mr. Sudhakar, Deputy Regisrtar, Academics and his helpful staff in the Administrative Block of the University of Hyderabad for the kind help they rendered to me.

My deepest feelings and obligations go to Dr. Soe Win, Associate Professor of Department of Economics and Statistics, Myanmar for the immense help he provided in enabling me to learn computer from the beginnings. His warmth, goodness and help was unparalleled and will always be remembered. Towards the end of my work, help also came from Dr. Tin Htwe, Dr. Myo Thein Kyam and Dr. Chit Htay Lwin, all from Myanmar.

I would also like to remember the names of my teachers and professors who have helped shaped my academic and intellectual outlook. My father, Late Professor Srish

Chandra Patnaik, Late Professor P. R. Brahmananda, Late Professor Bibekananda Das, Professor J C Sandesara, Professor D. M. Nachane, Prof. M. J. M Rao, Prof. Bharadwaj, Prof. Chinmoy Goswami, Prof. K.V.K. Nehru, Prof. R. C. Pradhan. Dr. C. R. Rao and Dr. B. Shobha of Department of Statistics, Univ. of Hyderabad also helped. Prof. Adwaita K. Mohanty and Prof. K.B. Das of Utkal University are especially remembered. Prof. C. R. Pathak, Prof. A.K. Mohapatro, Dr. Bidyadhar Nayak, Mr. Adi Vatcha, Mr. J K Patnaik, Dr. Ms. Basanti Patnaik, Mr. K.V. L. Kantha Rao have always been kind and helpful, at many moments of my life.

My obligations are due to Librarian, Directorate of Economics and Statistics, Andhra Pradesh for the massive data they provided me without reluctance. My appreciation also extends to the Librarians of, Centre of Economic and Social Studies (CESS), National Institute of Small Industry Extension and Training (NISIET), National Institute of Rural Development (NIRD), Hyderabad Library of Afzalganj, Institute of Public Enterprise (IPE), Library of Osmania University, Inter-Universities American Study Center, etc.

My stay in the University Hostel has been pleasant and acknowledgement for the kindness shown by the inmates, friends of the hostels and others whom I could but rarely meet, is due. Specifically, I would like to mention Dr. Bhagirath, Dr. Subrat Patnaik, Dr. R. K. Panda and his friends, Dr. D. Acharya, Ms. Sai Sailaja Bharatham, Ms. Pooja, Mr.Shine, Dr. Anuradha, Dr. Dippita Chakraborty, for being kind and helpful. Late Lokanath Mohapatra, Dr. Rajneesh Atre, Ms.Shalu Atre, Ms. Nita Patnaik and her family members, My Supervisors' family members, Shri. Chandrakanta Baba, Mr. Nani, my wife, Mrs. J. Bal, and her family members, my friends and colleagues of the Theosophical Society and J. Krishnamurti Centre, Badabapa's family and other members of our extended family, both from maternal and paternal sides, that have been factors of encouragement and inspiration at various stages of my research work. My prayers are for the souls of my family and circle of relatives who left us during my Research period are sent.

Finally, my acknowledgements would not be complete without mentioning my mother, *Professor Dr. Premalata Patnaik* who left no stone unturned to make my life financially secure and morally supportive enough to enable me to complete this study. There have been many others who have been kind towards me but lack of space constraints me from putting their names in print. Omissions are my responsibility and may kindly be excused.

CONTENTS

Chapter 1

Introduction

THEME OF STUDY

Industrial development is the fulcrum and an essential catalytic requisite for rapid pace of development. Kuznets' comparison of 50 countries has shown a marked increase in manufacturing output with rising per capita income. To him, marked increases in productivity are usually achieved in the face of population growth and rising labour force through major innovations that could be defined as 'application of new bodies of tested knowledge to the processes of economic production'[1]. Chenery[2] traced a statistically significant relationship between per capita income and degree of industrialisation [Also Kaur Kulwinder -Structure of Industries in India[3]]. All these studies stressed that without industrial development, economy cannot have progress; and will touch a low and/or a limited frontier of development. Development is to be noticed in growth of manufacturing industry resulting from opening up of new markets and new processes of deepening and widening of capital. Productivity growth in manufacturing industry is the major and sustainable propeller to economic growth and for structural transformation of now developed economies[4].

The current study absorbed the genesis of results of the above and similar studies that led to trace causal inter-relations between Industries' Growth, Partial and Total Factor Productivities, Regional Dispersal and Development of Industries in India. The theme of the study is titled "Productivity, Growth and Regional Dispersal of All-India Industries-1956-1995". The analysis relates to twenty industry groups at 2-digit level of aggregation on the basis of National Industrial Classification (NIC), 1987, that corresponds to International Standard Industrial Classification (ISIC). The Time Series Analysis of the study has been carried out over time periods of 4 decades, separately for each decade, and for the long period of 1956-95, together, wherever needed, for temporal comparison of results. Productivity, growth and dispersal measures of individual industries at national and regional levels are analysed for distinct size measures of industry. Regional dispersal analysis of size measures for each of the twenty two-digit industries has been carried out using states level data from 1959 on-wards, because states level data for the years 1956-1958 were not available.

While earlier authors and researchers have studied productivity, growth relations and regional dispersal of Industries separately, hardly any studies on regional dispersal of industries due to causal links with productivity and growth are noticed. This study is a contribution to knowledge of economic science and practice in attempting to find the causal links between productivity, growth and regional dispersal of industries.

Objectives of the Study

1. To analyse partial productivity ratios of factors; and Measurements of Total Factor Productivity of industry groups; and output elasticities of those factors as to infer returns to scale and to trace causal linkages between these measurements.
2. To analyse temporal shifts in industrial growth of the industry groups in India and to trace the causal relations with other variables, as in (1) above.
3. To trace the extent of industrial dispersal across states over time periods for (*i*) small states and Union Territories (UT), (*ii*) large states, separately and for (*iii*) All States and all UT taken together. Then to trace causal relationships of the dispersal measures of NVA and Employment at sub-national levels with the TFP, Partial Productivity of each Factor and Capital Intensity for each of the industry groups in the short-run and the long periods.
4. To draw policy guidelines based on Causal inter-relations analysed temporally for productivity, growth and dispersal indices of Indian industries.

Hypotheses and Research Question

(*a*) Whether Total Factor Productivity (TFP) manifesting Hicksian neutral technological progress and Partial Factor Productivities, influences and is influenced by Growth; and Whether Elasticities and Returns to Scale in Indian Industries leads to identification of Temporal Shifts in Scale Economies; and Whether Ranking of Industries in terms of the respective variables throws light on that variables' contribution to industries growth;

(*b*) Whether higher capital intensities in individual industries are reflected in higher growth rates of TFP and therefore Output growth of those industries;

(*c*) Whether industries at 2-digit level of aggregation having higher growth rates in output and employment have higher regional dispersal rates, revealed by both Herfindahl and Coefficient of Variation indices of regional dispersal of each industry group; and

(*d*) Whether Growth in Size Variables and Structural Ratios of Industries led to regional dispersal over time; and whether it implies testing Self-Perpetuation Hypothesis or

Williamson Hypothesis of Industrial Development that can reveal nature of Industrial Development in India as one of leading to Concentration initially and Diversification and Development ultimately over time; and whether all these results of analysis can be tested by Grossack's instruments of analysis to cause to infer evenness or unevenness of regional shares of Indian Industries' leading to further regional dispersal or concentration.

Importance and Relevance of the Study

More than 50 years of planning for development in India saw considerable increase in industrial base, diversification, structural changes, and changes in growth rates and short spells of stagnation/slow growth of industry. But much less is known regarding causal factors for regional dispersal of industries, extent of response to each of those causal factors, linkage measures of regional diversification and growth rate differential of distinct industries. Hence this study probes into the economic mechanism of causation to explain inter-relations of Regional Dispersal Measures and Growth Measures and also particularly of Returns to Scale, Capital Intensity, Partial and Total Factor Productivity Measures, linkages with each Regional Dispersal Measure. The three decades till mid-1980s onwards to date and particularly mid-1990s underwent Import Liberalisation, Privatisation, Globalisation and Economic Reforms of all Major Sectors including Monetary, Financial, Fiscal, Trade and Infrastructural Services in India. This accordingly needed an integrated approach to industrial planning that underwent structural adjustment and stabilisation policies or New Economic Policies for balanced regional growth of Indian industries. This in turn needed integration of productivity approach and regional equity approach; both to be fully supported by development of capital and human investment. This enables fulfilment of people's aspirations and participation of acquired skill base of local population and of skill mobility of labour force and ultimately convergence and divergence across states towards development of rural and backward regions and decentralised rural and urban industrial sector for balanced regional development. This analysis of dispersal measures associated with productivity and growth measures is a new addition to knowledge and would enable us to draw policy guidelines not merely for allocation of scarce resources but also to enable weaker sections to reap the benefits and to improve industrial skill spread quantitatively and qualitatively in rural areas.

Total Factor Productivity/measurement of technical change led to growth leading to cause for regional equity or imbalances otherwise in the long-run. Further, industrial employment and growth dichotomy that depends not only on the pace of technological change but also on social adjustments to exploit new products and processes[4] and learning effects[5]. All such hypotheses provide an adequate base for further research studies of industrialisation, competitiveness and causal factors thereof. Analytical results of this current study lead to further researches thus envisaged.

Review of Literature and Research Gaps

A brief review of a few major studies on productivity, growth but a few on regional dispersal of industries as carried out making use of both time series and cross section data led to find out the research gaps for the purposes of our study.

Ahluwalia's 'Industrial Growth in India—Stagnation since the mid-sixties' (1987)[5] analyzed long-term trends in industrial growth, focussing on causes of industrial stagnation in mid-sixties due to poor growth performance and dismal productivity achievements in industrial sector, resulting from slow growth in agricultural incomes, poor management and low investment in infrastructure sectors.

Goldar in his 'Productivity Growth in Indian Industry' (1986)[6] analysed trends in Partial Productivities, TFP and K-intensity at the aggregate level. He found a significant rising trend in L-productivity, K-intensity and a significant falling trend in K productivity. TFP growth rate of 1.3 per cent is low in relation to rate of growth in industrial output but a strong positive relationship between output growth and productivity growth is noticed. His study results for India are similar to findings in other countries' studies. The TFP growth in 'traditional' industries was marked positive but was not so for many 'modern' industries due to (*i*) incomplete 'learning effect' (*ii*) sharp fall in growth rate of fixed capital from 12.3 per cent p. a. in 1959-65 to 5.8 per cent p.a. in 1965-79 and (*iii*) fall in growth rates in real value added and labour. There was a reversal of the declining trend in K-productivity but K-deepening slowed down after 1970.

Goldar study did not address regional dispersal measures or to regional policies assessment but only to efficiency measures of national industries linkages.

Isher Judge Ahluwalia's 'Productivity and Growth in Indian Manufacturing' (1987)[7] pursues the issue of productivity growth in organised manufacturing over longer period (1959-86) and in detail. It found time series and pooled series estimates of statistically insignificant growth in TFP through estimation of Translog production function similar to earlier studies' estimates of TFPG during 1959-1983 but a reverse trend towards significant TFPG after 1982-83 for market use based industrial sectors, particularly high growth in productivity of consumer durables and capital goods sectors but not of intermediate goods sector unlike other countries' TFPG. Negative effect between higher capital intensity and productivity growth was due to policy distortions resulting into fragmentation of firms. Thus neither of the studies of I. J. Ahluwalia addressed to measures of regional dispersal of industries, leaving it as a Research gap.

Dhananjayan R.S. and N. Sasikala Devi (1998)[8] worked on objectives of estimating TFPG for 2-digit manufacturing and analysed the behavioural characteristics. TFP growth yielded low magnitudes but a spurt in TFP was noticed in mid 70s, late 80s and early 90s. The Study inferred that ad-hocism in policy programmes needed to be toned down and long- term policy directions devised and adhered to. Their study did not address to regional dispersal.

Oulton and Mahoney's study (1994)[9] of UK manufacturing for 1954-86 at three digit level of industrial aggregation to analyse Jorgenson's[10] growth of gross output dealt with evidence of increasing returns at industry level. It also tested Fabricant's law and whether capital was special in Romerian[11] sense of raising externalities. It did not trace regional dispersal of industries abroad.

Mehta S.S. (1974)[12] studied technological change in large-scale Indian industries from 1953-70 based on ASI census data. Till 1965, Indian industry expanded at a very high rate. The annual growth rates rose per annum. Industries studied by him also showed high rates of 6-7 per cent. But the main source of output growth was due to increased physical inputs and the role of technical change was minimal. Regional dispersal of Indian Industries was not analysed.

Somayajulu V. V. N. studies on 'Industrial Development of Andhra Pradesh: 1956-80 (1994)[13] examined the structural parameters of Partial and Total Factor Productivity for industrial development. It analysed at length the regional dispersal of industries at sub-regional district wise level and probed intensively the institutional constraints and how to overcome them for a more effective and comprehensive industrial development at all levels: national level and at a sub-national level of AP State economy. But causal linkages between dispersal and growth, TFP, etc. were not established.

There are many other studies [as in the Major comprehensive Review in Chapter 2] but regional dispersal measures, issues and Policy direction for the best regionally balanced industrial development were hardly analysed as to trace causal link relations with growth, productivity (TFP and Partial), Returns to Scale, factor intensity, etc.

Problem-setting for the Current Study

Studies relating to productivity and growth of Indian industries did not pin down causal and verifiable factors for economic weaknesses of industrial stagnation, recovery, growth, sluggishness and vicissitudes that manifested from time to time. No studies have been addressed to bring out an integrated industrial strategy, approach and policy across national, and inter-regional sectors and industrial development leading to regional dispersal of industrial growth in all states/UT of All India. The cited research gaps (Section 1.5) motivated to measure and relate growth, returns to scale, partial productivity measures, TFP measures and regional dispersal at national and state levels and trace causal relations between them in a framework of inter-relations between productivity, growth and dispersal measures as to test results and deduce policy guidelines as distinct contributions to industrial development studies in India. This current study also distinguished small states and UT from large states vis-a vis All India industries in the regional dispersal analysis.

Industrial growth and dispersal measures at 10-year and 40-year periods coverage reflecting different stages of industrial development of India had not been attempted in earlier studies. This study contributed to explain the causal factors for distinct periods analysis and tests whether size of states yielded distinct results of regional dispersal of industries caused by the relevant factors over time 1959-95. Such an integrated study of industrial development could provide new policy perspectives and future directions of research.

Data

Data classification problems, have been considered for adjustments on classification or coverage of units (wherever needed to) as to make comparable data from different sources, viz. CMI 1956-57, SSMI-1958, Statistical Abstracts from 1956-1971, ASI 1959 onwards and classification of 1970 NIC, 1987 NIC and 1998 NIC and then finally (Chapter 3) bringing out 3-digit and 4-digit ASI or NIC data in CMI and SSMI industries in a NIC-1987 framework. However, state level data was not available for 1956-58 at 2-digit level of aggregation and not considered.

Chapterisation

The *First Chapter* deals with Introduction, Objectives, Hypotheses, Research Questions, Research Gaps, Importance and Relevance of the Study that contributed to knowledge.

The *Second Chapter* deals with Literature Review revealing Research Gaps traced for the purposes of fulfilment of the Thesis' objectives.

The *Third Chapter* deals with Analytical Framework, Methodology of Analysis including Sources of Data and Adjustments.

The *Fourth Chapter* deals with Productivity Analysis of TFP Growth, Measures of Kendrick, Domar and Solow. Further, regressions of TFPs on K/L to measure contributions of capital-intensity to TFP growth are done. Analysis of size variables and structural ratios, their growth, partial and total factor productivities along with Cobb Douglas production function estimates of output elasticities of L and K for each industry, factor-intensity, etc. for 2-digit (NIC-87) industries over four decades were carried out. Whether growth, partial and total factor productivity measures move in tandem or in opposite directions were assessed as to reveal the causation mechanisms and linkages between productivity, factor intensity and growth in each industry.

The *Fifth Chapter* deals with Measures of Regional Dispersal of Indian Industries in All states and union territories together and separately for each of (*i*) large states and (*ii*) smaller states and UT as to assess their distinct region size effects on industrial development analysis. Barring Assam, all Northeastern states and Delhi were put in the third category. Sikkim, Arunachal Pradesh were omitted in the analysis for want of data. Herfindahl-Hirshman Index and Coefficient of Variation measures were used to analyze regional dispersal of size variables and structural ratios of industries to assess the extent and depth of industrialisation and regional dispersal in India and to provide inputs for regional policy thereof.

The *Sixth Chapter* attempts a Graphical Presentation of Long-term Trends of regional dispersal measures for each of the 5 Variables and Structural Ratios of the 2-digit Industries to find out which Industries' satisfy Williamson Hypothesis.

The *Seventh Chapter* deals with the Causal Links between productivity, growth and dispersal over 40 and 10-year time periods. This is to assess whether Total Factor

Productivity, Partial Factor Productivities been causal factors for growth and whether K/L contributes to productivity and in turn to regional dispersal of industries.

The *Eighth Chapter* deals with the Major Findings and Policy Guidelines.

REFERENCES

1. Kuznets, S. *Six Lectures on Economic Growth*, Free Press of Glenocoe, Inc, 1959, pp. 122.
2. Chenery, H.B.- Patterns of Industrial Growth-*American Economic Review,* 50, September 1960, p. 624-654.
3. Kaur Kulwinder in *"Structure of Industries in India: Pattern, Framework, Disparities"* also writes that that level of per capita income has been found to be correlated with degree of industrialisation, Deep and Deep Publications, 1983, Ch-1, pp. 18.
4. Kuznets, S. *Modern Economic Growth-Rate, Structure and Spread,* New Haven: Yale University Press, 1966, pp. 127.
5. Ahluwalia, Isher Judge *Industrial Growth in India-Stagnation in the Mid-Sixties,* Oxford University Press, Delhi, 1985.
6. Goldar B. N. *'Productivity Growth in Indian Industry',* Oxford University Press, (1986).
7. Ahluwalia' Isher Judge *'Productivity and Growth in Indian Manufacturing'* Oxford University Press, Delhi (1987).
8. Dhananjayan R.S. and N. Sasikala Devi *'TFP in Indian Manufacturing: 1973-93'* in *Productivity*, Vol. 39, No. 2, July-Sept-1998, p. 310-320.
9. Nicholas Oulton and Mary Mahoney's work on 'Productivity and Growth-A Study of British Industry-1954-86.*Occasional Papers-XLVI-National Institute of Social and Economic Research,* 1994. 10-Jorgenson D.W. 'Econometric Methods for modelling producer's behaviour' in Griliches, Z and Intriligator, M.D. (ed.) *Handbook of Econometrics, Vol. III*-Amsterdam, North Holland. 1986. 11- Romer P. –'Increasing returns and long run growth'—*Journal of Political Economy*, Vol.94, 1986- pp.1002-37.
12. Mehta S.S. *Productivity and Production Functions and Technical Change*—A Survey of Some Indian Industries, Concept Publishing House, 1974, 1980. pp, 10-20.
13. Somayajulu V.V.N. (1994) Industrial Development of Andhra Pradesh—*ICSSR Sponsored Study*-University of Hyderabad.

Chapter 2

Review of Literature

INTRODUCTION

This Chapter 2 reviews the literature of studies dealing with Partial and Total Factor Productivity, Factor Intensity, Growth and Regional Concentration and Dispersal of Industries and Inter-relationships between those concepts and measurements in theory and practice of India's industrialisation. Similar studies relating to international comparisons with other countries' industrialisation and micro-level foreign country case studies are also cited in the Review; that provided similar or divergent relationships leading to a few hypotheses for further empirical testing. This Review is also intended to trace research gaps as to fetch requisite hypotheses, or research questions. The Review is neither necessarily a full comprehensive survey nor claims to be a more refined or improved classification of themes based studies survey; but is intended for the cited purpose of examining the studies for causal relationships of growth, productivity and dispersal of the variables to trace research gaps for further works as not done in earlier studies. Hence, the Chapter is divided into following sections: Section 1 deals with initially those Studies dealing with International Comparison and Individual Foreign Country Case Studies. *Section 2* dwells upon a few Major Studies dealing with Indian Industries' growth, productivity, dispersal performance, etc. *Section 3* cites Studies focussing on discussion of relevant theoretical/technical and empirical verification issues dealing with Returns to Scale, Capital Intensity (K/L), Partial Productivity of Factors, Total Factor Productivity and Growth during long period and Period Wise Analysis till the Pre Reforms Period. *Section 4* deals with specifically those studies on Growth, Industrial Development and Regional Dispersal of Indian Industries. *Section 5* isolates the Research Gaps learnt from the Review of Literature cited above for further investigation of Indian Industries at national and sub-national levels with the experience of Post Reform Phase of Indian Industrialisation.

To cite an important Themes-based Review works of Indian industries' studies, Somayajulu V.V.N. and Jacob George[1] (1983) reviewed earlier, similar Research works on Indian Industries' economic issues and contribution of the studies to the themes under the current Review quoting authors' works. They also included production function studies in India because they can be distinguished by distinct objectives/themes, type of production function used, choice of variables, data used, etc. Such an improved classification adopted takes into account: 1-time series, cross section and pooled data studies; 2-state level and all India Industry studies, 3- micro-macro studies, where size and cluster of firms and industries define choice of variables, returns to scale, capital intensity, TFP measurements, sources of growth, etc. Later in 1990s, he estimated production function parameters in a major study of Andhra Pradesh Industries' development and relevant TFP and actual growth rates to trace inter-relations between sources of growth and development in AP industries, 1956-80.

The Classification undertaken in this Survey of Literature follows a chronological order of publication of studies under the themes in Respective Sections concerned.

INTERNATIONAL STUDIES

Ishaq Nadiri[2] (1970) in 'Some Approaches to the Theory and Measurement of TFP: A Survey' in - focuses on some basic hypotheses and empirical evidences but refrains from giving any conclusive answers regarding measurement and determinants. His Survey paper is limited to determinants of TFP in USA industry. He shows that Solow's TFP measure is similar to Kendrick's TFP proportional to changes in quantities of inputs and output given a production type of Cobb-Douglas type, characterised by Hick's neutral technological progress. He discusses the usage of value-added data, as to measure output on assumption that ratio of raw materials to total output remains constant[3] (Domar.-1963). Nadiri's evidence suggests that the cited ratio was neither constant for the whole economy nor for the individual industries. It declined due to improvements in technology, better inventory management, substitution of both raw materials and primary inputs. Gordon (1969)[4] viewed that omission of materials that influence production relations often leads to a positive bias in estimates of returns to scale and affects elasticity of substitution between L and K.

Irving Kravis (1976)[5] made a productivity comparison across countries to throw some light on causes of productivity differentials and to explain international differences in per capita GDP. Industry-wise comparisons have been made in terms of labour productivities. He did not pursue the industrial pattern of international differences in productivity as the industrial pattern differences were not significant. But Metals, Machinery and Chemicals revealed large productivity gaps in UK-USA comparative study Food Beverage, Tobacco, Apparel, Nonmetallic showed less gaps in productivity measurements.

Renuka Mahadevan (2002)[6] examined Australian 2-digit manufacturing for 1968-95. It decomposed TFP into technical progress and technical efficiency. And showed that trade liberalisation has a positive effect on technical progress but no significant gains in technical efficiency. She found that in textile clothing, footwear and leather, L-intensity was the most but with the lowest wage rates and lowest TP and TFP growth compared to other industries. Further, government protection led to more fall in productivity. Transport showed greater TP than textiles but there was scope for better use of technology. Petroleum, Coal and Chemicals were most K intensive but there were little gain from technical efficiency because these industries faced minimal competitive imports and catered to domestic demand.

Krishna K. L. (1992)[7] estimated a meta- production function as the envelope of all the efficient input-output points, for international comparisons. The difference between the observed and estimated growth rates of output [using the estimated coefficients] was the residual for the measure of TFP growth. It showed that relative sectoral growth rates of productivity were the important determinants of structural transformation in the economy. He reviewed some recent productivity studies with focus on TFPG. He compared TFPG in India versus South Asia and East Asia and assessed contribution of education to output growth. Then he discussed agricultural productivity, railways sector productivity and inter-state productivity differences, reviewed income convergence hypothesis and three sets of productivity measures for Andhra Pradhesh. TFP measurement was undertaken by using flexible functional forms of Production Function (PF) such as translog rather than restrictive types of Cobb-Douglas (CD) and Constant Elasticity of Substitution (CES).

First, Dougherty and Jorgenson (1998)[8] G-7 results are compared with Wolff (1991)[9]. In DJ and Wolff there is initial similarity in TFP levels but over time DJ index varies much. This is because p.f. of DJ allowed substitution possibilities at a much finer level along with data differences. In second part, TFP results are presented for 96 countries presented by Hall and Jones[10] and by Islam-1995. As regards 2nd set there are similarities at the bottom of the list than at the top but Islam index is more bottom heavy than H-J index. The difference in conclusion is due to difference in methodology and data.

Macro Studies showed that the TFP measures used to analyse issues of technological diffusion and convergence and the different approaches to TFP comparison have important roles for purposes of formulation of policy guidelines.

Islam Nazrul (1999)[11] makes a review of three main approaches to TFP analysis for international comparisons. They are 1- time series growth accounting (absolute and relative) approach of Kendrick, Denison (1967)[12], Jorgenson, etc. The absolute has been used by Kravis (1976)[13] and Nadiri (972)[14]. Jorgenson and Nishimizu (1978) initiated the relative form of time series approach to international TFP comparison.

Jorgenson distinguished between quality and quantity of inputs. Christensen, Cummings and Jorgenson (1981)[15] extended it to 9 countries and used the translog production function. This function allowed an expression for difference in TFP levels. But before conclusions about technological differences from TFP results can be drawn, it is necessary to decompose TFP into its different components. For Hall and Jones –1996, 1997, differencing is done in direction of cross section of countries but this depends on the way the countries are ordered. 3- Islam's Panel approach seeks better explanation of cross-country growth differentiation expression in a level equation form of Cobb Douglas Production Function (C-d p. f.) A_0 estimation is controlled well by Panel Approach. There is difference in scope of results produced by time series approach, cross section and panel regression. The results are presented in two formats.

Blakemore Arthur and Schlagenhauf Don (1983)[16] addressed the issue of switching regressions in the context of the USA productivity slowdown since 1950. A comparison of structural stability of these functional forms through Quandt's (1960) Most Likelihood Estimate (MLE) for testing null hypothesis that no regime switches have occurred was done. This was against the alternative that a change has occurred at unknown observation z*. In all three trends, when a simple linear time trend is utilised under assumption of single switch, ML occurs in 1973 II. This supports the opinion that a structural break occurred in US in 1973. But test for two switches is not definitive. This article was also important because it could enable comparison of possibly gradual productivity slowdown on global scale.

Power Laura (1998)[17] examines the relationship between productivity, investment and plant age for 14000 plants in USA manufacturing of 1972-88. Growth in productivity is systematically correlated with plant size in employment but there is no overall relationship between investment and productivity or productivity growth. In chemical industry, investment age coefficient is significant across plant regression but plant age is not. Fixed effects (accounts for cross plant and within plant variations and effects) and plant heterogeneity are more important determinants of observable productivity patterns than fixed costs of capital reallocation.

Hiau Looi Kee (2001)[18] provided some theoretical underpinnings of the issue of productivity growth in the context of East Asian NIC growth. 1-The endogenous growth theory stresses the role of productivity growth. Lucas[19] (1988) introduces the effect of trade on productivity growth through a learning-by-doing mechanism. But Young (1992)[20] using growth accounting techniques inferred there is no sign of productivity growth in Singapore. Krugman (1994))[21] claimed that growth was input-driven. 2-This second school led by Findlay (1996)[22] and Ventura (1997)[23] showed that in a general equilibrium setting, a small open economy can sustain high growth through Rybczynski effects of factor accumulation.

In Singapore, factor endowments accumulation plays a big role in many industries. Whereas in electronics factor productivity is the driving factor, in primary products industry both are equally important. Given nearly 60 per cent of value- added of manufacturing is generated in the electronics industry and primary products industry, the role of productivity is as important as factor endowments in estimations of translog revenue function for a panel of seven industries in 19 years from 1974-1992. Under assumptions of Constant Returns to Scale (CRS) and perfect competition the growth rate of TFP equals actual productivity growth. Growth of unskilled labour benefits rubber and wood industry. But primary products industry and manufacturing are skilled L intensive. Rybczynski elasticities measure growth of output due to growth of factor endowments in an economy. Since Capital (K) is intensively used in chemicals, electronics, machinery, petroleum and misc., where land and buildings are used intensively, productivity is a big factor of growth. For contributions of productivity is constructed as ratio of estimated effect of productivity to the total estimated effects of productivity, factor endowments, prices and fixed effect. Thus contributions of productivity, factor endowments prices and fixed effect are normalised such that the sum of the contributions equals to 100 per cent. Thus 46 per cent of the value-added of manufacturing sector derives from an industry that relies most heavily on productivity as a source of growth. 35 per cent of total value-added of sector is originated from industries that are driven from factor endowments.

SELECTED STUDIES OF INDIAN INDUSTRIES WITH THE SAME INTER-RELATIONS FRAME

Padma Desai (1969)[24] related study of industrial growth in context of export demand, domestic final demand, import substitution and intermediate demand at current prices. Shares in Gross Value Added and in gross output at market price and factor cost declined over 1951-63 but GVA of investment goods rose and GVA in raw material and intermediate category had constant shares of 35-40 per cent. In 1957-63, metals and chemicals (intermediate category) with large investment had started yielding outputs. Import substitution in 4 periods accounted for 5-9 per cent of additional output.

S. S. Mehta (1974)[25] in 'Productivity, Production Function and Technical Change—A survey of Some Indian Industries' measures TFP of technological progress in 27 large scale Indian Industries during 1953-65 and examines trends in productivity till 1970 in the neoclassical frame. He uses data from census sector and adjusts CMI with ASI data.

Trends in technical progress reveal diversity among industries. Labour productivity has increased significantly in most industries but K-productivity has not. K-intensity explains growth in L-productivity in cotton textiles, ceramics, tanning, sewing machines, etc. The rate of technological change in the growth process of Indian industries was not very significant. The components of technological change that seems to have affected the growth process are K-intensity and factor substitution. In 3-year rolling plan period 1966-68, rate of growth in industrial sector decreased to 1.6 per cent p.a. which increased slightly in 1969-70.

Vijay Bhasin and Vijay Seth (1980)[26] estimated CD and CES production functions for 27 3-digit and 4-digit major Indian manufacturing industries, commensurate with Dadi for 1950-65.

Brahmananda (1982)[27] deals with the productivity issue for the Indian economy, a sectoral perspective from classical, neoclassical and empirical points of view and presents a theory of productivity change suited to Indian industries considering the relevance of international productivity experience and its relevance to India. He also deals with controversies on development strategies from the productivity angle and so deals with allocation of factor quantities, relevance of CRS/LDR, disparities in wage ratios at sectoral and temporal levels, ratios of K/O, surplus/K, and the performances of private/public sectors.

He notes that the falling productivity trend is reflected in most commodity sectors and it has moved pari passu with the falling surplus/K ratio. No correlation was noticed between index of F-quantity change and index of TFP change. Sectors where K/O ratio was high showed more factor quantity accumulation, so it was no wonder that incremental K/O ratio rose very high in a short time. The productivity experience of developed countries does not show reversal of productivity index, unlike the case of India. Also, vis-à-vis them, India showed less concern with employment growth, the latter being less than population growth.

Goldar (1986)[28] estimated Cobb Douglas and translog production functions for large scale registered manufacturing from 1959-1979. His estimates indicate a significantly positive but low growth of 1.3 per cent p.a. in TFP in Indian Industry. This was low compared to rate of growth in industrial output; similarly low in comparison to similar estimates of other underdeveloped countries. The statistical analysis indicates a strong positive relationship between output growth and productivity growth that is consistent with evidence of other countries. TFP in some modern industries like Basic Metals, Chemicals, Petroleum and Rubber is negative while many traditional industries showed positive growth.

The objective was whether meaningful estimates could be obtained for returns to scale, substitution, distribution, efficiency parameters. They observed that: 1-there are inter-industry differences in rate of growth of technical change; 2-there is less scope for factor substitution and the elasticity of substitution is less than unity in most of industries 3-CES seems more appropriate specification for most Indian indsutries 4-most industries experienced decreasing returns to scale and 5-there are inter-industry differences in the pattern of income distribution among factors of production. CD is a better method in case of time trend with biscuit making and nonferrous metals. But ceramics, bicycles and electric lamps CD is better without time trend but CES is better with time trend in these cases. Choice between CD and CES varies from industry to industry.

K. L. Krishna's article (1987)[29] reviewed the trends in industrial production and productivity since 1950 to 1986. Industrial output grew 6-fold and average annual rate of growth works out to be 5.5 per cent within these 35 years. Within manufacturing, the organised sector grew at a higher rate than unorganised sector. So growth in industrial employment lagged behind output growth. Traditional industries show better performance than new industries in TFP growth. He points out 2 unsettled issues. They are: (1) Available estimates of TFP growth have to be reconciled. (2) Sources of TFP growth have to be analysed.

J. Ahluwalia's (1995)[30] 'Productivity and Growth in Indian Manufacturing analysed productivity and "Industrial Growth in India- Stagnation since the mid-sixties' analysed the trends in industrial growth and productivity across 20 two-digit industries and identified the factors for persistent industrial stagnation since the mid 60s. It revealed that a slowdown in growth of heavy industries and low growth in other industries. This observation was caused by low productivity performance in industries due to 4 factors that contributed to industrial stagnation.

They are: 1. slow growth in agricultural incomes and their effect in limiting demand for industrial goods, and in limiting supply of materials, power, etc; and 2. slow down in infrastructure investment, 3. poor management of infrastructure sector, 4. industrial policy framework impacting on a high cost industrial framework. She highlights the deleterious effects of industrial policy regime in 1970s and cites beneficial effects of policy liberalisation since mid-1980 when there was a break in manufacturing productivity mid-80s followed by New Economic Policies, reforms in industrial and trade policy.

Balakrishnan and Pushpangadan (1994)[31] argued in favour of a separate deflation of output and inputs as components of value added by their respective price indices. This method was critical enough to reverse Ahluwalia's conclusions of a 'turnaround in productivity growth'.

J. Mohan Rao (1996)[32] deals with method of growth accounting and econometric identification of the production function at any level of aggregation in the first article in 'Special Article Series'. He addresses critical issues of correspondence between theoretical measures and the indicators to measure it. It shows empirical relevance of B-P's revisions. They argue B-P procedure is also susceptible to bias but can be bias free through an alternative procedure. Secondly, when non-competitive conditions prevail a return to capital formation modifies bias in conventional productivity measure based on output or value added.

Pravin Krishna and Devashish Mitra (1998)[33] investigate effects of trade liberalisation after 1991 on productivity. They use an extended Hall methodology that corrects estimated TFP for Solow biases. Using firm level data (1986-93-CMIE data) from four industries electrical, non-electrical, electronics (3-6%), and transport and allowing for changing returns to scale they find some evidence of increase in growth rate of productivity-3-6 per cent in first 3 industries.

This happens through increased competition as seen in significant reductions in price marginal cost markups in post 1991 period. The traditional X-efficiency argument is invoked to justify these increases. Returns to scale got reduced probably because firms may be operating at smaller scale prior to reforms.

THEORETICAL AND TECHNICAL ISSUES EMERGING FROM PRODUCTIVITY FUNCTIONS, GROWTH, PRODUCTIVITIES AND DISPERSAL OF INDUSTRIES

Scale Economies and Technical Progress

Lakhwinder Singh and K. C. Singhal (1986)[33] investigates economies of scale and technical change and to locate sources of growth of Punjab large manufacturing for the period 1967-80 using ASI Census sector data. Capital (K) coefficient is found to be very small and is not significant for large manufacturing sector. So main source of growth is Labour (L). Basic metals and alloys industry registered high Capital (K) coefficient. But when a time trend as a proxy to Technical Progress (TP) was included, capital coefficient showed negative values. Neutral TP does not hold. While returns to scale was estimated to show increasing to scale. Electricity has a positive but insignificant coefficient. L coefficient is negative and significant in food products showing decreasing returns to scale. In cotton textiles, basic metals and transport, L-coefficient is negative and insignificant. However, only cotton textile, basic metals, transport and electricity reveal constant returns to scale. Final conclusion is large scale manufacturing shows constant returns. So output growth has been achieved through either one of factor inputs and not through returns to scale or TP. If this pattern and trend are repeated, then every increase in output would mean a greater strain in use of factors and resources and a proportionately higher dose of I is required for every additional unit of output.

What is needed is increasing efficiency of resources as to improve returns to scale and not greater K/L unless the increasing K/L and resources combination improves Technical Progress (TP).

Agarwal A L (1986)[35] estimated output elasticity of inputs, in turn their marginal productivities, (for example $a^\wedge\alpha$ (Q/K)), shares in total output (α/Sum of coefficients = $\alpha + \beta + \gamma$), where $a + b + c$ indicates returns to scale (S) , being increasing (S>1), decreasing (S<1)or constant (S=1) with gamma=1 (unitary elasticity of substitution) for estimated CDPF to 20 industries, with 7 industries of 1967-71 and rest 13 of 1975-80. In 1967-71, some estimated coefficients were negative indicating that increase in input use decreases output.

To overcome problems of multi-collinearity and other econometric problems, pooling of cross section and time series data was done. Regression coefficients computed simultaneously and/or due to fitting regression equations separately. In 1967-71 some estimated coefficients were negative that showed that increase in input use decreases output indicating vegetable and animal oil and fat, cement, etc. at 3-digit level. The estimated coefficients were positive for all Seven industries at 3-digit level. The coefficients of raw materials were positive in all industries but relatively the lowest in Repairs activity. Returns to scale was greater than 1 in Chemicals (IN31) and Transport (IN3). The efficiency parameter 'n' was 3.4946. In 1975-80, K-coefficient was negative in jewellery (IN38) and Water Supply (IN42) while being positive for 5 industries. In 1975-80, MP_L was positive in 5 industries of 1975-80 period, implying all 20 industries turned out to be raw material oriented.

Edward Wolff (1991)[36] found that K/L converged over long period though the process was much stronger after 1960. Lowering down of productivity convergence was associated with slowing down of K/L growth. The ratio of TFP to L-productivity growth is a rough measure of contribution of technical change to L-productivity growth. This was 0.57 and the remaining portion was attributable to capital deepening.

Results showed that there is a direct correspondence by period between the degree of K/L catch-up and TFP convergence. This was the strongest in 1950-79 but divergent in 1938-50. Secondly, thee is a direct correspondence by period between TFP convergence and average growth in K/L. This was the highest in 1950-79.

Wolff's paper hypothesized that convergence in L-productivity was due to convergence of K/L over time among the Seven industrialised countries. A positive correlation between TFPG and growth rate of K/L is deducible from the arguments of interaction between capital accumulation and technological advance. This is explainable from embodiment effect, vintage effect, learning by doing, potential technological advance and Verdoorn-

Kaldor effect whereby investment growth through demand growth leads to a favourable climate for investment and industrialisation. In Wolff, results showed a positive correlation of 0.79 between rate of TFPG and K/L over 1880-1979. Results based on regression and vintage model are mixed but support the existence of interaction effect between technological advance and capital accumulation. Many authors like Wolff, showed concern in possible interaction between processes of K-deepening and technological diffusion. Wolff's hypothesis is that TFP catch up depends on K-intensity catch up. He presents evidence for USA in terms of positive correlation between TFP growth rate and K- intensity growth rate. Also, after controlling for initial differences in TFP level, he regresses TFP growth rate on initial level of TFP and K-intensity growth rate and finds a positive coefficient. This is an indication of positive influence of capital accumulation on TFP catch-up.

Upender M (1996)[36] estimated elasticity of L productivity to find out substitution possibilities of L for K for 1973-90. The proportionate change in L-productivity due to unit or small change in wage rate (W/L) is the measure of elasticity of substitution $\sigma = 1/1+ \rho$ (where σ can take any value. $\sigma > 1$ means higher substitution possibilities). Returns to scale is 0.8 per cent and that shows Indian factory sector is subject to decreasing returns to scale. Results show that factory sector is K-intensive.

Elasticity is >1 and so there is greater possibility of substitution of L for K. The elasticity of L productivity with respect to wage rate is more than one and so substitution possibilities are high.

Krishna Kumar P. (2000)[37] undertook a study for selected five industries (Textile products, Leather, Rubber, non-electrical and electrical machinery, Chemical) at two digit level for time period 1973-93. Net fixed capital stock for different years was estimated by making adjustments for new investment and depreciation for respective years. It was found out that majority of industries faced increasing returns to scale. Electrical and non-electrical show Decreasing Returns to Scale (DRS) but significant rate of TP was 3 per cent. Leather faced Constant Returns to Scale (CRS) and TP was low at 0.0018. But for all the five industries rate of technical progress was positive and it had important contributions to value added.

Hasan Rana (2002)[38] uses panel data from 1976-87 on Indian manufacturing to determine the extent to which productivity is affected by both embodied (technology embodied in the capital goods that firms use) and disembodied technology (technical knowledge).

The productivity enhancing effects of new domestic capital goods however appear to be more broad-based. They are found to exist in a wide range of industries and not just the scientific or technology intensive ones as tends to be case for imported disembodied technology and imported capital goods. The analysis reveals that the productivity benefits of domestic capital goods appear to stem in least in part from the disembodied technologies imported by domestic capital goods producers.

Capital formation can exert two effects on L productivity. 1-by raising K/L ratio it will raise L-productivity even if there is no advance in technology use. 2-through interactions with technology advance K accumulation may be associated with gains in productivity over and above capital deepening.

Sengupta D. N. (1999)[39] reviewed the process of growth in Indian manufacturing in 1980-90 through Twelve three digit industries and examined the inter-linkages between growth and elements of productivity, demand, cost, prices, investment, employment, structural change and balance of commodity trade. Results showed that growth in the decade period was policy induced and that growth in consumer and non-consumer goods industries was demand induced growth that pulled up output of capital and intermediate goods. Productivity increased in response to output. After reaches 3.7 per cent pa, productivity increased by 1.4 per cent for every 1 per cent additional growth in output similar to I. J. Ahluwalia study (1991, p. 131-40).

STUDIES DEALING WITH INDUSTRIAL GROWTH AND DISPERSAL

V. Nath (1971)[39a] reviewed policies relating to regional development in the Five-year Plans especially in relation to state levels of economic development and rates of economic growth. He confined the analysis to states due to almost little availability of data for lower level administrative-economic units. His conclusion was pertaining to agriculture growth and modernisation, rather than industrial patterns. However, even there, the west and south states did rather well than the east and north-central states. He throws some light on industrial location and development of backward regions. Demands for additional resource allocations and special measures of relief of backwardness have come from an increasing number of backward regions.

But in the first 3 plans, despite 'intentional' roles given to infrastructures and social services, additional funds could not be provided. Financing was to be from state plans. In mineral resource belts, central investments wee made. But the backward regions of Bihar and UP, a total of 80 million people were in districts classified as being at the bottom or next level of development. These backward districts had 45 per cent of total all-India population of such districts.

These two states contiguous with MP and Orissa is the 'backward heart' of India. UP had the lowest per capita state plan expenditure under the first 3 Plans. Demarcation of backward regions using uniform criteria is essential for objective assessment of the magnitude of the problem of backwardness to remove complaints of differential treatment. The need for transfer of financial responsibility arises from the inability of states to undertake effective action.

In his first article in EPW, Nath showed the ambivalence of planners on locational problems. While advocating industrial dispersal, the planners avoided advocating licensing power to be used for locational purposes (table 2.1 col-16 Regional development in Indian Planning). He noted that the most rapid development had taken place in the developed states of Maharashtra, West Bengal and Gujarat. This was the case in 3rd and 4th plan periods. The flexibility due to new technological developments had made many industries footloose. It was noted that the large land requirements for assembly line production induced industries to seek locations in peripheral regions. But Maharashtra had sought to prevent concentration of industries in Bombay and direct industrial growth to less developed regions through construction of estates and financial incentives. Need for a comprehensive policy for industrial location was stressed in the study.

M. L.Pandit's (1974)[40] paper throws a new dimension into the dispersal issue. He divides the growth effect to regional effect and compositional effect and concludes that correlation between regional effect and state's industrial growth rates show a positive and strong relationship while no relationship emerges in case of compositional effect in relation with states' growth rates. Out of 17 states taken for study, regional effect is positive for 11 states in all time periods. But one of his policy conclusions that only when full employment is attained in each state was efficient allocation of industries a viable strategy. The reason is industrial dispersal itself must fulfil the goal of full and productive employment.

Kelkar V. L. and Kumar R (1974)[41] showed that the sustained period of inward oriented industrialisation was associated with high levels of concentration due to lack of medium range enterprises and a poorly developed SSI. The 1980s witnessed changes in industrial structure. Earlier, the metals related industries in north-eastern industrially underdeveloped regions dominated. But in 1980s, chemicals and consumer durables became engines of growth.

Somayajulu, V. V. N. (1980)[42] wrote a Resume of India's Industrialisation for a century of 1879-1978 that identified reasons and facts for distribution of industrial trends. Industrial Stagnation and Industrial Recovery were covered during the Pre-Planning and Five- Year Plan Periods including the Rolling Plan Period.

He wrote that industrial output on 1960 base was 5.5 per cent p.a. for a decade ending 1965-66, but later on pulled down to 0.2 per cent in 1966-67, 0.5 per cent in 1967-68 and a recovery of 6.2 per cent in 1968-69. Cotton textiles showed lower growth than all industries taken together. Silk and synthetic fibers increased their output faster. Import substitution of synthetic fibers caused decline in cotton textiles. Bank rates were reduced from 6 per cent to 5 per cent to ease industrial investment.

Industries were allowed to diversify their output up to 25 per cent of their licensed capacity without need to securing license. Tax incentives were provided in Central budget of 1968-69 to promote private investment and exports. But there was no increase in capital formation in private sector. Price index of raw materials rose after 1967 by 20.9 per cent. Steel shortage was a bottleneck to engineering production Demand for rail wagons decreased. In 1968-70, food manufacture, leather, footwear, made up textile goods, transport equipment faced recession. Supply bottleneck was noticed in oilseeds, raw cotton, steel, non-ferrous metals, coal, cement.

Somayajulu (1974 and 1976)[43&44] Structural Changes and growth rates in industrial sectors are reinforcing to each other over plan periods that value added in modern industries received later and greater importance than in traditional industries Output of tobacco, petroleum, chemical, showed higher growth in Small Scale Sector than those in Large Scale Sector in 1961-65. But textiles, food industries, electricity generation led the resurgence after 1965-67 (Somayajulu, 1974, 1976).

Dinesh Awasthi (1982)[45] used various measures of inequalities such as Standard Deviation of Logarithms, Gini Coefficient, Theil's Inequality Index and H-H Index for all years between 1961-1978 (except 1972) using ASI data for Fixed Capital, Employment, Value added. 1970-71 was taken as the base year and all the important states were covered. All indices showed reduction in inter-regional inequality though the trend was not smooth as in 1969 and 1978.

Uday Sekhar (1982)[46] examined trends in interstate distribution of industry in India during 1961-75 and determined whether disparities had been increasing over time or not. Comparing the ratios for 1976 he found that Maharashtra, West Bengal, Gujarat, Tamil Nadu had above average manufacturing value added/Net Domestic Product (VAM/NDP). In 1961, these states along with Delhi but not Tamil Nadu were more industrialised. During 1961-76, manufacturing sectors of other states have been growing at a faster pace relative to NDP and so a trend towards equalisation of state VAM/NDP is noticed.

Between 1961-1969, decline was manifested in Orissa, Madhya Pradesh, Bihar, Karnataka due to heavy investment in K-intensive public sector. In unorganised sector too, Coefficient of Variation. showed a decline of 84 per cent to 61 per cent between 1969 and 1978.

Another major study of industrially lagging state of Andhra Pradesh during 1956-1970s (nearly two decades of Planning) emerges from an ICSSR sponsored study by V.V.N. Somayajulu[58].

The study examined technical parameters of industries through estimation of Production functions, TFP and regional dispersal in large through large versus small and recast those findings for testing the explanation of mid-sixties Indian Industrial retrogression. His study shed light on the institutional financing aspects of AP Industrial development. He made an economic evaluation of the role of APSFC, APIDC, APSSIDC, APIIC, All-India Financial Institutions, Role of Central and State Investment Subsidies.

Small-scale industries contributed better than large industries in AP State and in backward districts of AP to regional dispersal, employment generation and growth after 1970s prior to which period of two decades no industrialisation took place. Large-scale industries in Metropolitan cities, hinterland picked up momentum of growth after 1980s. The fundings were supported by role of APSFC, APSIDC, APIIC and APIDC.

The study analysed the trends in sanctions and disbursements of finances to different industrial activities of small, medium and large-scale industries and to what extent of regional dispersal those lendings and priorities were given by APSFC. Similarly, the role of APIDC in respect of above aspects along with the aspect of entrepreneurial development is discussed. Despite the drawback in data coverage, it discussed plan allocations, production performance and an evaluation of study of joint sector units in equity participation problems of marketing and raw material procurement by APSSIDC and other corporations and financial institutions were analysed. Performance of APSSIDC depended on tact and alertness in co-ordination and in making the relevant Bodies understand the spirit of co-operation for small industry promotion, lack of co-ordination seems to be the cause of failure of APSSIDC. Despite the paucity of data, Industrial Estates (IE) and Industrial Development Areas (IDAs), their role for regional dispersal, occupancy ratios, voluntary loan contribution by APIIC along with suggestions for locational improvement were analysed. Role of All India Financial Institutions, the scheme-wise sanction of IDBI and IFCI for AP industries in backward areas, advances on project financing scheme by providing equity, modernisation, underwriting guarantees is noted. ICICI's promotional and investment role and Commercial banks industry-wise and district wise credit allocation to help SSI's and role of AP non-resident Indian Investment Corporation were also analysed. Role of central and state investment subsidies for tribal development blocks and backward areas, industry-wise disbursement, was analysed. A suggestion for all these explanation and studies was to prefer industries with higher regional linkages and its L-intensiveness for generating employment in backward areas too and industrial capital and material linkages to be preferred for overall growth of industries in AP.

R Nagaraj (1994)[48] studied relationship between employment, capital intensity and wage rate for 1973-87 for 42 three-digit registered manufacturing industries. His point of departure was from Isher Ahluwalia's 1992 study (p. 82-83) that identifies consumer non-durables as accounting for bulk of decline in employment with maximum increase in capital intensity and maximum increase in real wage rate in the relevant period.

Nagaraj differs in the explanation offered by Ahluwalia, Lucas and World Bank study. He believed that structural changes in favour of unregistered sector and also movement towards SSU within registered manufacturing were the cause of declining employment in registered factory sector.

Moreover, it postulated a compositional change in output towards L-intensive industries as overhang of employment in 1970s stagnation, restriction on fresh employment in large factories, contracting out and greater use of part time workers. Methodologically, in time series data of 42 three-digit industries, to minimize auto-correlation problems, the first difference in each series is correlated. In 9 of the 42 industries the postulated relationship is statistically valid with the expected sign for estimated coefficients.

But the results across the variants explored show lack of consistency with insignificant coefficient sign. Thus the results suggest that the relationship among the three variables is more complex than postulated.

Anuradha and AVVSK Rao (1995)[49] showed that the process of industrialisation was characterised by an inequality in its spatial distribution. Interstate disparities in relative terms tended to decline during 1971-86. Developed states experienced decline in their share of employment and productive capital while backward states showed increase. in Theil's index, while H-H Index showed a decline in value added, employment and value of output. Per capita productive capital, factory employment per thousand of population weighted and unweighted interstate CV also declined for all 15 states.

Jeemol Unni, N Lalitha and Uma Rani (2001)[50] analysed trends in growth and efficiency in utilisation of resources in Indian manufacturing before and after the reforms during 1978-95 with the break year at 1989-90. They gave a regional dimension to the repercussions of reforms by analysing organised and unorganised manufacturing in Gujarat during the same period.

They concluded that growth, value added and capital increased after reforms and especially so in the consumer durable goods sub-sector in organised sector. However, Total Factor Productivity Growth (TFPG) in Indian organised and unorganised manufacture showed decline. Growth in unorganised sector peaked in 1978-85 but decreased later. The authors concluded that perhaps large organised sector is better equipped to deal with competitive conditions arising out of the reform process. The pattern of growth in Gujarat's both sectors were similar. Gujarat did better in terms of value added for both sectors than all India. Employment growth in both sectors at regional and national levels was higher. But employment growth in unorganised sector in Gujarat was higher in India for both periods; though in case of organised sector result was different. Growth in capital intensity (K/L) ratio was relatively high in both sectors at national and regional levels leading to a negative growth in K productivity in the entire period. In the reforms period there was a sharp increase in K intensity in both sectors at All India levels and Gujarat. But in reforms period K/L declined leading to increase in K productivity in Gujarat.

However, TFPG in Gujarat for both sub-sectors was positive. Also basic and intermediate sub sectors grew rapidly in the reforms period. This was attributed to growth of physical infrastructure development in 1980s.

V. Surender (1986)[51] work on growth and dispersal took two points of time 1961 and 1978-79 and analysed Location Quotient and Coefficient of Localisation. His database is the three digit industries of ASI Census reports. Out of 21 industries, 11 were highly localised. Uneven distribution of industrial activities is ascribed to uneven distribution of productive resources and lack of cheap transportation facilities. Agro-based industries were located mostly in south and non-agro in Bihar, Maharastra, West Bengal and Union Territories. Localisation Quotient showed wide dispersal. They are in electric light and power, non-ferrous basic, electrical machinery and industrial machinery. LQ of >1 is seen in transport and rubber. Basic and capital goods showed tendency towards backward locations. His hypothesis that the higher the growth of industries, higher the dispersal and vice versa was empirically verified. But cement and petrol also show high dispersion but low growth and so LQ studies are not deemed conclusive. Combined effects of initial concentration and growth of industry is significant at 18 degrees of freedom.

Rohit Desai (1986)[64] analysed results over two points of time—1964 and 1980-81 using census level data. He wrote that the process of diversification has gained ground across states. He also related the level of diversification with economic development by estimating rank correlation coefficient between indices of urbanisation, infrastructure, investment in mining, manufacturing, small-scale units at state level. State level industrial diversification was studied by analysing state level coefficient of specialisation by using employment data for organised manufacturing. His conclusion was that there was no significant change in spatial industrial diversification in 1981 over 1964. Majority of states showed specialisation. But regional development indicators were positively related with spatial diversification.

Jayadevan C M (1995)[53] analysed interstate variations in the rates of growth of employment in organised industry as a whole and in 17 individual organised manufacturing industries in India during 1976-88 for 15 states and tried to explain causes of interstate variation in employment. He studied 195 three-digit industries. Large employment growth rate differentials across states were noticed due to disparity in the growth of real output. No significant impact of real wages per worker on the employment growth rate was noticed except in cotton textiles for 1976-77 and beverage, tobacco and nonmetallic mineral products for 1987-88. Interstate variations in value added growth rates are significantly explained by varying magnitudes in industrial disputes and consequent number of man-days lost in various states. Employment in organised industry can be promoted by removing labour market distortions.

K. Rana (1988)[54] writes of uneven development at inter-state level. There was centralisation or concentration of industries till 1976 when Maharashtra, Gujarat, West Bengal and Tamil Nadu contributed 57.37 per cent of value added. ASI 1978-79 revealed the domination of developed states in industrialisation. On the criteria of domestic consumption of electricity per capita, Punjab showed 29.8 kwh followed by Maharashtra at 28.4Kwh and Haryana at 19.9 kwh but in HP it was 15.5 Kwh in spite of fact that it was used for temperature regulation. In backward states, the most serious constraint on development was constraint of finance.

Vijay Seth (1987)[55] used data on CMI-ASI from 1951-81 to test convergence hypothesis and interstate spatial pattern of industries. He used relative share of the region in total population as proxy for size of states. He used Hoover measure, Zelinsky-Fuch measure, Grossack's measure and the measure of changes in the significance of regions. These measures showed that process of industrialisation was accompanied by inter-state convergence in India. Finally, it was pointed out that institutional and technological spread of agriculture is important for spread of industry.

Sunil Kumar (1999)[56] analysed productivity variations across states and found that there is no convergence in Indian manufacturing in a regional context in the period 1969-94 using ASI factory sector data. The fall in Total Factor Productivity (TFP) in industrially developed states may be due to obsolete capital aging infrastructure, deteriorating urban environment and failure to upgrade technology. But the deregulatory framework in 1980s helped impart positive effect on TFP growth at aggregate and regional levels except West Bengal and Orissa. Results also suggested that the government policy of balanced regional development has helped the lagging states in raising their manufacturing productivity.

RESEARCH GAPS AND POST REFORM PHASE

Mohan Rao (1996)[57] made many methodological changes. His real productive capital is measured as a sum of working capital deflated by manufacturing WPI at 1960-61 prices and fixed capital at replacement values also at 1960-61 prices. He showed that the trend rate of growth of TFP was 2 per cent for entire period. But it was high at 5.5 per cent in 1973-81 and –2.2 per cent in 1981-93. The contribution of productivity growth to value added growth was 33 per cent for 1973-93 but 52 per cent for 1st period and – 96 per cent for the 2nd period.

Thus he differs from Ahluwalia's conclusions in that there is a turnaround in 1980s in the negative direction. But TFPD for Mohan Rao and Ahluwalia is same. Mohan Rao's TFPD shows movement from positive to zero growth. In the Indian manufacturing TFPG with double deflation showed less bias though this may not hold true in general.

Mohan Rao uses Gross Value Added to find out Total Productivity Growth (TPG) for 1973-93. The results of aggregated manufacturing differ from earlier studies in that industrial performance in 1980s did not show improvement compared to 15 years before. Real value of output growth based on ASI data show growth rate of 6.9 per cent pa for 1973-93. But real value added growth rates are much different when this period is divided into two sub-periods though this is not the case in real value of output growth rate calculations.

Sandeep Kumar (1999)[58] confines his analysis to intra-state and inter-district analysis of industrial development and dispersal. Over the time period of study (1971-91) in 1988, only chemical product groups exceeded other major industry groups in terms of labour productivity and capital intensity. Agro-based industries showed increase in their share of total factory workers but the share of capital investment and value added declined. Size structure showed shift in favour of small and medium size industries in general (86% in 1988). Analysis of H-H and Theil's index showed upward trend in the concentration in value added over 1967-68. The author has also shed light on fiscal incentive structure and institutional financing both for backward and non-backward districts.

Sumit Majumdar (1999)[59] analysed productivity trends in Indian Industry for 1950-93. Productivity is measured using a linear programming based technique called Data Envelopment Analysis (DEA). His results showed that in 1950s, industrial efficiency was relatively high; in the 1970s there are retrogression and in 1980s, patterns reversed to a great extent. But in 1990s efficiency peaked showing that reforms were working well.

Dhananjaya R. S. and Sasikala Devi, N. (1998)[60] provided and assessed behavioural characteristics of TFPG in an 18 2-digit inter-industrial framework to see how efficient use of technology accounts for rapid growth in certain categories than others. Kendrick, Solow and Divisia indices are estimated for 1973-94. While overall trends in TFP growth rates affect output expansion with lag of 1 or 2 years depending upon nature of policies adopted, Divisia index of TFP has yielded better rates of technical efficiency and so higher rates of output growth.

In 1980s, Divisia did not show better in any group vis a vis other periods. But in 1990s, Divisia showed higher results in two digit industry numbers such as 23—25-26 in traditional sector and 30-31—32-33-35-36-37 in non-traditional sector. For overall case, Divisia showed higher in 32-38-23—36-25-35-30-31. But generally, TFP contributions to output growth have yielded low magnitudes though during inflationary spurts in mid 70s, late 80s and early 90s TFP showed higher magnitudes, expansion in the rest was higher in early 90s than previous periods. Only in 35 group, Solow indices showed higher than base year's unitary magnitude. Among 3 estimates, Divisia index recorded values greater than one in most years of study for all non-traditional categories. Kendrick index of TFPG showed higher rate of output expansion (>than base year value of 1) prevailing in 70s, 80s, 90s. w. r. t. 20-21, 25, 26, 38 industry groups. Using Solow, TFP in 70s was higher than 80s and 90s in all traditional categories except 20-21 and 29 groups. Non-traditional groups showed higher values in all except 35, 37.

Kaplinsky Raphael's (1997)[61] paper reviews changing strategic perspectives from inward orientation towards a liberalised scenario (in two phases) and the consistent performance of the Industrial sector in post 1947 period. It concludes that given poor productivity performance, most studies that have been undertaken of Indian Industrialisation have been macroeconomic in nature and that there has been a poor tradition of microeconomic research into the determinants of industrial competitiveness.

Some forms of industrial development especially those based on cheap labour are only sustainable with a depreciating exchange rate as countries engage in a competitive process of devaluation to lower dollar wage rates. This does not lead to income growth. So also is the case when production is performed behind closed doors. The border price value added in industry, i.e. value of industrial output, when calculated at the cost of imported equivalents, can be much lower than when it is computed at domestic prices and then converted into international units of account through exchange rate. Given India's commitment to distribution concerns that has long been a central objective of industrial development. This poses challenges in balancing needs for sustained income growth, international competitiveness and equity in distribution that led to the policy framework towards 1-Development of heavy industries; 2-State to control monopolies; 3-Import substitution to be a key strategy 4-promotion of SSI. 5-The trend towards opening of industry's economy that requires change in pace and quality of industrial development. It is seen that competition in product markets is no more based on costs than on a combination of costs and product quality differentiation and innovation.

The divergent nature of results from Studies of Mohan Rao, Sandeep Kumar, Sumit Majumdar, Dhananjaya and Sasikala is an incentive to probe further into the problem of Industrial Productivity to understand the causes thereof. TFP in Indian Industry in these above cited studies shows a rising trend. To Kaplinsky, lower TFP figures has not enabled researchers to develop a strong micro-economic foundation of productivity studies in India. While the differential TFP figures of many researchers on Indian Industries is an incentive to further probe into nature of TFP figures obtainable in Indian Industries, this thesis probes further into the possible links between productivity, growth and dispersal measures in Indian Industry that can be one of the foundations to develop a tradition of micro-economic research in productivity and growth in Indian Industry for fulfilment of objectives of regional equity in Indian Industry.

REFERENCES

1. Somayajulu VVN and George Jacob in 'Production Function Studies of Indian Industries: A Survey' in *Artha Vijnana,* V-25, N-4, Dec 1983, pp. 402-418.
2. M. Ishaq Nadiri 'Some approaches to the Theory and Measurement of TFP'—A Survey—*Journal ofEconomic Literature* Vol. VIII—*American Economic Association*, Pennyslyvania, 1970, p. 1137-1177.
3. Domar Evsey 'On Total productivity and All That', *Journal of Political Economy,* Dec, 1962.
4. Gordon R J- '$45 Billion of US Private Investment has been mis-laid'-*Amer. Econ. Rev.* 59 (3), June 1969, pp. 221-238.
5. Kravis Irving 'Survey of International Comparisons of Productivity' in *The Economic Journal*, No. 86; March 1976; pp. 1-44.
6. Mahadevan Renuka 'Trade Liberalisation and Productivity growth in Australian Manufacturing Industries' *Australian Economic Journal*, Vol. 30, No. 2, June 2002, pp.170-18.
7. Krishna K. L. (1992) booklet "What do we learn from productivity studies?" in his *Presidential Address to the Tenth Annual Conference to AP Economic Association in Andhra University*, Waltair, 8-9 February, 1992.
8. Dougherty C. and Jorgenson D.W.—International Comparison of Sources of Growth, *American Economic Review (AER)*-Vol. 86, May 1996, pp. 25-29.
9. Wolff E.N. and Dollar D-Capital Intensity and TFP Convergence in Manufacturing-1963-1985 in Baumol WJ, Nelson W.W. and Wolff E.N ed- *Convergence to Productivity—Cross National Studies and Historical Evidence*-New York, Oxford University Press, 1994.
10. Hall and Jones—Levels of Economic Activity Across Countries- *American Economic Review (AER)*-Vol. 87, 1996-97, pp. 173-4.
11. Islam Nazrul—'International Comparisons of TFP- A Review'-*Review of Income and Wealth*, Series 45, December 1999, N. 4.
12. Denison E- why Growth Rates Differ—*The Brookings Institution-Washington* DC-1967.
13. Kravis, *op.cit.*
14. Nadiri Ishaq M—Some Approaches to the Measurement of TFP-A Survey—*Journal of Economic Literature*-1970.
15. Christensen L, Cummings D, Jorgenson D—*New Developments in Productivity Measurements and Analysis in Kendrick J.W. and Vaccara B (ed.) Studies in Income and Wealth*, Vol. 41—University of Chicago Press, 1980.
16. Blakemore and Schlagenhof Don—'Estimation of the trend rate of growth of productivity' in *Applied Economics*, 1983, 15, 807-814. Quandt's (1960)—Tests of hypothesis that a linear regression obeys two separate regimes, *Journal of American Statistical Association*, 55, 324-30.
17. Power Laura (1998) in 'Missing Link: Technology, Investment and Productivity' in *Review of Economics and Statistics*, Vol. 80, 1998, pp. 1300-312. She explains the weak link between investment and productivity saying that high productivity is not the motive for rise in investment.
18. Hiau Looi Kee-*Policy Research Working Paper 2702*—'Productivity versus Endowments—A Study of Singapore's Sectoral Growth, 1974-92'—*World Bank Development Research Group Trade*—Nov., 2001.
19. Lucas 'On the Mechanics of Economic Development'—*Journal of Monetary Economics*, Vol. 22-1988, pp. 3-42.

20. Alwyn Young—'A tale of Two Cities: Factor Accumulation and Technical Change in Hong Kong and Singapore' *NBER Macroeconomics Annual*, 1992, pp. 13-53. & Young A.—'The Tyranny of Numbers-Confronting the statistical Realities of East Asian Growth Experience'—*Quaterly Journal of Economics-* Vol. 110, No. 3, 1995, p. 641-668.
21. Paul Krugman—'The Myth of Asian Miracle'—*Foreign Affairs*, Vol. 73, No. 6, 1994, pp. 62-78.
22. Findlay Ronald—Modelling Global Interdependence: Centres, Peripheries and Frontiers' *American Economic Review (AER)*-86, 1996 No. 2, pp. 47-51.
23. Jaume Ventura—Growth and Interdependence—*The Quarterly Journal of Economics* (*QJE)*—Vol. 112, No. 1, 1997, pp. 57-84.
24. Desai Padma—'Growth and Structural Change in Indian Manufacturing Sector: 1951-1963 in *Indian Economic Journal* (IEJ), Vol. XVII, No. 2, Oct.-Dec., 1969.
25. Mehta S. S. (1974) 24 in 'Productivity, Production Function and Technical Change—A Survey of Some Indian Industries'.*Concept Publishing House*, 1974.
26. Vijay Bhasin and Vijay Seth (1980) 'Estimation of Production Functions for Indian manufacturing Industries'-Jan 1980, *Indian Journal of Industrial Relations*, No. 3, Vol. 15.
27. Brahmananda P.R '*Productivity of the Indian Economy—Rising Inputs or Falling Outputs*' (1982).
28. Goldar B.N.-*Growth and Productivity in Indian Industries*—OUP-1995.
29. K L Krishna's article—*'Industrial Growth and Productivity in India'* in Professor Brahmananda's book '*The Development Process of the Indian Economy*' 1987.
30. Ahluwalia I.J. 'Productivity and Growth in Indian Manufacturing'-OUP-1995.
31. Balakrishnan and Pushpangadan—'TFP Growth in Manufacturing Industry—A Fresh Look—*Economic and Political Weekly (EPW)*, March-1994.
32. J. Mohan Rao- in 'Manufacturing Productivity Growth—Method and Measurement. *Economic and Political Weekly (EPW),* Vol. XXXI, No. 44, Nov-2, 1996.
33. Pravin Krishna and Devashish Mitra (1998)'Trade Liberalisation, market discipline and productivity Growth: New Evidence from India' in *Journal of Development Economics*, Vol. 56, pp. 447-462).
34. Lakhwinder Singh and K C Singhal—'Economies of Scale and Technical Change' in *Productivity-* 1986, XXVII, 1, 55-60.
35. Agarwal A. L. 'On estimation of Cobb Douglas Production Function in Selected Indian Industries' in *Artha Vijnana*, June 1986, V-28, N. 2, 152-170.
36. Wolff Edward-'Capital Formation and Productivity Convergence Over the Long Term' in *American Economic Review (AER)*—Vol-81, June-Dec., 1991, p. 565-579.
36. Upender M. 'Elasticity of L-productivity in Indian Manufacturing' in *Economic and Political Weekly (EPW),* 25 May 1996.
37. Krishna Kumar P. (2000) (Ch-16-pp-264-271 titled 'Returns to Scale and Technical Progress in Indian Manufacturing' in book by VVN Somayajulu's *"Econometric Studies of Economic Reforms in India"* published by Academic Foundation-2000.
38. Hasan Rana (2002)—'The impact of imported and domestic technologies on the productivity of firms: panel data evidence from Indian manufacturing firms'—*Journal of Development Economics-* 69-2002, pp. 23-49.
39. Sengupta D. N.—'Indian Manufacturing Industry—Growth Episode of the Eighties' in *Economic and Political Weekly (EPW),* May 29, 1999, pp. M-54-M62.
39[a]. Nath V. 'Regional Development Policies', *Economic and Political Weekly (EPW)*—Special Number July 1971, pp. 1601-1608.
40. Pandit M. L.- 'Industrial Income in the States-1960-69' *(Indian Journal of Regional Science,* Vol. VI, No. 2, 1974, p. 124-136. *("Spatial variations in Rates of Industrial Development in India" for M. Phil degree* at Centre for Studies in Regional Development, Jawaharlal Nehru University).

41. Kelkar V. L. and Kumar R. Industrial growth in 1980s- Emerging policy issues-*Economic and Political Weekly (EPW)* January 27 pp. 209-222, 1974.

42. Somayajulu V.V.N. –Industrial Development in India 1878-1978*'Productivity'*, 1980, No. 1, 1980, p. 9-66.

43. Somyajulu VVN—Structural Changes and Growth in Indian Industries –1946-1970, *Asian Economic Review*, December-1974, Vol. 17, No. 1, 2, 3.

44. Somayajulu V.V.N. Measurement of Structural Changes in Small versus Large Industries, 1965-1975, *Economic and Political Weekly (EPW)*, 1976.

45. Dinesh Awasthi—'Trends in regional Dispersal Inequalities in India 1961-1978'-*Anvesak*, Vol. 19, Nos: 1 and 2.

46. Uday Sekhar—Trends in Interstate disparities in Industrial Development in India 1961-1975—*Indian Economic Journal*—Oct. - Dec., 1982, Vol. 30, No. 2.

47. Somayajulu VVN—"Industrial Development of Andhra Pradesh-1956-1980"—*ICSSR Sponsored Study*. 1994. Of this, Industrial Stagnation and growth in Indian Industries of Andhra Pradesh, 1956-1985-Re-Examining Mid Sixties Explanations for India's Industrial retrogression, *Artha Vijnana*, Vol. 13, pp. 127, 140. Strategies of Industrialisation in Small Scale and Large Scale Industries of Andhra Pradesh..." In Indian Economy in I-O Framework. Regional dispersal of Industrial Incentives in Andhra Pradesh, 1982-1997. Production functions, TFP, growth and Employment Implications of Khadi and Village Industries, regional Diversification versus Convergence Hypothesis-retested for AP, *Economic Evaluation of APSFC-PRAJNAN.*

48. Nagaraj R (1994) 'Employment and Wages in Manufacturing Industries—Trends, Hypothesis and Evidence' in Special Article in *Economic and Political Weekly (EPW)*—Jan 22, 1994, p. 177-186.

49. Anuradha and AVVSK Rao—'An Analysis of Interstate Industrial Disparities in India 1970-71-1985-86'—*Indian Journal of Regional Science,* Vol. 27, 1995.

50. Jeemol Unni, N Lalitha and Uma Rani in a Special Article—'Economic Reforms and Productivity Trends in Indian Manufacturing', *Economic and Political Weekly,* Oct. 13, 2001.

51. V. Surender *'Indian Industries'* BR Publishing Corporation in Ch. 5, 1986.

52. Desai Rohit-Changing Pattern of Regional Industrial Diversification—A comparison over time—*Indian Journal of Regional science (IJRS),* Vol. 18, No. 1, 1986.

53. Jayadevan C M of National Labour Institute, Noida—*Indian Journal of Regional Science (IJRS),* p. 41-56, Vol. XXVII, Number 1 & 2, 1995.

54. K. Rana in *'Industrialisation of Hill States in India'* Deep and Deep Pub. Chapter VIII (1988).

55. Vijay Seth 'Industrialisation in India—A Spatial Perspective'—*Commonwealth Publications,* New Delhi-2, 1987.

56. Sunil Kumar 'Inter-state Variations in Productivity in Indian Manufacturing Sector: A Translog Approach'-*Indian Journal of Regional Science (IJRS),* Vol. XXXI, No. 2, 1999, pp. 82-94.

57. Mohan Rao—for 1973-93—*Economic and Political Weekly (EPW)*—Nov. 2, 1996.

58. Sandeep Kumar's published Ph.D. work on 'Regional Disparities in Industrial Development' (*Pub-Classical Publishing Company),* New Delhi-15, 1999.

59. Majumdar Sumit—'Fall and Rise of Productivity in Indian Industry- Has Economic Liberalisation Had an Impact?' in *Economic and Political Weekly (EPW)*-1998-99 (p-M-46- M-53).

60. Dhananjaya R. S. and Sasikala Devi, N. 'Total Factor Productivity in Indian Manufacturing: 1973-93', *Productivity Journal,* Vol. 39, No. 2, July-Sept 1998, pp. 310-320.

61. Kaplinsky, R-'India's Industrial Development: An Interpretative Survey' *World Development,* Vol. 25, No. 5, 1997, pp. 681-694.

Chapter 3

Materials and Methodology

INTRODUCTION

Abramovitz Moses, a pioneer in the field of productivity growth measurement demonstrated Total Factor Productivity (TFP) to be one of the main sources of measurement of output growth[1], as to serve for economic efficiency leading to welfare. The objective of industrialization being growth with efficiency and/or productivity leading to regional equity, this Chapter deals with the requisite framework of analytically sound Materials specification and Methodologies for demonstration of productivity-growth linkages. Such analytical framework and methodologies have to be verified empirically. This chapter intends to establish and empirically test measures of Partial and Total Factor Productivity to establish links between productivities and of growth and then to trace linkage with measures of regional dispersal of Industries. Thus this Chapter provides an Analytical Framework, Specifications, Materials and Methodologies for tracing inter-relations among partial and total factor productivity, capital intensity, growth of output and regional dispersal of Industries. This Framework serves to use both cross-section data of states and time series data of industrially significant periods of anlysis (medium term of each decade and long term of four decades, 1956-95).

A meaningful contribution is also expected from the TFP measures in the analysis of the role and rate of technological progress and in turn growth of Indian Manufacturing output resulting into regional industrial dispersal as to ensure equitable regional development towards rural backward regions.

This Chapter is divided into Four Sections as below: 1. Data- Bases, Materials and Measurement, Rationale for Formulae: 2. Adjustments Needed for and a Brief Review: 3. Classification, Aggregation and Adjustments and Data Limitations and Problems: 4. Analytical Framework for Growth and Regional Dispersal.

DATA-BASE, MATERIALS AND MEASUREMENT, RATIONALE FOR FORMULAE USED

Annual Survey of Industries (ASI) for data availability from secondary sources are to compute annual Growth Rates, Partial and Total Factor Productivity ratios through estimation of Cobb Douglas (CD) production function for each of the 20 two-digit industries based on National Industrial Classification—1987 over 1956-95 and for decadal periods, such as 1956-65, 1966-75, 1976-85 and 1986-95. Monthly Statistics of Production of Selected Industries were also used to cross checking, whenever necessary, that include data and results of research studies of Scholars, Institutes and Planning Commission's reports including those sponsored by Central and State governments. For State and Union Territory Dispersal analysis, *ASI-1973-1997- Data republished by EPW Research Foundation, Mumbai (2002)* was used to compute measures of Regional Dispersal. A Time Series Data of Annual Survey on Industries (1959-1971)[2] was also used for computing measures of Regional Dispersal.

Rationale for Time Period Chosen

Distinct decadal sub-periods and total 40 years period analysis were done. Those periods data fulfil Fabricant Law that period effects carry a common explanation to remain independent of cross industry correlations and a positive relationship between output growth and productivity growth.

Selection of Twenty 2-digit Industries

Selection of 20 two-digit manufacturing industries cover comprehensively total industrial sector. Choice of Electricity Gas and Steam (IN40 + 41 = 41) separately was needed for taking growth, productivity, dispersal of this major infrastructure sector, whose low performance could impede industrial growth. A more dis-aggregative industries classification would cause for problems of non-comparability over a long (40 years) time span and for distinct sub periods (each 10 years or less).

Data-Base

The Census of Manufacturing (CMI) data was published each year from 1946 till 1957 with details of input, output, capital and labour for 29 industries. The data was adjusted into 2 or 3-digit classification frame of Annual Survey of Industries (ASI). In the year 1958 only, Sample Survey of Manufacturing Industries (SSMI) was done and SSMI data was available for 3-digit ASIC industry groups. From 1959 onwards CSO-ASI developed a data- base for 63 industries in 3-digit for 200 industries in 7-digit industry groups and 5-digit industry groups of ASIC available for each of the calender year with effect from (w.e.f) 1959 to 1966 that led to adjusting them to the financial year. From ASI 1966 onwards the financial year-wise data came into vogue. In 1972, ASI data was not published.

The CMI[3] and ASI[4] were the databases for all industry studies[5]. But CMI and ASI data are not comparable because of differences in coverage and classification of industries.

Many studies in the first decade (1949-1957) of independence were restricted to use CMI data (S. S. Mehta). Some studies ASI data from 1959 onwards could not take into account the industrialisation phase of the Second Five-Year Plan period. Studies that used CMI and ASI data and adjusted for changes in classification were by Raj Krishna and S. S. Mehta[6] but some other studies[7] ignored these differences. M .M. Dadi and S. R. Hashim[8] took note of adjusted changes in coverage and in classifications in industrial statistics (1946-64) for each industry group at 2-digit level of aggregation.

ADJUSTMENTS NEEDED FOR AND A BRIEF REVIEW

Definitions, Measurements, Coverage and Scope of usage must satisfy consistency for policy-relevant analysis as otherwise non-comparability over time and space due to differences in definitions of units, classifications and coverage will not fulfil any meaningful analysis, interpretation and policy conclusion.

Census of Manufacturing (CMI) sector covered under registered (under Factories Act 1948) units employing 20 or more workers and using power for the period 1946-58 and confined to 29 out of 63 industry groups. From 1959 onwards, ASI dealt with 63 industry groups. ASI census covered all registered firms employing 50 or more workers with the aid of power (or 100 or more workers without power) and sample Part of ASI covered all registered firms employing 10-49 workers with power use and 50-100 workers without power use.

S. S. Mehta[9] (1980) traced comparable industry groups in both to be 27 groups of industries. Two groups that cannot be identified by S. S. Mehta were the 22nd group of CMI (aluminium, copper, brass) and 28th group of CMI (general engineering and electrical engineering). To make CMI and ASI comparable, two adjustments are necessary—one on industrial classification and the other on definitions of units covered as to be on a uniform basis, both needed for industry study. In between ASI and CMI SSMI, 1958 data cover factories employing 10-49 workers using power on any day of 1958 only with the result of non-uniform definitions and inconsistent classification making the three sets of data of industrial statistics of distinct periods non-comparable without adjustments appropriately.

Another problem has been that the composition of product mix has been undergoing a sharp, rapid structural change[10]. The derived composition of proportions, distinct growth rates and structural ratios show big jumps over 1960s and 1970s above the 1956-60 frame due to import substitution policy, export led strategy plus an outcome of indigenous enterprise in large, medium and small scale industries.

Data of CMI and SSMI were cross checked with the data from Statistical Abstracts of 1956, 1957, 1958, 1959, 1960 and tried to fit the 3-digit/4-digit factory-units into a two digit frame of NIC-1970 and NIC-1987 and structured our data to fit NIC-1987.

There was an additional problem. CSO-ASI inter-changed the Industry No. 30 representing Rubber and its products[11] into Industry No. 31 representing Chemicals and its products group from 1989-90. So the necessary corrections that had to be into the data set done for comparability and uniformity. To avoid similar nomenclature problems due to transition from NIC-1970 to NIC-1987 industries IN35 and IN36 were clubbed and called IN36. A similar procedure was followed when IN40 and IN41 was clubbed into IN41. IN39 was excluded from the analysis due to lack of consistent data. Industry number 20 and 21 was clubbed and called Industry Number-21.

Classification, Aggregation and Adjustments for Concordance

ASI Industries comparable to CMI industries[12] (Reference is given in the end of this Chapter).

S. No	CMI Industries	Comparable ASIC Code
1.	Wheat flour	205-1
2.	Rice milling	205-2
3.	Biscuit making	206
4.	Fruits and Vegetables	203
5.	Sugar	207-1
6.	Distilleries & Breweries	211+212+213
7.	Starch	209-7
8.	Oilseeds crushing	209-2+312-1
9.	Edible & hydrogenated oil	209-3
10.	Paints and Varnishes	313
11.	Soaps	319-6
12.	Tanning	291
13.	Cement	334
14.	Glass and Glassware	332
15.	Ceramics	333
16.	Plywood and tea-chest	251-2
17.	Paper and paper-board	271
18.	Matches	319-8
19.	Cottton Textiles	231-3
20.	Woollen Textiles	231-3
21.	Jute Textiles	231-2
22.	Non-ferrous metals	342
23.	Iron and Steel	341-1
24.	Bicycles	385
25.	Sewing Machines	360-11.5
26.	Electric Lamps	370-1.4
27.	Electric fans	370-1.3

Twenty industry groups at the 2-digit level of NIC-87 (National Industrial Classification-1987) have been chosen for classification and grouping with NIC-70, NIC-87, NIC-98 the various industries as given in our data-set in the 1956-95 period and compared.

The International Standard Industrial Classification (ISIC) and NIC-87 are comparable at each one's 3-digit classification[13].

Data Limitations and Adjustments

Without proper aggregation one cannot interpret properties of an aggregate production function that governs behaviour of TFP because of heterogeneity properties.

For the missing gaps in data sets, as in the year 1972, interpolation was resorted to since time series technique demanded a continuous data set. For some other missing values due to distortion in numerical values at its source of physical availability, one nearby point average of two nearby, where necessary was adopted. However, such cases were a few.

Major Group	Aggregated Industry
20-21:	Manufacture of Food Products
22:	Manufacture of Beverages, Tobbaco and Tobacco Products.
25:	(23 - Manufacture of Cotton Textiles) + (24- Wool, Silk and Synthetic Textiles)+(25: Jute, Hemp and Mesta Textiles).
26:	Manufacture of Textile Products (including Wearing Apparel, Other than Footwear)
27:	Manufacture of Wood and Wood Products, Furniture and Fixtures.
28:	Manufacture of Paper and Paper Products and Printing, Publishing and Allied Industries.
29:	Manufacture of Leather and products of leather
30:	Manufacture of basic chemicals and chemical products (except products of petroleum and coal) (includes inedible oils and fats-315 of NIC-70. surgical cotton and bandages.
31:	Manufacture of rubber, plastic, petroleum and coal products and processing of nuclear fuel.
32:	Manufacture of non-metallic mineral products (includes optical glass-321.5. of NIC-70)
33:	Basic metal and Alloys industries.
34:	Manufacture of metal products and parts, except machinery and transport equipment (includes stoves, hurricane lanterns-345; springs-349 of NIC-70)
35:	Manufacture of machinery, machine tools and parts except electrical machinery
36:	Manufacture of electrical/electronic machinery, apparatus, appliances and supplies and parts (includes 366.2-electronic control instruments)
36=35+36.	
37:	Manufacture of Transport equipment and parts.
38:	Other Manufacturing industries (includes 265.1-umbrellas, 321.5-optical glass, and 366.2-electronic control instruments from NIC-70)
40:	Electricity generation, transmission and distribution

Source: Concordance tables from NIC-87 to NIC-70 (at 3-digit table) in NIC-1987 document.

CSO evolved the SIC in 1962 but subsequent revisions were undertaken in NIC-1970, NIC-1987, NIC-1998. For purposes of comparability of time series a correspondence across these classifications was established with one-to-one correspondence. Wherever it is 'difficult' to establish, the criteria of pre-dominant activity was applied to prepare the concordance tables with NIC-1998[14].

Concordance of NIC 1987 from NIC 1970 at 3-digit level was as per concordance Tables NIC 1987 from the Expanded version of National Industrial Classification (NIC)-India 1970

Concordance table prepared to make NIC 1987 with NIC 1998

Sl.No.	NIC 1987 Code and Nomenclature of Industry Grouping	NIC 1998 Code and Nomenclature of Industry Grouping
1	2	3
1.	20+21	151 (Prod, Process, Preservation of meat,fish, fruit, vegetable, oils and fats)+152(Manf. of Dairy Products)+ 153 (Manf. of Grain Mill Products)+ 154 (Manf. of other food products)
2.	22	16 (Manf. of Tobacco Products) + 155(Manf of beverages)
3.	26	172 (Manf of Other Textiles)+173 (manf. of knitted and Crocheted Fabrics)+161(Manf. of Wearing Apparel except Fur apparel)
4.	27	20 (Manf. of Wood and products of Wood and Cork except furniture +Manf. of articles of straw and plating material)+ 361(Manf. of Furniture and manufacture NEC)
5.	28	21 (Manf. of Paper and paper Products) +22(publishing, printing and reproduction of recorded media)
6.	29	182 (dressing and dyeing of fur, manf. of articles of fur)+19 (tanning and dressing of leather, Manf. of luggage, handbags, saddlers and footwear)
7.	30	24 (Manf. of Chemical and Chemical Products)
8.	31	23 (Manf. of Coke, refined petroleum and refined fuel) +25(Manf. of rubber and plastic products)
9.	32	26 (manf. of non metallic mineral products)
10.	33	27(manf. of Basic metals)+371(Recycling of waste and scrap)
11.	34	2881(Manf. of structured metal products,tanks, reservoirs, steam generators, manf of structured metal products)+ 2812(mnf. of container of metals, whether or not fitted with tops, metal for LPG mnf. of radiation boilers)+ 289(mnf. of other fabricated metal products)

...(Contd.)

1	2	3
12.	35+36	2813(mnf. of steam generator except central heating hot water boilers) + 29(mnf. of machinery equipment, NEC)+ 30 (mnf. of office, accounting and computing machinery)+ 31 (mnf. of electrical apparatus and machinery) + 32 (mnf. of radio, TV, communication equipment and apparatus)
13.	37	383 (mnf. of motor vehicles)+385(mnf. of motor cycle and bicycle) + 389(mnf. of transport equipment and NEC)
14.	38	33(mnf. of medical precision and optical instruments) + 369(mnf. of NEC)
15.	40+41	401(collection, distribution and purification of water)

Industries from 1956-59 data set of CMI (1956-58) included in NIC 87 classification:

Sl.No.	CMI(1956-59)	NIC 1987
1.	Wheat Flour, Rice milling, biscuit baking, fruit, vegetable processing, sugar and gur, starch, vegetable oils	20+21
2.	Distilleries and breweries	22
3.	Textiles, Dyeing, Bleaching,Finishing and processing including Mercirising, Finishing, Calendering, Glazing, Proofing, etc.	23
4.	Wool Baling, and Pressing (239.3)	24
5.	Varnishes, matches, paints	30
6.	Glass (321), Ceramics(323),Cement (324, 327)	32
7.	Aluminium, Brass and Copper	33
8.	Sewing machines and fans	35
9.	Bicycles	37

1960 Classification-Statistical Abstracts[15]

NIC 1987(two digit level)	3-digit level of NIC 1987
1	2
20+21	201 + 202 + 203 + 204 + 205 + 206 + 209 + 212 + 219
22	220 + 221 + 222 + 224 + 225
23	230 to 236

...(Contd.)

1	2
26	260 + 261 + mnf of wearing apparel except footwear
27	270 + 273 + 275 + 276 + 279
28	280 + 281 + 289
29	290 + 293 + 295
30	300 + 301 + 303 + 309
31	310 + 311 + 312 + 314 + 315 + 316 + 319
32	320 + 321 + 322 + 323 + 324 + 329
33	330 + 331 + 332 + 339
35	350 + 351 + 352 + 353 + 357 + 358 + 385
36	360 + 361 + 362 + 363 + 364 + 365 + 366 + 367 + 369
37	370 + 371 + 372 + 375 + 376 + 377 + 379
38	380 + 381 + 382 + 383 + 386 + 389
40 + 41	400 + 401 + 410 +

For the Year 1965

NIC1987 in 1965 year	3-digit level of NIC 1987
20 + 21	202.1 + 203 + 204 + 205.1 + 205.3 + 206 + 207.1 + 207.2 + 208 + 209.1 + 209.10 + 209.2 + 209.3 + 209.4 + 209.5 + 209.6 + 209.7 + 209.8 + 209.9 + 312.1
22	211 + 212 + 213 + 214 + 220.1 + 220.2 + 220.3 + 220.4 + 220.5 + 220.6 + 204 (mnf. of ice)
23	231.7 + 231.1 + 239.1
24	239.3 + 231.3 + 231.4 + 231.5
25	239.2 + 239.4
26	231.6 + 231.8 + 231.9 + 232 + 233 + 239.3 + 239.5 + 239.6 + 239.8
34	260.2 + 260.3 + 350.1 + 350.2 + etc.

For the year 1968

Sl.No.	NIC 1987 (2-digit level)	1968 (3-digit level)
1.	20+21	202.1+207.1+209.10
2.	22	399.6 (mnf. of Ice)

For the Year 1969

1981-1969 year on (2 digit level)	Statistical Abstracts-1969 correspondence of 1987 (3-digit taken into account)
	201 + 202 + 203 + 204.1 + 205 + 206 + 208 + 209 + 312
	211 + 212 + 213 + 214 + 220
	232 + 233 + 239 + 243 + 244
	251 + 252 + 259 + 260
	280 + 271
	291 + 293 + 241
	311 + 313 + 319
	300 + 329 + 321
	331 + 332 + 333 + 334 + 339
	341 + 342
	350
	360 + 370
	381 + 382 + 383 + 385 + 386 + 389
	391 + 392 + 393 + 394 + 395 + 399
	511

For 1970

NIC 87(2-digit level)	NIC70(3-digit level)
30	311.1.1 + 311.1.2 + 311.1.3 + 311.2.1 + 311.1.1 + 311.4 + 311.9 + 311.10 + 311.5 + 311.6
31	319.9 + 319.10 + 321 + 300.1
32	399.17 + 331.10 + 331 + 332 + 333 + 334 + 339
34	260.2 + 350 (–350.9 + 350.1)
37	381 + 382 + 383 + 385 + 386 + 389
38	391 + 399 + 392-393 + 394 + 235

Theoretical and Analytical Framework

The theoretical and analytical framework of our study integrates two strands of knowledge relating to measures and measurements, Growth and of Regional Dispersal and their causal relationship. First, it analyses and interprets Growth Measures of Size Variables and Structural Ratios of Partial Productivities of Factors and Total Factor Productivity

(TFP) and relates Returns to Scale, Total Factor Productivities of 2-digit Indian Industries. Then it finds out Herfindahl-Hirshman Index and Coefficient of Variation of 5 size variables and Structural Ratio of Capital Intensity (K/L), across different identified States and UT wise. It also uses Grossack's method of determining and understanding the process evenness or otherwise of regional dispersal over four decades and through cross- checking results. Finally, causal analysis as to whether dispersal of Industries is caused by TFPG, K/L, Capital Productivity and Labour Productivity or a combination of them was done.

The concept of the Production function specifies the technical relationships between attainable outputs and a specified set of inputs for a given technology with the relevant parameters of production function providing all possible [feasible and/or efficient] outputs for a given combination of inputs and factor use. An optimum capacity output is the most efficient unique one corresponding to the unique combination of input and factors employed. Scale of operation increases upto that optimum capacity with minimum average cost of production, given fixed market prices of inputs, factors and outputs. Cobb Douglas production function was estimated to get parameters which are exponents of Labour and Capital, since those coefficients are output elasticities of Labour and Capital respectively used as weights for TFP measurements in Domar TFP measures for individual industries at two-digit level of disaggregation[16].

The study adopts Cobb Douglas Production function due to its easy adaptability for both embodied and disembodied capital with its assumption of unitary elasticity of substitution. This facilitates analysis of measures of returns to scale, changes in factor intensities, output elasticities of factor inputs and analysis of TFP as in Domar. The output elasticities of factors are used as weights for factors while computing TFP. This analysis helps in inferring growth and employment implications of different industries assuming unitary elasticity of substitution as given for Cobb Douglas production Function. Every production function can yield four inter-linked parameters. They are; Elasticity of Substitution, returns to scale, efficiency and capital intensity. K/L reveals the capital intensive-ness of technology while elasticity of substitution determines the specification of the production function.

CDPF estimation provides returns to scale parameter as sum of output elasticities of factors/inputs that could be estimated directly as regression coefficients of log-linear transformation of CDPF.

The constant returns to scale continuous production function (CRSCPF) is another form of aggregate production function expressing the factors and outputs in per capita terms and is widely used in Theoretical models of economic growth with/or without technical progress.

The theoretical framework and policy implications of Neoclassical Economic growth and production function can be extended to include the role of technical progress or TFP. If such changes in technology result in changes in ratio of marginal products, technological change is non-neutral, otherwise it is neutral. Technology is Hicks neutral. If K/L constant, ratio of marginal productivity is also constant.

The Arithmetic Index of TFP:

The Arithmetic Index was introduced by Abramovitz[17] (1956) and J.W. Kendrick[18] (1961). $\Delta A^k t = \Delta Q_t / Q_0 \div [\, s_0 (\Delta L\, ^t/L_0) + (1\text{-}s^0)\, \Delta K\, ^t/K_0]$

where $s_0 = PL_0 / P_0 Q_0$ where s_0 is share of Labour in Net Value Added in base year '0'. P_{k0} and P_{L0} are prices of Capital and Labour in base year '0'.

Kendrick Index of TFP has an implicit production function whose output is linear combination of appropriately weighted shares of factors.

Similarly, Solow[19] method of finding TFP provides scope for analysis of capital deepening and capital widening possibilities through the Solow Fundamental equation: $6\text{ K} = s\, f(k) - n\, k$ where 6 K is rate of accumulation per L or capital intensity which is positive for a capital deepening industry. $sf(k)$ are investible resources per capita, out of internal savings to meet labour force growth rate (n) determined exogeneously and 's' is savings rate that is amenable to monetary and fiscal manipulation. The policies of subsidy, incentive, controls regulation can be obtained if their consequences for influencing 6K to draw guidelines for industrial investment planning.

Evsey Domar[20] said that in Kendrick's formulation, marginal products change proportionately to TFP and so are not independent of TFP. Thus MRTS did not vary when price or quantity varied. Thus it represented a case of circular reasoning. But Kendrick countered this by continuously changing weights but it did not change the nature of the problem encountered. So very acute interpretation is necessary in case of Kendrick results.

Domar preferred the Geometric Index as rates of growth are directly measured in a multiplicative production function of Cobb Douglas type $V_t = A_t^D\, L_t\, K_t$). So, $6A_t^D / A_t^D = 6V/V - (\alpha 6L/L + (1 - \alpha)\, 6K/K)$ is the rate of TFPG.

Domar also suggested fixed weights that are output elasticities of Labour and Capital similar to Kendrick weights (*i.e.*) shares of L and K in Value Added and both assumed Constant Returns to Scale (CRS) providing the necessary conditions for competitive equilibrium as in the CD form of p. f.

Solow's Geometric Index of TFP

In a pioneering contribution, Solow allowed the factor prices and marginal products to change continuously over time and presented his Geometric Index as an improvement over Kendrick and Abramovitz.

Solow started with a more general pf. $Q = A_t^S\, F(\text{K.L.})$.

Since $A^S\,(t)$ varies with time and independent of K and L, technological change is by assumption, disembodied and Hick's neutral. Under competitive conditions, $6Q/Q = 6A^S/A^S - (\alpha 6K/K + \beta\, 6L/L)$.

Assuming CRS and defining $q = Q/L$, $k = Q/K$, Production Function turns out to be Constant Returns to Scale Continous Production Function (CRSCPF), then

$\therefore\; 6q/q = 6A^S/A + \alpha\, 6K/K$ where $6q/q$ is the rate of increase in output per worker.

The Solow growth rate is also derived from the following:

$$G\,A_t^S = g_Q\,(t) - [s_t\,(g_L(t) + (1 - s_t)\,g_K(t)$$

Where g's are annual growth rates in the respective variables and s_t is income share of Labour at time t.

A_t^S index can be computed assuming A_0 =100 for the base period '0' and setting up

$$A_t^S = A_t^{S\text{-}1}\,[1 + g_A(t)],\ \text{for } t = 1, 2, 3\ldots$$

Solow Index uses shifting weights, unlike Kendrick and Domar that use constant weights for the total time period under consideration.

Analytical Framework for Regional Dispersal

Herfindahl-Hirshman Index ($HHI = \Sigma X_i^2 - [\Sigma X_i]^2$)[21] and Coefficient of Variation (C.V. = SD/ Mean of C) formed the measures of dispersal of 5 variables and structural ratios for each of the 2-digit industry of which the two measures together taken as the first stage of analysis for the Study of industries over space/regions or states. But based on HHI or HI and CV alone, whether expansion in industries is evenly shared by all spatial units cannot be inferred because these two provide the extent of concentration/dispersal in aggregate for all States/UT over All India. So in this study, Grossack's method[22] is used to explain the evenness or otherwise of regional dispersal/concentration of industries. Grossack derived a method of analysing the process of concentration of economic power by use of regression techniques and Herfindahl Index.

To begin with, HI_{xi} (where x in this analysis pertains to size variables or structural ratios in some particular year) where i =1......n. For Grossack, X_i is the market share of the ith firm as a ratio and n is the number of firms in the industry. If x_i is the deviation of the ith firm's share from the mean, then the above equation can be written as $HI_x = \Sigma x_i^2 + 1/n$.

Grossack identifies the two parts comprising the HI (*i*) sum of squared deviations and the (*ii*) reciprocal of the numbers of firms. Then he defines an initial permanent HI for a particular, say, base year 0 and since 'n' is independent of both base and terminal years, the permanent index can be distinguished from the observed index in the sum of squares term. He then substitutes sum of squares of the permanent components in the observed index and proceeds to infer a value for the sum of squares index[23].

Grossack distinguished permanent and transitory components by identifying firms that have large shares of a particular market in a particular period i.e. beneficiaries of a set of advantages relative to the smaller firms in that market. Among these advantages are patent holdings control of scarce resources, good trade conditions access to favourable financing, etc. Some of these advantages are permanent and some transitory. He hypothesized that these advantages are the ultimate bases of the market power of larger firms. However, the inference of market power shares of large versus small firms is of no concern to our regional dispersal analysis of each industry group wherein there is no further breakup or disaggregation of either industry group of state or UT of India as to have units of measurement and to check for further analysis of nature of and extent of shares in the aggregate (s) concerned.

VARIABLES, DEFINITIONS AND CONCEPTS

FACT = Factories FC = Fixed Capital

NW = No. of workers TI = Total Inputs

GVA = Gross Value Added NVA = Net Value Added

NW/FACT = Employment/per factory O_2F = NVA/FACT= Output Growth per Factory

KI2 = FC/NW= Capital Intensity

K2P = NVA/FC = Measure of Capital Productivity (Technical Coefficient or Partial Productivity Measure)

K1P = GVA/FC = Measure of Capital Productivity (Technical Coefficient or Partial Productivity Measure)

L1P = NVA/NW = Measure of Labour Productivity

L2P = GVA/NW= Measure of Labour Productivity (Structural Ratio)

KF = FC/FACT = Growth of Capital Employed per Factory (Structural Ratio)

OIF = GVA/FACT = Output Growth per Factory at Current Prices = Measure of Industrial Growth (Structural Ratio)

CMI data by size define the following thus:

Fixed Capital : This is the aggregate book value of land, buildings, plant, machinery and transport equipment. Other fixed assets such as furniture and fixture are in current prices. Book value is not given separately and so no adjustment in capital data is possible. This is deflated by the Wholesale Price Index of Machinery and Transport at 1981-82 prices.

Working Capital : Working Capital, also in money terms, consists of aggregate money value of materials, stores, fuels, semi-finished goods and by-products, cash in hand at the bank and algebraic sum of sundry creditors.

Productive Capital : It consists of both fixed and working capital both added to arrive at total productive capital in real terms.

Number of People Employed (L) : It consists of workers and persons other than workers.

Definitions and Concepts[24] (ASI-1995-96):

Gross Output: Defined to include ex-factory value of products and by-products manufactured during the accounting year. It also includes receipts for non-industrial services rendered to others, receipt for work done for others on materials supplied by them, value of electricity sold and net balance of goods sold in the same condition as purchased.

Gross output =Value of output = Total output = GVA.

Net Value Added (NVA) – is increment to value of goods and services that is contributed by factory and is obtained by deducting the value of total inputs and depreciation from value of output.

Therefore, NVA = Value of output- total input- depreciation.

Total Inputs (TI) – comprises total value of fuels, materials consumed (as defined below) as well as expenditures such as 1. Cost of contract and commission work done by others on materials supplied by factory. 2. Cost of materials consumed for repair and maintenance of a factory's fixed assets including cost of repairs and maintenance work done by others to factory's fixed assets. 3. inward freight and transport charges; rates and taxes excluding income tax, postage, telephone and telex expenses, insurance charges, banking charges, cost of printing and stationary.

Capital: Value of capital refers to gross value of fixed capital plus inventories. The value of fixed capital as reported in CMI and ASI represent the written down (book) values (where depreciation is calculated according to the rates allowed by the income tax authorities) and hence do not reflect the true value of capital. *Actually it is the replacement cost of capital that is congenial to production functions.* The empirical evidence would suggest that the relationship between replacement cost of new K and output is more stable because efficiency of assets does not decline as accounting procedures show.

The gross value and purchase price (suitably adjusted for price variations) is the closest to capital theory.[26] So far as the value of inventories is concerned, since it is available in current prices, it is simply added to the adjusted value of fixed capital to arrive at the figure of total capital.

Productive Capital (PC)- Fixed Capital (FC) + Working Capital (WC)

Invested Capital (IC) = Fixed Capital (FC) + Physical Working Capital (PWC)

FC refers to land, building, plant, machinery, furniture, etc.

WC refers to stocks of materials, fuels, semi-manufactured products, etc.

WC = PWC + cash deposit in hand and at bank + net balance receipts over amounts payable. It excludes unused overdrafts facility, fixed deposits, advance for fixed assets, loans and advances, long-term loans.

Physical Working Capital (PWC) = defined to include all physical inventories, owned, held or controlled by factory such as fuel, materials, stores, etc. It includes stock of materials, fuels, stores,etc. purchased for re-sale, semi-finished goods and work in progress on account of others, and goods made by factory ready for sale at end of accounting year. It also includes finished goods processed by others from raw materials supplied by factory and held by them. However, it excludes finished goods processed by factory from raw materials supplied by others.

Fixed Capital (FC)- represents depreciated value of fixed assets owned by the factory as on the closing day of the accounting year. It includes fixed assets of head office allocable to factory and also full value of assets taken on hire-purchase basis (whether fully paid or not) excluding interest element. Fixed assets are those that have a normal productive life of more than one year. It excludes intangible assets and assets solely used for post-manufacturing activities such as sale, storage and distribution.

Workers = Excluded are persons holding positions of supervision or management or employed in administrative office, store keeping and welfare sections, sales department as those engaged in purchase of raw materials, etc. and in the production of fixed assets for factory and watch- and- ward staff.

It included all persons employed directly or thro' any agency whether for wages or not and engaged in any manufacturing process or in any kind of work incidental/committed to manufacturing. Also included are labour engaged in repairs and maintenance or production of fixed assets for factory's own use or labour employed for generating electricity or producing coal, gas are included.

ASI defines workers as those that are employed in the manufacturing processes (or any other kind of job incidental to or connected with the manufacturing process).

REFERENCES

1. Abramovitz Moses: Welfare Quandaries and Productivity Concerns-Presidential Address delivered at the Ninety-third meeting of American Economic Association, September 6, 1980, Denver, Colorado-*American Economic Review*-March 1981, Vol. 71, No. 1, pp. 1-17.
2. Annual Survey on Industries (1959-1971) published by the *Central Statistical Organisation* (CSO), Government of India (GOI), Kolkata.
3. *Census of Manufacturing Industries*—GoI, Directorate of Indian Statistics, 1946-58, Manager of Publications.
4. ASI-GoI, CSO, ASI-1959-65, Department of Statistics, Cabinet Secretariat, Calcutta.
5. Mehta S.S., *Productivity and Production Functions of Selected Indian Industries*, Concept Publishing House, 1974, p. 18.
6. Raj Krishna and S. S. Mehta- Productivity Trends In Large Scale Industries, *Economic and Political Weekly (EPW)*, Oct. 26, 1968;
7. Chatterjee, Anil Kumar- Productivity in Selected Manufacturing, *Economic and Political Weekly (EPW)*, Nov 24, 1973; RR Singh- Productivity Trends and Wages-*Eastern Economist*, April 29, 1966). Chatterjee and Singh ignored these differences.
8. Dadi and Hashim—An adjusted capital Series desired for Indian Manufacturing 1946-64 *Anvesak*, December-1971 takes note of and adjustments for both. At industry level, Dadi and Hashim have adjusted the data at only two- digit level of aggregation in Dadi M. M. and Hashim S. R. - *Capital-Output Relations in Indian Manufacturing*, Dept of Economics, Faculty of Arts, M. S. University of Baroda, Baroda.
9. S. S. Mehta S. S., *op.cit.*, pp. 20.
10. Mehta S.S., *op.cit.*
11. *Summary Results for the Factory Sector-ASI Reports,* 1989-90.
12. Source: M. M. Dadi 1973—*Indian Economic Journal;* 1980-81, Vol. 28; Oct. - Dec. 1980; Vol. 2, pp. 28; Note: Both CMI and ASI use the same definition for 'workers' and 'other than workers' as used in Factory Act 1948. (Previous Page in this Chapter)

13. Balance Robert and Sinclair Stuart—*Collapse and Survival: Industry Strategy in a Changing World;* 1983-George Allen and Unwin—UK. Ch. 1, pp. 12.

14. Industrial Classification in terms of NIC 1987: (Source) *EPW Research Foundation*—A Data Base on Industrial Structure in India-ASI 1973-74-1997-98, p. 1096-1108.

15. Data Gaps in these early years till 1965 were filled up by making a study of the Statistical Abstracts.

16. Sims C. A -'The Dynamics of Productivity Change—A Theoretical and Empirical Study' *(Unpublished dissertation, Harvard Univ,* Aug 1967), suggested contribution of K and L to gross output separately from contribution of material input. But a separability assumption, though unrealistic, is required such as: $Q^1=f(K,L,K)=g(h(K,L),M)$ where Q^1 is gross output, M is material input and h(K,L) would be real value added). Susanta Basu in *Quaterly Journal of Economics (QJE),* Vol. 111, pp. 639-1268, 1996 (Pro Cyclical Productivity: Increasing Returns or cyclical utilisation?) also says that material inputs do not have variable utilisation rates and materials are likely to be used in fixed proportions with value added.

17. Abramovitz M-Resource and output trends in USA since 1870-Papers and Proceedings of *American Economic Association (AEA),* 1956, pp. 5-23.

18. Kendrick J.W.-Productivity in the USA—*NBER,* Princeton.

19. Solow- Technical Change and Aggregate Production Function—*Review of Economics and Statistics,* Vol. 39, 1957, pp. 312-20.

20. Domar (1962) 'On Total Productivity and All That'—*Journal of Political Economy,* Dec. 1970.

21. HI is computed as : $H=\Sigma X_i^2 - [\Sigma X_i]^2 = \Sigma X_i^2 - [n\,\bar{X}_i]^2 = \Sigma X_i^2 - n^2\,\bar{X}_i^{\,2} = \Sigma X_i^2/n - n\,\bar{X}_i^2 = \Sigma X_i^2/n^2 - X_i^2$

22. Grossack I. M.—"One Concept and measurements of permanent industrial concentration"—*Journal of Political Economy,* Vol. 60 (A) 1970, pp. 745-760.

23. Grossack I .M.— "Towards integration of static and dynamic measures of concentration" *Review of Economics and Statistics,* Vol. 48, 1965, pp. 301-308.

From the product moment form of the regression coefficient $b = r\,\sigma_y/\sigma_x$ where r is the coefficient of correlation of the market shares in the two years and σ_y and σ_x are the standard deviations of the shares in the subscript years.

24. Annual Survey of Industries (ASI)-1995-96.

26. Dadi and Hashim—Adjusted capital series for Indian Manufacturing, *Anvesak* -1946-1964)p-236-248, Vol. 1.

Analysis of Growth Rates and Determinants

INTRODUCTION

This Chapter 4 analyses 1-growth rates of 2-digit (SIC*) industries over a 40-year period from 1956 to 1995 and ranking the industries; 2- Total Factor Productivity Growth (TFPG) of the 2-digit industries by Kendrick, Domar and Solow measures with relevant weights to labour and capital growth rates, for which purpose Cobb Douglas (CD) production function (pf) was estimated to find out output elasticities (exponents) of labour and capital. The estimated Cobb Douglas production function exponents sum provides to check for returns to scale (increasing, decreasing, constant) for each 2-digit group of Indian industries for 40 year period of 1956-95 and 10-year time periods each covering in sequence a total period of 1956-95.

This Chapter has another section bringing out causal factors as determinants of growth rates linking with partial productivities of factors, similarly with Capital Intensity (K/L) and with TFPG; so as to show whether growth in output is propelled by growth in partial productivities of factors, Capital Intensity (K/L) ratio and TFPG in each of the industries in the relevant periods of study.

The analysis of growth rates and of their causal factors indicated relative importance of industries so that policy-guidelines can be better inferred. Growth rates are the estimated

* SIC: Standard Industrial Classification of India is closely similar, at two digit level, to Annual Survey of Industries Classification (ASIC) 1959 (onwards), as followed in ASI (Census Part) and NSS (Sample Part of ASI) Reports, Published by Central Statistical Organisation (CSO), NSS Organisation (NSSO), Government of India, New Delhi. Accordingly, 2-digit level Industry Groups in all these Reports had the same/similar names, for each of Industry Groups; hence the two digit industry classification is justified for comparability.

regression coefficients of Semi log form: $log\ Y = a + bt$. The results and the major findings of this Chapter 4 are further investigated in the following chapters: to find out as to whether they can serve as causal factors to explain the regional dispersal of 2-digit industries and to understand the economic mechanism involved for the purpose (s) and to trace the desired linkages of dispersal, growth, structural ratios and of size variables.

ANALYSIS OF GROWTH RATES OF VARIABLES AND STRUCTURAL RATIOS

Analysis of Growth Rates of Factories

Table 4.1. Growth Rates of Factories of 2-digit Industries in 1956-95 (in the order of ranking)

Ind. Name	Ind. No.	Gr. Rt.(descend.order)
Food Prd.	21	33.1%
Leath Prds	29	19.2%
Met.Prd	34	18.9%
Tex	25	17.5%
Ru-Pet-Co	31	14.5%
Bever'g	22	12.6%
NmMp	32	10.4%
Paper	28	10.1%
Trans. Eq.	37	9.4%
Wood Prd.	27	9.2%
Chem.	30	9.2%
Basic MA	33	8.8%
M. o. t. T.	36	7.9%
Tex Prd.	26	7.7%
OMI	38	5.8%
EGS	41	1.2%

Food Products (Industry No. 21 = 20 + 21) grew at 33.1 per cent p.a. (maximum) over the years 1956-95 which is a non-durable essential for high growth and base population with their high daily consumption norm of MPC (APC) and Engel Elasticity. Then followed the many User and Intermediate (Input) Industries whose growth rates were: 19.2 per cent growth rate in case of Leather Products (IN29), 18.9 per cent in Metal Products (IN34), 17.5 per cent for Textiles in Silk, Woollen, Cotton and Jute (IN25=23+24+25), 14.5 per cent in Rubber, Petroleum and Coal (IN31) and 12.6 per cent in of Beverages (IN22).

Paper Products (IN28) grew at 10.1 per cent and Non-Metallic Mineral Products (IN32) at 10.4 per cent. They serve as material inputs to economic and social overhead sectors and in services like construction, education, electronics and software development in the country. In turn many sunrise industries get developed for government consumption and investment goods industries.

Wood and Wood Products (IN27) is an intermediate good serving the housing activity and its growth at 9.2 per cent is due to high wage rate. Chemical and Chemical Products (IN30) at 9.2 per cent, a sunrise industry since 1970s and 1980s, had little/no growth in 1950s and 1960s Pharmaceuticals grew in 1990s as new sector capable of further growth.

Similarly noted is Growth of Transport Equipment and Parts (IN37) at 9.4 per cent, a key infrastructure and capital goods industry.

But Intermediate Industry like Basic Metals and Alloys (IN33), growing at a low of 8.7 per cent and a User Industry like Textile Products (IN26) at 7.7 per cent growth lagged behind due to lack of production planning though in the latter context, material of textile products for garments was high.

Capital goods industries like Electrical and Non-Electrical Machinery other than transport comprising IN35 and IN36, a key sector for enhancing industrial growth in an economy planned on basis of heavy industry strategy, grew at 7.9 per cent, showed a slowdown in the latter 3 decades.

Other Manufacturing Industry (IN38) at 5.8 per cent revealed the second lowest growth rates while Electricity, Gas and Steam (IN41 = 40 + 41) at 1.2 per cent shows the lowest growth rate.

The long-term trends in this comparative study of growth rates factories of 2-digit industries in India speak of likely weak forward and backward linkages and non-conformity of industrial units in numbers with lack of planning to raise the requisite number(s) of units that generate materials, capital, infrastructures and industrial output growth rates needed for final consumption goods, investment goods and exports of Indian economy. However, the earlier analysis should take into account the differential scale of operation of the units. These two together is reflected in their final result of net Value Added of industries.

Table (4.2) shows growth in NVA being the highest in case of Electricity, Gas and Steam (IN41) at 18.1 per cent followed by 17.2 per cent growth rate in Textile Products (IN26) and 17.1 per cent in Leather and Leather Products (IN29). This was followed with growth rates ranging between 12.6 per cent in case of Food Products (IN21) and 15.9 per cent growth rate in case of Chemical and Chemical Products (IN31). The second lowest is seen in Wood and Wood Products (IN27) at 11.1 per cent and the lowest NVA growth rate has been recorded by Textiles (IN25) at 10.1 per cent. However, Textile Products grew at one of the highest rates at 17.2 per cent but textiles showed the lowest growth at 10.1 per cent. This indicates lack of production planning possibly due to shortages, bottlenecks, lack of demand and weak linkages.

Analysis of Growth Rates in Net Value Added (NVA) of Individual Industries for 1956-95

Table 4.2. Net Value Added (NVA) Growth Rates (in descending order)

Ind. Name	Ind.No.	Gr. Rt (in descend.order)
EGS	41	18.1
Tex Prd	26	17.2
Lea.Prd	29	17.1
Ru-P-Co	31	15.9
Bever'g	22	15.9
TransEq	37	14.9
MotT	36	14.9
Met.Prd	34	13.7
Ba MA	33	13.7
Paper	28	13.3
NmMp	32	13.2
Chem.	30	13.2
OMI	38	13.1
Food Prd	21	12.6
Wood Prd	27	11.1
Tex	25	10.1

Analysis in Growth Rates in Gross Value Added (GVA)

Compared to NVA growth rates, the GVA growth rates were usually higher or marginally lower or the same. For example, in case of Textile Products (IN26) where GVA growth rate was lower at 16.5 per cent compared to NVA growth rate of 17.2 per cent Electricity, Gas and Steam (IN41) GVA growth at 18 per cent was similar to 18.1 per cent of NVA growth in that industry. In Textiles of Cotton, Woollen, Silk and Jute (IN25), lowest GVA as well as lowest NVA is recorded. Rubber, Petroleum and Coal (IN31) had the highest growth rate in GVA at 18.2 per cent while NVA growth rate in IN31 was moderately high at 15.9 per cent. Leather and Leather Products (IN29) GVA growth rate was 18.1 per cent while NVA growth rate showed 17.1 per cent. Wood and Wood Products (IN27) with GVA growth of 12.9 per cent but growth in NVA was 11.1 per cent, though both values were on lower in their respective categories. So is the case with Electrical and Non Electrical Machinery other than transport (IN36) where NVA recorded 14.9 per cent growth but GVA showed 16.4 per cent. Paper showed NVA at 13.3 per cent but GVA at 15.3 per cent. While wider differences in growth rates in GVA and NVA of a few industries like Paper, Wood, MotT, could be due to growth of capital depreciation or capital replacement or both, in all other industry groups shown above, growth in capital depreciation and replacement may not be too high to be accounted for.

Table 4.3. Growth Rates of GVA of 2-digit Industries in 1956-95 (in their order of rankings)

Ind Name	Ind No.	Gr. Rt. (in descend. Order)
Ru-P-Co	31	18.2
Lea..Prd	29	18.1
EGS	41	18
Tex Prd	26	16.5
Bever'g	22	16.4
MotT	36	16.4
Chem.	30	16.3
Tran.Eq	37	15.6
Paper	28	15.3
Met.Prd	34	15.3
Bas. MA	33	15.2
NmMp	32	14.8
OMI	38	13.9
Food Prd	21	13.2
Wood Prd	27	12.9
Tex	25	11.8

ANALYSIS OF GROWTH RATES IN EMPLOYMENT OR NUMBER OF WORKERS (NW) ABSORBED IN RESPECTIVE INDUSTRIES

In the following subsection, growth analysis of employment or number of workers (NW) absorbed in industries is done (Table 4.4) because the employment growth variable may differ from the result of output growth.

The low growth rates in employment of number of workers (NW) in most of the 2- digit manufacturing industries confirms that industries except Food Products (14.7% growth rate) are in general low labour-intensive ones in large scale, medium scale industries and in some small scale industries too. Employment growth rates ranged from 5.1 per cent in Textile Products (IN26) to 7.7 per cent in Rubber, Petroleum and Coal (IN31). Beverages (IN22) at 7.7 per cent is followed by Leather and Leather Products (IN29) at 6.9 per cent and Electricity, Gas and Steam (IN41) at 6.7 per cent, while Paper

Table 4.4. Growth Rates of NW of 2-digit Industries in 1956-95 (in the order of their rankings)

Ind Name	Ind No.	Gr. Rt. (in descend. Order)
Food Prd	21	14.7
Ru-Pe-Co	31	7.7
Bever'g	22	7.1
Leath.Prd	29	6.9
EGS	41	6.7
Tex Prd	26	5.1
NmMp	32	4.3
TransEq	37	4.3
Tex	25	2.3
Met.Prd	34	3.1
Wood Prd	27	2.2
Paper	28	3.8
Chem.	30	3.8
Basic MA	33	3.9
MotT	36	3.9
OMI	38	1.8

and Paper Products (IN28), Chemical and Chemical Products (IN30), Non-Metallic Mineral Products (IN32), Basic Metals and Alloys (IN33), Metal Products (IN34), Machinery Other than Transport (IN36) and Transport Equipment and Parts (IN37) ranged in employment growth rates between 3.1 per cent and 4.3 per cent. It also reflects of heavy industry strategy since 1956 to 1980s and no employment planning motivations on the part of industries (both large scale and small scale and even to date). But influence of globalisation and import liberalisations of capital inflows during the last two decades and Economic reforms of Industry, Trade, etc. New Economic Policies or Structural Adjustment and Stabilisation Policies- all addressed to emergence of capital Markets, Stock Markets with lower interest rates for financial, and physical fixed, working capital use, capital intensive speculative activities of real Estates, Five Star Elite Culture. No skilled, unskilled employment planning for implementation is envisaged in practice to employ them, particularly due to the last two decades brain drain of the trained and technically and professionally educated at huge costs in Indian Higher and Vocational courses Learning Centres, financed, encouraged and helped by Globalisation, Import Liberalisation of Capital Inflows, Unutilisation and Underutilisation of capital/ capacities.

Low employment growth rate figures in Beverages (2.2%), textiles (2.3%) and other manufacturing industries (1.8%) point to lacunae in employment planning and if properly planned can reveal far more substantive employment absorption capacity.

Analysis of Growth Rates in Another Employment Variable, i.e. WF defined as NW/FACT Described as Number of Workers per Factory in each Industry

Table 4.5. Growth Rates in Employment Per Factory in 2-digit Industries for 1956-95

(in descending Order)

Ind Name	Ind No.	Growth Rates (in descend.Order)
Tex	25	7.2
Wood Prd	27	6.9
Ru-Pet-Co	31	6.7
Leath.Prd	29	6.2
Paper	28	6.2
NmMp	32	6.1
Food Prd	21	5.8
Met.Prd	34	5.7
Bever'g	22	5.5
EGS	41	5.4
Chem.	30	5.3
TransEq	37	5.1
OMI	38	4.9
Basic MA	33	4.8
MotT	36	4.1
Tex Prd	26	2.6

The results of growth rates of work force per factory is the least in Textile Products while the rest are co-terminus with employment of workers growth rates in many cases, i.e. Machinery other than Transport (IN36), Transport Equipment and Parts (IN37), Electricity, Gas and Steam (IN41), Basic Metals and Alloys (IN33), Rubber, Petroleum and Coal (IN31), Leather and Leather Products (IN29) and Wood and Wood Products (IN27). However, employment of workers per factory (WF) growth rates were higher compared to growth in Number of Workers (NW) of Beverages (IN22), Textiles (IN25), Textile Products (IN26), Paper (IN28), Chemicals (IN30), Non-metallic mineral (IN32), Metal Products (IN34) and Other Manufacturing Industries (38). Labour Intensity is expected to be better in daily used household necessities like Food Products and Textile Products Industries but is found to be the least with respect to criteria of workers per factory growth in Textile Products (IN26).

Analysis of Growth Rates in Fixed Capital (FC)

Table 4.6. Growth Rates of FC of 2-digit Industries in (in the order of their rankings)

Ind Name	Ind No.	Gr. Rt(descending order)%
EGS	41	14.4
Basic MA	33	12. 7
Chem.	30	12.4
MotT	36	11. 8
Leath.Prd	29	11 .4
NmMp	32	11.2
Ru-Pet-Co	31	10 .9
Bever'g	22	10.7
Paper	28	10.4
TransEq	37	10.4
Food Prd	21	9.7
Met.Prd	34	8.3
Tex Prd	26	7.6
Tex	25	10.2
OMI	38	5.1
Wood Prd	27	4.4

The growth rate of FC is the highest in Electricity, Gas and Steam (IN41) at 14.4 per cent, it being a capital and fuel-intensive or their infrastructure intensive industry followed by higher growth rates of Basic Metal and Alloys (IN33), Chemical Products (IN30), Metal Products (IN34), Leather (IN29) and Non-Metallic Mineral Products (IN32) at 12.7 per cent and 12.4 per cent, 11.8 per cent, 11.4 per cent and 11.2 per cent respectively. These are all capital intensive intermediate input based industries. This is followed by similar intermediates like Rubber, Petroleum and Coal (IN31) and further followed by consumer goods industries like Beverages (IN22), Paper (IN28), Textiles (IN25) and Capital Good like Transport Equipment and Parts (IN37) with growth rates of 10.9 per cent, 10.7 per cent, 10.4 per cent, 10.1 per cent and 10.4 per cent respectively.

This was followed by Metal Products (34), Textile Products (IN26), Other Manufacturing Industries (IN38) and Wood Products (IN27) recording low growth rates in FC at 8.3 per cent, 7.6 per cent, 5.1 per cent and 4.4 per cent respectively. These are of consumer goods and intermediates due to low intensity of fixed capital that resulted in low growth in fixed capital stock and low pace of fixed capital formation.

Analysis of Growth Rates in Capital Per Factory (KF)

All Industries growth rates in KF were admittedly low because Factories growth rates were better than fixed capital growth which were facing shackles of license permit economic set-up. This is seen in case of Wood Products (IN27) at 4.9 per cent (FC growth rate. was less at 4.4%), this being a labour-intensive industry. Similar Labour Intensive Textile Products (IN26) KF growth rate was at 4.7 per cent (FC growth rate was at 7.6%). Electricity, Gas and Steam (IN41) had the highest growth rate in KF at 13.3 per cent (as 14.4% in FC growth rate), being a high capital intensive fuel input, less in number of plants/ factories but a key to infrastructure and end use industries sectors.

Table 4.7. Growth Rates of KF of 2-digit Industries in 1956-95 (in the order of their rankings)

Ind Name	Ind No.	Gr.Rt(des)%
EGS	41	13.3
Met.Prd	34	5
Wood Prd	27	4.9
Basic MA	33	3.6
MotT	36	3.8
Ru-Pet-Co	31	3.5
Food Prd	21	3.5
Chem.	30	3.2
Leath.Prd	29	2.9
Tex Prd	26	2.6
Tex	25	2.6
Bever'g	22	1.9
Paper	28	1.8
OMI	38	1.7
TransEq	37	0.9
NmMp	32	0.7

Analysis of Growth Rates in Capital Intensity (KI2=FC/NW)

The higher growth rates in capital intensive (KI2=FC/NW) range from 9.8 per cent of Textiles, followed by Basic Metals (IN33) at 8.7 per cent and Chemicals (IN30) at 8.6 per cent, all being Intermediates. Machinery Other Than Transport (IN36) at 7.8 per cent and Electricity, Gas and Steam (IN41) at 7.8 per cent are the other higher growth industries, both being Capital intensive. Textile Products (IN26) follows next at 8.5 per cent. High capital intensity took place for Textiles and Textile Products due to forward linkage. Chemicals and Basic Metals' high capital intensities growth resulted due to heavy industry strategy especially in these two, and for overall growth due to both forward and backward linkages for the new sunrise industries of pharmaceuticals, Electrical and Electronics Machinery other than transport (36) that are capital goods industries.

Table 4.8. Growth Rates in KI2 for 2-digit Industries for 1956-95

Ind Name	Ind. No.	Gr.Rt. (descend)%
Tex	25	9.8
Basic MA	33	8.7
Chem.	30	8.6
Tex Prd	26	8.5
MotT	36	7.8
EGS	41	7.8
NmMp	32	6.8
Paper	28	6.5
Food Prd	21	6.4
TransEq	37	6.1
Met.Prd	34	5.3
Leath.Prd	29	4.5
OMI	38	4.2
Bever'g	22	3.6
Ru-Pet-Co	31	3.2
Wood Prd	27	2.2

The medium growth industries are Non-Metallic Mineral Products (IN32) at 6.8 per cent, Paper Products (IN28) at 6.5 per cent, Food Products (IN21) at 6.4 per cent, Transport Equipment and Parts (IN37) at 6.1 per cent and Metal Products (IN34) at 5.3 per cent. Food Products showing some capital intensity is due to increasing use of agricultural machinery, tractors, HYV seeds, fertilisers, irrigation pump-sets of new technology.

The low growth industries are Leather Products (IN29) at 4.5 per cent, Other Manufacturing Industries (IN38) at 4.2 per cent, Beverages (IN22) at 3.6 per cent, Rubber, Petroleum and Coal (IN 31) at 3.2 per cent and Wood Industries at 2.2 per cent of both Intermediate and Consumer Goods.

Analysis of Growth Rates of Output measured in terms of GVA/FACT and NVA/FACT

Textile Products (IN26) alone is a specific single industry group as capital intensity grew at a high of 8.5 per cent similar to employment per factory growth unlike low employment growth in terms of NW. This indicates growth in skilled, technical and professional category with unskilled labour being replaced or substituted by capital intensification and concomitant technology advancements.

Table 4.9. Growth Rates of Output Measured in terms of GVA/FACT and NVA/FACT

O1F Ind Name	O1F Ind No.	O1F Gr.Rt(des)%	O2F Ind Name	O2F Ind No.	O2F Gr.Rt(des)%
EGS	41	16.8	EGS	41	16.9
OMI	38	9.1	Tex Prd	26	9.8
Leath.Prd	29	8.8	OMI	38	8.2
Tex Prd	26	8.8	Leather	29	7.4
MotT	36	8.8	MotT	36	7.0
Chem.	30	7.2	Food Prd	21	6.3
Food Prd	21	7.0	TransEq	37	5.5
Basic MA	33	6.4	Ru-Pet-Co	31	5.2
Met.Prd	34	6.4	Basic MA	33	5.1
TransEq	37	6.2	Met.Prd	34	4.8
Paper	28	5.8	Chem.	30	4.1
Tex	25	4.4	Bever'g	22	3.3
NmMp	32	4.4	Paper	28	3.2
Wood Prd	27	3.7	Tex	25	3.0
Ru-Pet-Co	31	3.7	NmMp	32	2.7
Bever'g	22	3.7	Wood Prd	27	1.9

Exceptions apart, growth rates in NVA seen to be sound for purpose of analysis of comparative growth rates of Industries in India contributed by capital, labour and factory growth rates [as in the above pages]. Growth rates of factories in Beverages, Food, Non-Metallic, Wood and Textiles were all on the higher side that it gave lower NVA per factory growth rates over the long term because of lower commensurate gains in outputs.

PARTIAL PRODUCTIVITY MEASURES: THIS SECTION DEALS WITH ANALYSIS OF GROWTH RATES IN LABOUR PRODUCTIVITY AND CAPITAL PRODUCTIVITY OF 2-DIGIT INDIAN INDUSTRIES OVER 1956-95

This Sub-section Deals with Growth Rates in Capital Productivity Measures

Growth Rates of K1P (= GVA/FC) and K2P (=NVA/FC) of 2-digit Industries in 1956-95

Both K1P and K2P give similar results in respect of growth rates and ordering of industries, though differing marginally. Capital Productivity growth of Textile Products (IN26) influenced positively its NVA and GVA growth rates. Similar inferences of positive impact of capital productivity growth rates on NVA and GVA growth rates can be drawn for OMI (IN38), EGS (IN41), Leather (IN29), Wood (IN27), Rubber, Petroleum and Coal (IN31), Beverages (IN22), Transport (IN37), Metal Products (IN34), Chemicals (IN30), Machinery other than transport (IN36), Basic Metals and Alloys (IN33), Paper (IN28), NmMP (IN32), Textiles (IN25)—all nearly but not strictly in that order of industries.

Table 4.10. Growth Rates of K1P and K2P of 2-digit Industries in 1956-95 (in the order of their rankings)

K1P Ind Name	K1P Ind No.	K1P Gr.Rt.(des)	K2P Ind Name	K2P Ind No.	K2P Gr.Rt.(des)
OMI	38	9.8	Tex Prd	26	9.600
Tex Prd	26	8.9	OMI	38	8.900
Wood Prd	27	8.6	Wood Prd	27	6.700
Ru-Pet-Co	31	7.4	Tex	25	5.600
Leath.Prd	29	6.5	Leath.Prd	29	5.600
Bever'g	22	5.8	Met.Prd	34	5.400
Met.Prd	34	5.2	Ru-Pet-Co	31	4.900
TransEq	37	5.2	TransEq	37	4.600
Paper	28	4.8	Bever'g	22	5.300
Tex	25	4.8	EGS	41	3.500
MotT	36	4.7	MotT	36	3.100
Chem.	30	3.9	Food Prd	21	2.900
NmMp	32	3.7	Paper	28	2.900
EGS	41	3.6	NmMp	32	1.900
Food Prd	21	3.5	Chem.	30	1.800
Basic MA	33	2.4	Basic MA	33	1.100

This finding signifies the role of Fixed Capital, its intensity and its Productivity in all registered large, medium and small industries, while increasing scale of operation might influence positively each other's capital, its intensity and productivity, also due to upgraded technology absorption, modernisation, forward and backward linkages improved over time of planning and markets for capital (physical and financial) and commodity trade, globalisation, liberalisation, economic reforms applicable to All Industries without distinctions of process, input or end use bases.

Growth rate of Labour Productivity Measured in Terms of L1P (=NVA/NW) and L2P (=GVA/NW) for 2-digit Indian Industries in the Period 1956-95

Labour Productivity (L1P and L2P) contributed to NVA and GVA growth in Other Manufacturing Industries (IN38), Electrical and Non-Electrical Machinery other than Transport (IN36), Metal Products (IN34), Transport Equipment (IN37), Textile Products (IN26) etc. This contributed to work force growth, these in turn to labour intensity, irrespective of their being distinctive in input base and market base character. This finding is also due

Table 4.11. Growth rate of Labour Productivity measured in terms of L1P (= NVA/NW) and L2P (=GVA/NW) in 2-digit Indian Industries in 1956-95 (in the order of their rankings)

L1P Ind Name	L1P Ind No.	L1P Gr.Rt(des)%	L2P Ind Name	L2P Ind No.	L2P Gr.Rt(des)%
OMI	38	19.1	OMI	38	14.4
Tex Prd	26	12.2	Chem.	30	12.5
EGS	41	11.5	MotT	36	12.5
MotT	36	11	Met.Prd	34	12.3
Met.Prd	34	10.6	Tex	25	11.6
TransEq	37	10.5	Tex Prd	26	11.5
Leath.Prd	29	10.1	Paper	28	11.5
Basic MA	33	9.9	EGS	41	11.4
Tex	25	9.7	TransEq	37	11.3
Paper	28	9.4	Basic MA	33	11.3
Chem.	30	9.4	Leath.Prd	29	11.1
Food Prd	21	9.2	Wood Prd	27	10.8
Bever'g	22	9	NmMp	32	10.5
Wood Prd	27	8.9	Ru-Pet-Co	31	10.4
NmMp	32	8.8	Food Prd	21	9.8
Ru-Pet-Co	31	8.1	Bever'g	22	9.4

to economies of increasing scale of operation of all Registered Industries labour absorption intensity (both skilled and unskilled) and influenced positively by their capital intensity. This analysis leads to the conclusion that scale of operation might lead to both factor intensification and to both factor productivities and in turn to NVA and GVA growth rates in all industries as experienced in India since 1948-50 that includes 35 years of centralised (direct and Indirect) planning regime and two decades of liberalisation, globalisation, privatisation, economic reforms New Economic Policies (Structural Adjustment and Stabilisation), Market friendly regime that caused for capital intensification complementary to labour absorption of skilled category.

It is learnt from the earlier analysis of growth rates of industries' size variables, factor intensity and factor productivities in Indian Industries during 1956-95, all being complementary and reinforcing each other without enabling a major distinction between process based or input based industries and market based industries (end-Use) based industries and /or for a choice between centralised planning regulated regime (1950-80) and /or recent two decades of market friendly, liberalisation, globalisation, privatisation. However, all the results of growth rates analysis envisage the significant role and impact of technical progress or TFP in many sectors associated with all industries, sub-sectors during 55 years. Accordingly, analysis is extended to trace growth differentials in TFP measures of Kendrick, Domar and Solow for 2-digit industries in 40 years period i.e. 1956-95.

TFP Growth Rates Measured in terms of Kendrick, Domar, Solow

Total Factor Productivity arises only when output growth is more that what is /are contributed growth in each factor input of all inputs/factors together. It means an additional output growth caused by an unknown factor termed Technical Progress that can be/is due to change in combination of inputs or factors or output process change or to technology change.

Thus TFP growth is due to Technical Progress in processes or to technology advancement/ up-gradation/modernisation in technical processes constituted in Industry.

Wood Industry (IN27) showed maximum TFP growth rate due to Kendrick (9%) and Domar (7.3%). While its rank has fallen due to Solow at a growth of 1.3 per cent, [this may be due to changing current year weights in Solow different from the comparable fixed base year weights in Domar and Kendrick formula] the highest TFPG was reached by Rubber Petroleum and Coal Industry (IN31) at 2.3 per cent. IN31 was in second position in Kendrick and Domar. Growth in TFP differed due to three authors' measures in Non-Metallic Mineral Products (IN32), Wood (IN27), Transport (IN37).

The lowest TFP growth was seen in Chemicals (IN30), Textiles (IN25). While Chemicals was a sunrise industry, Textiles growth spurted in 1970s and 1980s. Since Chemicals being a capital-intensive industry does have further scope to raise growth; it thus may become a 'leading' industry if TFPG can be further exploited. Textiles (IN25) is subject to further capital injection and efficiency as this being a Labor-intensive industry and is actually the highest in rank in capital intensity in our study, hence is a cause for growth. Ambiguous or inconsistent result is seen in Paper (IN28) and Food (IN21).

Table 4.12. TFP Growth Rates of Kendrick, Domar, Solow of 2-digit Industries in 1956-95 (in the order of their rankings)

Ind Name	IndNo.	Kendrick (%)	Ind Name	Ind No.	Domar (%)	Ind Name	Ind No.	Solow (%)
Wood Prd	27	9.0	Wood Prd	27	7.3	Ru-Pet-Co	31	2.3
Ru-Pet-Co	31	6.44	Ru-Pet-Co	31	4.17	Tex Prd	26	2.1
EGS	41	4.9	BM&A	33	3.45	EGS	41	1.9
NmMP	32	4.6	Paper Prd	28	2.74	BM&A	33	1.8
BM&A	33	4.5	Tex Prd	26	2.51	TrE&P	37	1.7
Food Prd	21	4.46	Leath Prd	29	2.26	Met Prd	34	1.6
Tex Prd	26	4.32	EGS	41	2.1	MotTr	36	1.5
OMI	38	4.31	MotTr	36	1.94	OMI	38	1.4
Beverage	22	4.28	Food Prd	21	1.91	NmMP	32	1.4
Leath Prd	29	3.84	Beverage	22	1.55	Wood Prd	27	1.3
MotTr	36	3.58	Textiles	25	1.47	Textiles	25	1.3
Met Prd	34	3.51	Met Prd	34	1.43	Paper Prd	28	1.0
TrE&P	37	3.4	TrE&P	37	1.38	Beverage	22	1.0
Paper Prd	28	2.97	OMI	38	1.37	Food Prd	21	1.0
Textiles	25	1.96	Chem	30	1.32	Leath Prd	29	0.8
Chem	30	1.91	NmMP	32	1.11	Chem	30	0.6

Paper Industry (IN28) had good growth due to Domar but, along with Beverage, Food, all three being labour intensive, and less relatively capital intensive in our study, showed scant TFP growth due to Solow. Managerial deficiencies are likely prime reason for low TFPG in labour intensive industries. The culture of high labour turnover, holidays, seasonal character of agriculture both in food crops and cash crops, high disguised unemployment in agriculture, high population and dependency burden, all these mar rise in productivity in these L-intensive industries.

Wood Industry (IN27) TFPG is highest in Kendrick and Domar. As wage rates in forest based products are abysmally low and tribal population being a high percentage of total population in India, cost of procurement of forest produce for Wood Industry is very low and consequently, the value attached to growth in money terms turned out to be high.

Rubber Petroleum and Coal (IN31) showed High TFPG, this being a high K intensive industry and petroleum being found short in extraction leading to high prices may not be able to meet high demand growth and its capacity to act as a leading sector in India's economic and industrialisation may be limited.

Electricity, Gas and Steam (IN41) showed higher growth well but will need further power reforms with greater decentralisation and expansion. Textile Products (IN26) need input-output linkages between Textiles and Textile Products, with their capital intensity providing a case for augmenting Labour intensity and for capturing Asian, European and American markets. Basic Metals and Alloys (IN33) is also another promising Intermediate industry can be another leading industry if wage costs are kept down at reasonable levels. Smaller states are coming up and demand in those directions increasing, Basic Metals and Alloys (IN33) will be one of the best leading Industries for growth in Indian Industry and economy followed by Other Manufacturing Industries (IN38) and Electrical and Non Electrical machinery other than Transport (IN36).

Transport Equipment (IN37) and Metal Products (IN34) though not causing alarm, can raise themselves up to serve as effective channels of growth.

THIS SECTION DEALS WITH RESULTS AND ANALYSIS OF RELATIVE RANKINGS OF INDUSTRIES IN TERMS OF GROWTH RATES OF FACTORIES, EMPLOYMENT, FIXED CAPITAL, NET VALUE ADDED, GROSS VALUE ADDED VIS-À-VIS ALL INDUSTRIES GROWTH RATES IN THE CORRESPONDING VARIABLES

Food Products (IN21) and Electricity, Gas and Steam (IN41) tops the rankings of concerned variables such as Factory growth rate, Workers, Fixed Capital, NVA, GVA of Industries vis-à-vis All India Industries, though first two variables and latter three variables grew in opposite ways.

EGS Industry tops rank in FC, NVA, GVA but is ranked 13th in factory growth rate and 5th in Employment (NW) growth rate. EGS being capital intensive does well in output growth rates that were fuelled by higher Fixed Capital Input.

Food Products (IN21), a Labour Intensive Industry did grow well with high employment (NW) growth particularly due to horizontal, decentralised spread of factories though NVA and GVA of IN21 was low due to lower productivities even with increasing capital, both Fixed and Productive. Measures to improve Labour productivity will go a long way to improve NVA and GVA growth rates.

Next in order of rankings in NVA growth were, Textile Products, Leather, Beverages, Rubber, Petroleum and Coal. Textile Products being a labour Intensive Industry had shown remarkable consistency in showing higher Labour productivity growth of both L1P and L2P and in turn particularly of Labour Productivity (L1P) on employment Growth rate. Despite a lower FC growth rate rankings, those industries had high ranks of NVA and GVA growth rate.

Though Leather (IN29) and Beverage (IN22) are traditionally Labour Intensive Industries, they had FC growth more than Factories growth that propelled to higher output growth rankings. Rubber, Petroleum and Coal (IN31) being Capital-Intensive had higher Output growth ranks due to higher FC growth. Employment Growth rates in Rubber, Petroleum and Coal (IN31) and in Transport Equipment (IN37) raised NVA and GVA growth rates in these industries due to their higher Capital Intensities and TFPG.

Table 4.13. Ranking of Industries in terms of growth rates of Factories, Emp, FC, NVA, GVA vis-à-vis All Industries growth Rates in the corresponding variables (in the order of higher to lower for each variable growth rates)

Fact I..Name	Fact Ind No	Fact $\hat{\beta}$	Emp I.Name	Emp Ind No	Emp $\hat{\beta}$	FC I.Name	FC Ind No	FC $\hat{\beta}$	NVA I.Name	NVA Ind No	NVA $\hat{\beta}$	GVA I.Name	GVA Ind No	GVA $\hat{\beta}$
Food	21	33.1	Food P	21	14.7	EGS	41	14.4	EGS	41	18.1	EGS	41	18.1
Leath.	29	19.2	Ru-P-Co	31	7.7	B.M&A	33	12.7	Tex Prd	26	17.2	Tex Prd	26	17.2
Met.Prd	34	18.9	Bev	22	7.1	Chem	30	12.4	Leather	29	17.1	Leather	29	17.1
Tex	25	17.5	Leather	29	6.9	MotT	36	11.8	Bev	22	15.9	Bev	22	15.9
Ru-P-Co	31	14.5	EGS	41	6.7	Leather	29	11.4	Ru-P-Co	31	15.9	Ru-P-Co	31	15.9
Bev	22	12.6	Tex.Prd	26	5.1	NmMP	32	11.2	MotTr	36	14.9	MotTr	36	14.9
MnMP	32	10.4	Tr.Eq	37	4.3	Bev	22	10.7	Tr.Eq	37	14.9	Tr.Eq	37	14.9
Paper	28	10.1	B.M&A	33	3.9	Ru-P-Co	31	10.9	OMI	38	13.1	OMI	38	13.1
Trs Eq.	37	9.4	NmMP	32	4.3	All-Indus	All-Indus	10.5	All-Indus	All-Indus	13.9	All-Indus	All-Indus	13.9
Chem	30	9.2	MotT	36	3.9	Tr.Eq	37	10.4	B.M&A	33	13.7	B.M&A	33	13.7
Wood	27	9.2	Chem	30	3.8	Paper	28	10.4	Met.Prd	34	13.7	Met.Prd	34	13.7
B.M&A	33	8.8	Paper	28	3.8	Tex	25	10.2	Paper	28	13.3	Paper	28	13.3
All-Ind	All-Ind	8.8	All-Indus	All-Indus	3.2	Food P	21	9.7	Chem	30	13.2	Chem	30	13.2
EGS	41	1.2	Met.Prd	34	3.1	Met.P	34	8.3	NmMP	32	13.2	NmMP	32	13.2
OMI	38	5.8	Tex.	25	2.3	Tex.Prd	26	7.6	Food P	21	12.6	Food Prd	21	12.6
Tex Prd	26	7.7	Wood	27	2.2	OMI	38	5.1	Wood	27	11.1	Wood	27	11.1
MotT	36	7.9	OMI	38	1.8	Wood	27	4.4	Tex.	25	10.1	Tex.	25	10.1

However, lower growth rates in some Intermediates and Consumer Goods industries were due to low factor productivities and low TFP growth.

The desired need and rational principle lie in both capital and skilled and unskilled labour intensification in all industries of all states, union territories and in their rural backward regions as to minimise unemployment underemployment, regional disparities and to increase industrial growth of small, medium and large scale industries, with high linkages [forwards and backward,] of ancillary and parent units that provide wage goods to reduce inflation, poverty, inequality. Next in importance come the capital goods, Basic Goods and Intermediates to enable high rate of capital formation, economic growth and development followed by household durable consumer goods, house construction materials, electricity gas and water supplies to households of lower middle income, and to enhance levels of living of masses. Durable goods of the elite, top rich group consumption in five star hotels, scandals of brokers, speculators, politicians, top bureaucrats and corporate managers and professional executives in governments and MNCs Business Houses, Banks, Companies, etc should receive the lowest priority.

Industrial and Trade Policies should address to issues pertaining to generation of employment of labour, balanced regional development, even distribution of assets, income work opportunities to all in India to meet social and economic goals of Five year Plans. The current decades export led import liberalisation strategies of industrialisation, and need for reduction of brain drain and skills trained at huge costs in higher education in India that fetches better growth and amenities for developed countries at cost of underdeveloped ones.

CAUSAL RELATIONS TO INFLUENCE TFP GROWTH, GVA, NVA, EMPLOYMENT GROWTH AND THEIR DETERMINANTS IN INDIAN INDUSTRIES

This Section 4.5 traces the causal relations between TFP Growth, GVA and NVA Growth and each one's determinants through estimated linear regressions of TFP= f (K/L), NVA = f(TFP), GVA = f(TFP), GVA = f(Labour Productivity), NVA = f(Labour Productivity), GVA = f (Capital Productivity), GVA = f (Capital Intensity), NVA = f (K/L), NVA= f(Capital Productivity), Employment (NW) = f (K/L), NW= f(TFP), NW= f(Labour Productivity), NW= f(Capital Productivity). TFP is of Solow as mentioned earlier.

Analysis of Influence of Capital Intensity (K/L) on TFP of Solow

The TFPG influenced by Capital Intensity were in Beverages (IN22) at 24.861 per cent, followed by Textile Products (IN26) at 12.461 per cent and Wood Products (IN27) at 11.22 per cent, Textiles at 10.58 per cent, leather Products at 10.55 per cent, then followed by Food Products (IN21) at 8.6 followed by Metal Products (IN34) at 6.097 per cent and Other Manufacturing Industries (IN38) at 4.879 per cent.

The influence of Capital Intensities on TFPG were lower in Electricity, Gas and Steam (IN41) at 4.46 per cent followed by Transport Equipment (IN37) at 3.94 per cent, Paper (IN28) at 3.77 per cent and Machinery other than transport (IN36) at 3.7 per cent with

Table 4.14. Growth in TFP of Solow in response to capital intensity for 1956-95

Industry Name	Industry Number (IN)	$\hat{\beta}$
Beverages	22	24.861
Textile Products	26	12.461
Wood and Wood products	27	11.22
Textiles (23+24+25)	25	10.575
Leather and Leather Prd.	29	10.549
Food Products	21	8.613
Metal Products	34	6.097
Other Manf. Industries	38	4.879
Electricity, Gas and Steam	41	4.45
Transport Equip. Parts	37	3.941
Paper and Paper Products	28	3.778
Machinery o.t. Transport	36	3.704
NmMP	32	2.927
Chemicals	30	2.288
Rubber-Petroleum & Coal	31	1.75
Basic Metals and Alloys	33	1.102

Non metallic Mineral Products at 2.93 per cent, Chemicals at 2.99 per cent and Rubber, Petroleum and Coal at 1.75 per cent, followed by the lowest in Basic Metals and Alloys (IN33) at 1.1 per cent. These findings are contrary to usual notion that higher the capital intensity growth higher will be the TFPG in capital intensive industries, followed by less influence in Intermediates and very much less TFPG in consumer goods industries. However, the empirical verification indicated contrary results that consumer goods like Beverages, Textile Products, Wood Products, Textiles, Leather products, Food Products, EGS, OMI TFP growth were influenced better by their capital intensity than in capital goods and intermediate goods Industries in India which is a welcome trend to clear wage goods shortages.

Influence of TFP on NVA, GVA and Employment in Indian Industries for 1956-95 Growth in NVA and GVA in Response to TFP by Solow

Electricity, Gas and Steam (IN41) NVA growth had maximum influence of TFP growth (Solow) with b^ at 2.557 followed by Textile (IN25) at 2.48 and then by Electrical and Non-Electrical Machinery Other Than Transport (IN36)) at 2.47, Basic Metals and Alloys (IN33), Rubber, Petroleum and Coal (IN31) in that descending order.

Table 4.15. Growth in NVA and GVA in Response to TFP by Solow for 1956-95
NVA= a +b (TFP); GVA= a +b (TFP)

NVA Ind Name	NVA INCode	GVA $\hat{\beta}$ in NVA	GVA Ind Name	GVA INCode	GVA $\hat{\beta}$ (GVA)
EGS	41	2.557	Met. Prd.	34	1.914
Tex	25	2.484	Beverage	22	1.816
MotTr	36	2.466	OMI	38	1.576
BM&A	33	2.436	Leather	29	0.806
Ru-Pet-Co	31	2.433	Mac.otTr.	36	0.768
Food	21	2.354	Transport	37	0.626
Chem	30	2.351	R-Pet-C	31	0.579
TrEq	37	2.335	Food Prd	21	0.528
NmMP	32	2.24	Paper	28	0.526
Paper	28	2.215	EGS	41	0.519
Met Prd	34	2.179	NmMP	32	0.462
Bev	22	2.138	Chemical	30	0.45
OMI	38	1.977	Bas M&A	33	0.434
Tex.Prd	26	1.846	Textiles	25	0.426
Wood	27	1.846	Tex Prd	26	0.357
Leather	29	1.773	Wood Prd	27	0.118

The lowest influence was revealed in Leather (IN29) where b^ was the lowest at 1.77, only preceded by Wood (IN27) and Textile Products (IN26) at 1.85.

Influence of TFPG on GVA growth had the maximum influence in Metal Products Industry (IN34), followed by Beverages (IN22). However, Leather takes the 4th position whereas Electricity, Gas and Steam (IN41) takes the 10th position.

Wood (IN27) and Textile Products (IN26) had the lowest influences of TFPG on growth of both output (GVA and NVA) measures.

Analysis of Influence of TFP on Employment of 2-digit Industries for 1956-95

The influence of TFP on employment growth measured in terms of number of workers (NW) was the highest in case of Metal Products (IN34), followed by Manufacturing other than Transport (IN36) and Beverages (IN22). So TFP influence for raising employment growth is imperative both in capital intensive and labour intensive industries. The lowest influence is seen in case of Wood (IN27) followed by steadily better in case of Basic

Metals and Alloys (IN33), Paper (IN28), Textiles (IN25) employment growth in these industries.

Table 4.16. Growth in Employment in Response to TFP in 2-digit Industries for 1956-95

Ind.Name	Ind	$\hat{\beta}$
Metal Prd	34	1.612
MotTr	36	1.425
Beverage	22	1.372
Chem	30	1.309
Food	21	1.249
Ru-Pet-Co	31	1.047
OMI	38	0.739
EGS	41	0.682
Leather	29	0.583
Tex.Prd	26	0.553
NmMP	32	0.374
Tr.Eq	37	0.361
Textiles	25	0.241
Paper	28	0.145
BM&A	33	0.106
Wood	27	0.092

Analysis of Influence of Capital Productivity on Gross Value Added, NVA and Employment in Indian Industries for 1956-95

The influence of capital productivity on growth of GVA was the highest in case of non-metallic mineral products (IN32), followed by Paper (IN28), Beverage (IN22), Leather (IN29) and Food (IN21), Chemicals (IN30), Rubber, Petroleum and Coal (IN31) and Other Manufacturing Industries (IN38).

The lowest influence of capital productivity on GVA growth was seen in case of Electricity, Gas and Steam (IN41), in spite of its capital intensity. Similarly, Textile products (IN26) and Transport Equipment (IN37) are also on the lower side, inspite of capital intensity of IN37 and Labour Intensity of IN26.

Table 4.17. Growth in GVA in response to capital productivity

Ind.Name	In	$\hat{\beta}$
NmMP	32	1.64
Paper	28	1.581
Beverage	22	1.135
Leather	29	0.971
Food Prd	21	0.803
Chem	30	0.768
Ru-P-Co	31	0.559
OMI	38	0.557
Textile	25	0.476
MotTr	36	0.44
Metal Prd	34	0.318
Tr.Eq	37	0.315
Tex.Prd	26	0.266
BM&A	33	0.18
Wood	27	0.067
EGS	41	0.041

Table 4.18. Growth in NVA in response to Capital Productivity in 2-digit Industries for 1956-95

Ind.Name	Ind	$\hat{\beta}$
Beverage	22	1.511
Leather	29	1.275
Ru-Pet-Co	31	1.162
Paper	28	0.972
Food	21	0.87
Met.Prd	34	0.834
Chem	30	0.75
OMI	38	0.686
BM&A	33	0.482
NmMP	32	0.32
Tex.Prd	26	0.293
Textiles	25	0.232
Wood	27	0.079
Tr.Eq	37	0.065
MotTr	36	0.064
EGS	41	0.048

Analysis of Influence of Capital Productivity on Net Value Added (NVA)

The influence of capital productivity on NVA was maximum in case of Beverages (IN22), followed by Leather (IN29), Rubber, Petroleum, and Coal (31), Paper (IN28) and Wood (IN27), followed by Metal Products (IN34), Chemicals (IN30), Other Manufacturing Industries (IN38), Basic Metals and Alloys (IN33) and Non-Metallic Mineral Products (32) respectively in descending order.

Analysis of Effect of Capital Productivity on Industries' Employment for the period 1956-95

Leather (IN29) shows the maximum influence of capital productivity on growth rate of employment (NW) followed by Beverages (IN22), Rubber-Petroleum and Coal (IN31) and Food (IN21) in descending order. So, employment in Labour -intensive industries also need to be enhanced through increase in efficiency of capital productivity.

Chemicals (IN30) takes the 9th position, followed by Basic metals and Alloys (IN34) and Wood (IN27).

The lowest influence was in Electricity, Gas and Steam (IN41) and Transport Equipment (IN37), showing b^ of 0.058.

Table 4.19. Growth in Industries' employment (NW) in response to capital productivity in Indian Industries for 1956-95 (in Descending Order)

Ind.Name	Ind	$\hat{\beta}$
Leather	29	1.375
Beverage	22	0.924
Ru-Pet-Co	31	0.477
Food	21	0.396
Paper	28	0.383
NmMP	32	0.373
MotTr	36	0.33
Textiles	25	0.318
Chemicals	30	0.316
BM&A	33	0.281
Wood	27	0.098
OMI	38	0.096
Metal Prd	34	0.079
Tex.Prd	26	0.063
EGS	41	0.058
Tr. Eq	37	0.058

Analysis of Influence of Capital Intensity on Gross Value Added, NVA and employment in Indian Industries in 1956-95

The influence of capital intensity on growth of output in terms of GVA is the highest in case of Electricity, Gas and Steam (IN41), followed by Textile Products (IN26), Leather (IN29) and Other Manufacturing Industries (IN38) in that descending order.

The least influence is seen in Metal Products (IN34).

Capital intensive industries such as Chemicals (IN30), Rubber-Petroleum and Coal (IN31) and Basic Metals and Alloys (IN33) show least influences of capital intensity on GVA growth.

Table 4.20. Growth in GVA in response to Capital Intensity in Indian Industries for 1956-95: (in Descending Order)

Ind.Name	I.N.	$\hat{\beta}$
EGS	41	1.346
Tex.Prd	26	1.296
Leather	29	1.272
OMI	38	1.255
Tr.Eq	37	1.229
MotTr	36	1.128
Beverage	22	1.051
NmMP	32	1.001
Food Prd	21	0.991
Paper	28	0.982
Textiles	25	0.925
Wood	27	0.821
Chem	30	0.682
Ru-Pet-Co	31	0.556
BM&A	33	0.547
Metal Prd	34	0.475

Analysis of effect or influence of Capital Intensity on Net Value Added

The growth in NVA is most influenced by capital intensity in case of Leather (IN29), followed by Textile products (IN26), Electricity, Gas and Steam (IN41).

Food (IN21) occupies 9th position in the descending scale. Beverages (IN22) is 6th while, Chemicals (IN30) is 15th. The lowest position is in Rubber-Petroleum and Coal (IN31) i.e. is in 16th position.

Table 4.21. Influence of KI_2 (FC/NW) on Net Value Added (NVA) in each of the 2-digit Industries for 1956-95 (in Descending Order)

Ind.Name	I.N.	$\hat{\beta}$
Leather	29	1.346
Tex.Prd	26	1.32
EGS	41	1.19
Tr.Eq	37	1.16
OMI	38	1.088
Beverage	22	1.077
MotTr	36	1.059
BM&A	33	1.03
Food	21	1.002
NmMP	32	0.927
Metal Prd	34	0.871
Wood	27	0.854
Textiles	25	0.792
Paper	28	0.767
Chem	30	0.63
Ru-Pet-Co	31	0.565

Analysis of Influence of Capital Intensity on Employment

Transport Industry (IN37) shows maximum growth in employment (NW) in response to capital intensity with b^ showing 1.16, followed by Textile Products (IN26) and Rubber, Petroleum and Coal Industry (IN31). So capital intensity is important for employment growth even in capital intensive industries as in IN37 and IN31. The need of K/L increase in EGS is also vindicated here even in context of need for higher employment growth.

The lowest influence of capital intensity on employment (NW) growth is in textiles (IN25). Wood (IN27) and Manufacturing other than transport (IN35+36=36) also show low influences of capital intensity on employment growth. Thus the need of the textile sector for employment increase is less on raising in capital intensity.

Table 4.22. Growth in employment (NW) in response to capital intensity for 2-digit All India Industries for 1956-95 (in Descending Order)

Ind.Name	Ind	$\hat{\beta}$
Tr.Eq	37	1.161
Tex.Prd	26	0.656
Ru-Pet-Co	31	0.646
EGS	41	0.515
Leather	29	0.501
Beverage	22	0.418
OMI	38	0.412
NmMP	32	0.386
Metal Prd	34	0.353
Paper	28	0.349
BM&A	33	0.264
Chem	30	0.229
Food	21	0.224
MotTr	36	0.149
Wood	27	0.055
Textile	25	0.041

Table 4.23. Growth in Industries output (NVA) in response to L-productivity for 2-digit Industries for 1956-95

Ind.Name	Ind	$\hat{\beta}$
Ru-P-Co	31	1.727
Tex.Prd	26	1.372
Beverage	22	1.284
OMI	38	1.263
Leather	29	1.248
Tr.Eq	37	1.189
Met Prd	34	1.166
Paper	28	1.157
MotTr	36	1.129
BM&A	33	1.12
NmMP	32	1.034
Wood	27	1.025
Textile	25	0.969
Food Prd	21	0.855
Chem	30	0.739

Analysis of Influence of Labour Productivity on Net Value Added, GVA and Employment-analysis is done here for Results showing growth in NVA, GVA and NW due to the influence of Labour Productivity.

The influence of labour productivity on NVA growth rate was the maximum in case of Rubber-Petroleum and Coal (IN), followed by Textile Products (IN26), Beverages (IN22) and Other Manufacturing Industries (IN38). The lowest influence is in Chemicals (IN30) as it was in case of influence of labour productivity on GVA growth rate. Food Industry, Textile, Wood also showed lack of influence of labour productivity on NVA growth, these being L-intensive industries.

Influence of Labour Productivity on GVA Growth in Indian 2-digit Industries for 1956-95

Other Manufacturing Industries (IN38), Transport Equipment (IN37), EGS (IN41) though capital Intensive, the growth rates in GVA were influenced to the maximum by their Labour Productivities. Food products assumed the 15th Position, though it is a Labour Intensive Industry. Its productivity is not a concern for units selling in a local market Rubber, Petroleum and Coal (IN31) showed the lowest influence of Labour productivity on GVA growth, being a Capital Intensive Industry.

Table 4.24. Growth in GVA in Response to Labour Productivity for Indian Industries for 1956-95 (in Descending Order)

Ind.Name	IN	$\hat{\beta}$
OMI	38	1.331
Transport	37	1.261
EGS	41	1.246
Tex.Prd	26	1.221
Met.Prd	34	1.203
Beverage	22	1.197
Paper	28	1.158
Leather	29	1.15
M.ot.Tr	36	1.107
Textile	25	1.086
Ba.M&A	33	1.078
NmMP	32	1.06
Wood	27	1.026
Chemical	30	0.989
Food Prd	21	0.756
Ru-P-Co	31	0.661

Analysis of Influence of Labour Productivity of 2-digit Industries on Employment for 1956-95

The influence of labour productivity on employment (NW) growth was the maximum in case of Leather (IN29), followed by Textile Products (IN26) and Rubber-Petroleum and Coal (IN31). Food (IN21) takes 10th position.

The least influence was in Textiles (IN25), though this is a L-intensive industry. Its Employment growth recorded a low figure too. Transport Equipment (IN37) and Wood (IN27) also showed low influence of L-productivity on growth of employment in terms of NW. These two need more infusion of capital and greater increase of capital productivity and TFP.

Table 4.25. Growth in Industries' employment (NW) in response to Labour productivity in 2-digit Industries for 1956-95

Ind.Name	Ind	$\hat{\beta}$
Leather	29	0.697
Tex.Prd	26	0.648
Ru-Pet-Co	31	0.483
NmMP	32	0.396
EGS	41	0.379
Chemical	30	0.378
Beverage	22	0.361
Paper	28	0.352
OMI	38	0.324
Food	21	0.318
MotTr	36	0.309
Metal Prd	34	0.288
BM&A	33	0.283
Tr.Eq	37	0.166
Wood	27	0.072
Textiles	25	0.013

ANALYSIS OF RETURNS TO SCALE THROUGH COBB-DOUGLAS PRODUCTION FUNCTION ESTIMATION FOR 2-DIGIT INDUSTRIES FOR 1956-95

Returns to Scale is an aggregate performance of Factors and Inputs in terms of sum of output elasticities of factors and inputs whichever are employed and contributed to output.

Table 4.26.

1956-95	1956-95	1956-95	1956-95	1956-65	1956-65	1966-75	1966-75	76-85	76-85	1986-95	1986-95
Ind. Name	IN	a+b	Ind.Name	IN	a+b	IN	RS	IN	a+b	IN	RS
Textiles	25	1.88	Tex.Prd	26	5.13E+00	33	3.8	33	4.34	31	7.69
Chemical	30	1.777	Leather	29	1.48E+00	25	2.68	41	2.67	32	5.61
NmMP	32	1.646	Beverage	22	1.44E+00	28	2.54	36	2.6	28	4.68
Mac.Ot.T	35+36	1.346	NmMP	32	1.33E+00	26	2.15	25	2.35	36	3.28
MetalPrd	34	1.309	Chemical	30	1.18E+00	22	1.13	31	2.33	25	2.81
Food	20+21	1.286	Textile	25	1.13E+00	27	1.55	27	2.3	30	2.76
Transport	37	1.24	MetalPrd	34	1.06E+00	38	1.84	34	2.12	27	2.17
Wood	27	1.239	Food	21	1.05E+00	34	1.7	30	1.79	33	1.8
OMI	38	1.2	Paper	28	9.66E-01	32	1.52	38	1.69	34	1.79
EGS	40+41	1.197	Transport	37	9.18E-01	30	1.51	32	1.67	41	1.67
Tex. Prd.	26	1.157	EGS	41	8.94E-01	36	1.48	29	1.42	29	1.41
Leather	29	1.123	Wood	27	7.98E-01	21	1.41E+0	26	1.19	26	1.38
Beverage	22	1.11	Mac.ot Tr.	36	7.21E-01	29	1.24	37	1.22	37	1.32
Paper	28	1.0581	Bas M&A	33	6.84E-01	31	1.19	22	1.06	21	1.27
Ru-P-Co	31	0.808	OMI	38	6.24E-01	41	1.15	21	0.699	38	1.1
Bas.M&A	33	0.57	Ru-P-Co	31	5.97E-01	37	0.767	28	0.601	22	0.818

Note: IRS—Increasing Returns to Scale. CRS—Constant Returns to Scale. DRS—Decreasing Returns to Scale.

These elasticities are independent of their scale, origin and Unit (s) measurements, hence the sum, each being a pure number can be obtained by adding them. Thus we get >1(IRS), <1(DRS) and =1(CRS)

Increasing returns to scale in 40 yr period 1956-95 was noted by Textiles (IN25), followed by Chemicals (IN30), Nonmetallic Minerals (IN32) and Machinery other than transport (IN36), Metal Products (IN34), Food (IN21), Transport Equipment and Parts (IN37), Wood (IN27), Paper (IN28) in descending order. But scale economies do not necessarily reflect growth in NVA, GVA or Employment growth or factories growth rate. Thus scale economies are a factor for entry and exit of firms in the industry. The rest of the industries had Constant Returns to Scale (CRS).

The decades show temporal shifts in the industries' relative scale economies. Textiles (IN25) was 6th from above in descending order, but it shifted to 5th position in 1966-75. In the next two decades it got relegated to 5th and 6th position respectively. Thus Textiles has been reaping scale economies constantly and the recession period did not dampen scale economies.

In the period 1956-65, Textile Products (26), Leather and Leather Products (IN29), Beverages (IN22), Non-Metallic Mineral Products (IN32), Chemical and Chemical Products (IN30), Textiles of Cotton, Wool, Silk and Jute (IN25), Metal Products (IN34) and Food Products (IN21) showed Increasing Returns to Scale, rest showing constant returns to scale.

In the second decade, all showed increasing returns except Transport Equipment and Parts Industry (IN37) that showed Constant Returns to Scale (CRS).

In the 3rd decade, Basic Metals and Alloys (IN33), Electricity, Gas and Steam (IN41), Machinery other than Transport (IN36), Textiles (IN25), Rubber-Petroleum and Coal (IN31), Wood and Wood Products (IN27), Metal Products (IN34), Chemical and Chemical Products (IN30), Other Manufacturing Industries (IN38), Non-Metallic Mineral Products (IN32), Leather (IN29), Textile Products (IN26), Transport Equipment (IN37), Beverages (IN22) showed Increasing Returns to Scale. Food Products (IN21) and Paper (IN28) showed Constant Returns to Scale(CRS).

In final decade, Rubber-Petroleum and Coal (IN31), Non-Metallic Mineral products (IN32), Paper (IN28), Machinery other than Transport (IN36), Textiles (IN25), Chemicals (IN30), Wood (IN27), Basic Meals and Alloys (IN33), in fact all, except Beverages (IN22) showed Constant Returns to Scale (CRS).

The perennially low scale economies were in Basic Metals and Alloys (IN33) and Rubber, Petroleum and Coal (IN31), Beverages (IN22) and Other Manufacturing Industries (IN38). Basic Metals though did show high scale economies during 1966-85 and slipped back in the last decade due to onslaught of economic reforms that left this industry to fend for its own, this being an Intermediate Industry.

Food, Leather, Metal Products, Textiles show high scale economies in the first decade, but Food slipped into DRS in 1976-85.

MAJOR FINDINGS AND CONCLUSION

An Analysis of Growth Rates of Factories revealed Food Products Industry (IN21) growing at a maximum growth rate of 33.1 per cent, followed by User and intermediates Industries. The Comparative Study of Industries' growth rates of Factories brought out possible weak forward and backward linkages and lack of implementation in terms of numbers corresponding to planning goals.

Net Value Added (NVA) growth rate was the highest in Electricity, Gas and Steam (EGS) at 18.1 per cent followed by growth rate on Textile Products (IN26), with lowest growth rate being recorded by Textiles (IN25), indicating lack of appropriate production planning and weak linkages.

Low growth rates in employment in number of workers in most of the industries except Food Products Industry (IN21) confirmed that most industries in India are low labour intensive ones. Low employment growth rate figures n Beverages (2.2%), Textiles (2.3%) and OMI (1.8%) pointed to lacunae in employment planning and thereby hinted at greater employment absorption capacity.

Growth Rate in Fixed Capital (FC) was the highest in Electricity, Gas and Steam (IN41) that is also inferred to be the cause of recording highest NVA growth rate in EGS (IN41). But Intermediates showed low FC growth rate and bolstering FC in these with proper Regional Input Output Planning can alter the overall investment climate.

The highest growth in Capital Intensity was shown in Textiles (IN25) and Capital productivity Growth Rate in Textile Products (IN26) influenced positively its NVA and GVA growth rates. Higher Labour Productivity growth rates in many industries (OMI recorded the highest) contributed to work force growth and in turn to labour intensity, hinting at scale operation leading to both factor intensification and factor productivities and that in turn to NVA and GVA growth. All these results envisaged greater role for Total Factor Productivity (TFP).

TFPG was the maximum in Wood Industry (IN27) and with Chemicals (IN30), Textiles (IN25) and Basic Metals (IN33) also showing higher growth rates, meant Smaller States can grow faster.

Ranking revealed that Food and EGS ranked high in Factories and NW growth rates. Textiles showed remarkable consistency in both Labour Productivity and Employment growth rates. Leather and Beverage, though Labour Intensive, had high FC growth rate that contributed to high output growth.

A Causal Analysis showed highest TFPG due to K/L was in Beverages, but lowest in Basic Metals, contrary to common understanding. Influence of TFPG on NVA showed maximum influence in EGS (IN41), followed by Textiles (IN25) and Machinery other than Transport (IN36). On GVA growth, maximum influence of TFPG was in Metal Products (IN34), followed by Beverages (IN22) and OMI (IN38). Similarly, TFP influence on Employment growth rate showed maximum effect on Metal Products (IN34), followed by Machinery other than Transport (IN36) and Beverages (IN22). Thus TFPG influence was seen in both Labour Intensive and Capital Intensive Industries. Lowest TFPG influence in Output (GVA) and employment growth rates was noticed in Wood (IN27).

Influence of Capital Productivity on GVA was the highest in NmMP (IN32), followed by Paper (IN28), Beverages (IN22) and Leather (IN29). Influence of Capital Productivity on NVA was the maximum in Beverages (IN22), followed by Leather and RPC (IN31). Influence of Capital Productivity on employment was highest n Leather (IN29), followed by Beverages (IN22) and RPC (IN31). So improvement in Capital Productivity may be the key to raising the Labour Intensive-ness of Industries.

Labour Productivity is high in generally those industries were Capital Productivity was low. But highest Labour Productivity influence on NVA was in Transport Equipment (IN37) followed by RPC (IN31). Highest Labour productivity influence on GVA growth was in OMI (IN38) followed by Transport Equipment (IN37) and then by EGS (IN41). On Employment, highest influence of Labour Productivity was in Leather (IN29), though Textile Products (IN26) and RPC (IN31) also ranked higher, though it recorded lower figures.

An Analysis of returns to Scale decadal period wise showed that recession did not dampen higher scale economies in Textiles (IN25). In 1966-75, all industries showed IRS except Transport Equipment (IN37). Food slipped into Diminishing Returns to Scale in the third decade of 1976-85. In the fourth decade (1986-95), all industries except Beverages showed CRS. Increasing Returns to Scale in Textiles (IN25), Chemicals (IN30), NmMP (IN32) and MotTr (IN36) in the long run period of 40years. But such scale economies do not necessarily reflect growth in NVA, GVA, Employment, and Factories' growth rates.

Thus despite high growth in Units, to reap scale economies, a proper agricultural environment and high expectations need to be maintained and nurtured which slackened during the decade of New Economic reforms period. Transport is another industry that showed inconsistent scale economies largely due to inadequate planning. Also, higher growth rate in units does not necessarily bring about scale economics. To improve scale economies, an enabling environment, innovative marketing techniques, development of support infrastructure are necessary. These are conspicuous by their absence in a developing economy due to inadequacy of resources for balanced development of industries and of regions/states/districts; rural vs urban diversity and forward vs backward states/regions. Hence, the following Chapters address to regional dispersal of industries, measures and causal factors for regional dispersal vs. growth, TFPG, Capital Intensity, Factor Productivities, Returns to Scale of Industries, etc. Increasing returns to scale in many industries was noted independent of TFPG. This could be due to higher factor productivities, accrued in turn from output elasticities to those factors/inputs, which was again independent of factor intensities and growth rates of Industries concerned. It may be further concluded that TFPG and output growth and factor productivities caused for increasing returns to scale in many and constant returns to scale in a few; but the converse necessarily hold good in the sense that returns to scale may remain independent of TFPG of disembodied (Neutral TP) and embodied type.

REFERENCES

1. The ASI data covers all factories registered under Sections 2m (*i*) and 2m (*ii*) of the Factories Act of 1948, i.e. those employing 10 or more workers with the aid of power; and those employing 20 or more workers without the aid of power, respectively, on any day of the preceding 12 months.
   (*a*) The ASI covers Bidi and Cigar Workers Act 1966, Registered Factories. employing 10 or more and using power and 20 or more if not using power.
   (*b*) All the electricity undertakings registered with the CEA are covered under ASI irrespective of their employment size. Certain services and activities like cold storage, water supply and repair of motor vehicles and of other consumer durable like watches are also covered under the ASI (pages 19 & 20, Ch. 3, EPWRF).
2. Sources- Herfindahl O.C., "*Concentration in Steel Industry*". Ph. D. Thesis, Columbia University, M. A. Adelman, "Comments on 'H' Concentration measures and Numbers equivalent: *Review of Economic and Statistics*, Vol. 51, 1969, pp. 99-101.
3. The Coefficient of Variation (CV) is a measure of dispersion suggested by Carl Pearson-Sources-'*Fundamentals of Statistics*' by S C Gupta, Himalaya Publishing House, Bombay, 1987, p. 415-17.
4. Employment was used by F. B Graver, F. M Baddy and A. J Niron in "*The Location of Manufactures in USA*", University of Minnesotalas, Minneapolis, 1933.
5. Value added was used by Linge G.J.R in "Concentration and Dispersal of Manufacturing in New Zealand"2- *Economic Geography*, Vol. 36-1960, pp. 326-343.
6. *EPW Research Foundation*—Data Base-Annual Survey of Industries, 1973-98.
7. Gupta S.C. Fundamentals of Statistics, *op. cit.*, pp. 416.
8. Allen, RGD *Statistics for Economists*, pp. 110.
9. William, Jeffrey, "Regional Inequality and the Process of National Development", *Economic Development of Cultural Change,* Vol. XIII, No. 4, Part-II, pp. 3-84, July 1965.
10. Somayajulu V V N—*Industrial Development of Andhra Pradesh-1956-86,* ICSSR Study, University of Hyderabad, Hyderabad-500046; (p. 4.3) 1993.
11. Chowdhury M.D.—*Behaviour of Spatial Income Inequality in a Developing Economy: India, 1950-70"* Paper presented at the 9th Conference of the Indian Association for Research in National Income and Wealth-January 1974.
12. Venkataramiah P. "Inter-State Variations in Industry, 1951-1961: A comment"—*Economic and Political Weekly (EPW)*, 4-August, 1969, pp. 1280-1.
13. Nair, K. R. G., "A Note on Inter-State Income Differentials in India-1950-51 to 1960-61", *Journal of Development Studies*, 7 July 1973, pp. 441-447.
14. Pathak C. R., "Regional Disparities in Industrial Development in India" Chapter-6, pp. 113-124; in the book "*Economic Liberalization and Regional Disparities in India-Special Focus on the North-Eastern Region*" edited by A. C. Mohapatro and C.R. Pathak, *Star Publishing House*, Shillong, 2003.
15. Dhar P. N. and D.U Sastry, "Inter-State Variations in Industry, 1951-61, *Economic and Political Weekly (EPW)*, 4, March-1969, pp. 535-538

16. Mahajan O.P.—*Regional Economic Development in India-1950-66*, Ph. D. Dissertation Kurukshetra University, 1972.
17. Lahiri R.K- "Some aspects of Interstate Disparity in Industrialization in India", *Sankhya*, 31, Series B, Dec. 1969.
18. Rao Hemlata, "Identification of Backward regions and the Study of Trends in Regional Disparities in India", Paper presented at the Regional Imbalances Seminar, *Indian Institute of Public Administration (IIPA)*, New Delhi, 1972.
19. Mathur Ashok, "Regional Development and Income Disparities n India: A sectoral Analysis-*Economic Development and Cultural Change*, Vol. 31, No. 3, April 1983, pp. 475-505.
20. Somayajulu V V N, *op. cit.*

Chapter 5

Analysis of Measures of Regional Dispersal of Indian Industries (1956-95) in All States and UT together and separately for Large States and for Small States and UT

INTRODUCTION

The objective of this Chapter is to analyse the nature and extent of regional dispersal of two-digit industries reflecting dispersion vis-à-vis concentration in India during the forty years of industrialisation from 1956 to 1995-6. It brings out trends over time periods of industrial growth or of retrogression during which concentration of industries or of regional dispersal took place, evenly or unevenly. In this context, Perpetuation hypothesis implies that growth in less developed countries might increase concentration and regional disparities, while Williamson hypothesis of industrialisation speaks of decrease in regional disparities after a certain period of concentration. But these two hypotheses are not tested empirically in this chapter because the data details are not available at micro-units of industries to connect multi-level space units like districts. However, a meaningful analysis due to industry (two-digit level) group for all large states together and all small states together and All States (large and small) together using State-UT wise data for each industry group is done here.

This chapter is divided into the following sections: Section 5.2 deals with Conceptual and Data details.

Section 5.3 deals with Analytical Framework (Review of Analytical Tools).

Section 5.4 deals with analysis of HH and CV results of All States and UT taken together, covering each industry group with respect to each of the variables during 10-year periods, followed by a similar analysis of a total of 40years, a similar analysis being done for Small States and UT and for Large States separately.

This would trace and deduce the differences in measures of regional dispersal arising due to each industry over distinct time periods and helps to understand how industrialisation is region-specific in the process of growth and development. This in turn helps in drawing policy guidelines and recommendations.

CONCEPTUAL AND DATA DETAILS

Measures of regional dispersal of industries are the measures of Hirshman-Herfindahl Index (HHI) and Coefficient of Variation (CV). The states and union territories are taken as units of analysis to measure the dispersal of 2-digit industries of Registered Factory Sector[1]. Summary Results of Registered Factory Sector are provided in the Annual Survey of Industries (ASI) Census Reports and in National Sample Survey (NSS) Sample Part of ASI Reports published by the Central Statistical Organization (CSO). This database is reproduced in the Economic and Political Weekly (EPW) Research Foundation Reports (ASI Census and Sample Part.

For the purposes of ASI, Census of factories were surveyed that consisted of employing 50 or more workers and using power, and those employing 100 or more workers but not using power. Besides, all the electricity undertakings irrespective of their size of employment, as also Bidi and cigar establishments were enumerated on census basis. The remaining factories, i.e. those employing 10-49 workers and using power, and 20-99 workers but not using power constituted the non-census (sample) sector and were fully covered but over a period of two years. The sample thus constituted 50 per cent of the factories each year in such a way that a factory is surveyed every alternate year (page20, Chapter-3, EPWRF).

The two measures of dispersion, i.e. Herfindahl Index (HHI)[2] and Coefficient of Variation (CV)[3] are used to measure regional dispersal of industries in terms of each of the five size variables, viz., Number of factories, Productive capital (PK) as proxy for Capital, Number of Workers as proxy for Labor[4], capital-labour (K/L) for capital intensity and output measured in terms of Net Value Added (NVA)[5], separately.

The 40-year time period is sub-divided into four sub-periods: 1959-1965, 1966-1975, 1976-86 and 1986-1996. 1965-66, 1975-76 and 1985-86 are the break points of very slow growth or trough years of industry. Data for 1956, 1957, 1958 were not uniformly available. Similarly, data for 1971, 1972, 1975, 1977-78 also was not available, hence neglected for analysis. So for the missing data of the states and of all-India in 1970s an averaging two preceding and two succeeding years data was used to interpolate the missing value.

All the factories in ASI frame have been classified into their appropriate industry groups as per NIC 1970 from 1973-74 to 1988-89 and as per NIC 1987 thereafter. Accordingly, classification is done on the basis of values of the principal products manufactured by them. But to comply with the secrecy clause of Collection of Statistics Act, the results of some industry groups were not published. If the number of units is 1 or 2 or 3, they were clubbed with each other for non-identity, except for industry groups 400 and 401 (electricity generation and distribution (p. 22, Ch-3, EPWRF[6]).

Computation of HH and CV, for all states and union territories (UTs) data were taken together, distinctly from two other groups data, each separately in categories of 17 large states and 12 small states including a few hill states and Union Territories, for each of the five variables. Data for Sikkim and Arunachal Pradesh was not available for all or for most of the years. Data for other hill states of Mizoram, Meghalaya, Nagaland, Manipur; and for coastal & island UTs of Pondicherry, Andaman & Nicobar, Dadra & Nagar Haveli, Daman & Diu, Chandigarh were not available for many initial years of four decades. The newly formed states like Chattisgarh, Jharkhand, Uttaranchal have been excluded.

Section 5.3 Analytical Framework Drawn from a Brief Review of Studies

Coefficient of Variation (C.V.)[7] is a relative measure of dispersion, defined as by $\sigma/\bar{x}$. It is a pure number, independent of units of measurement and is suitable for comparing the variability as a ratio mean of distributions. Karl Pearson defined it as percentage variation in mean[8]. A smaller CV is understood to mean homogeneous consistency better or more than the other. C.V. is a static ratio method and is useful for comparative statics only.

The findings and results of dispersal measures is to test the Perpetuation Hypothesis and the Williamson Hypothesis[9] leading to study of linkage effect differences that may lead to policy guidelines. The self-perpetuation hypothesis says that regional disparities widen in the process of development due to concentration of activities in a few pockets. On the contrary, Williamson states that regional inequalities increase in the beginning but ultimately lessen in the course of development. Many studies that test these hypotheses show differing results. Yet this is an extension of Hirshman's unbalanced growth model as explained and empirically tested by VVN Somayajulu[10].

VVN Somayajulu pointed out that in his study of Industrial Development of Andhra Pradesh pattern of change in regional inequalities depend not merely on variables and structural ratios but also on dis-integration of space studies such as districts, Blocks, villages, etc. Somayajulu concludes that India's experience in the 55 years of industrial planning could not decrease regional inequalities and this negated Williamson's hypothesis.

Location coefficients are silent regarding inter-temporal shifts and hence could not form part of our current study. This study intends to establish a link between technical progress, growth rates and dispersal that could provide insights into the processes of industrial development and the changes in industrial equity (regional and individual) and in efficiency of industries.

Studies by M.D. Choudhury[11], Venkataramaiah[12] (criticism of Dhar & Sastry), K G Nair[13], C.R Pathak.[14], all pointed out to increasing disparities. However, Dhar & Sastry[15], O. P. Mahajan[16], R.K. Lahiri[17] and Hemlata Rao[18] saw convergence. Ashok Mathur[19] analyzed sectoral disparities for 25 years and stated that initially there is a narrowing down but later inequalities increased. He said that no state except UP contributed to narrowing down. But VVN Somayajulu[20] pointed out that primary sector's disparities (since it originated in rural decentralised sector and out-migration of rural labour activities caused to reduce disparities in rural activities but led to increase disparities in secondary sector activities or urban metropolitan cities) are open to testing at various spatial levels in micro state level industrial development studies as in AP Studies of the author.

ANALYSIS OF RESULTS, FINDINGS RELATING TO CV AND HH OF VARIABLES AND STRUCTURAL RATIOS OF INDUSTRY GROUPS OF LARGE STATES, ALL STATES AND UNION TERRITORIES TAKEN TOGETHER VERSUS SMALL STATES AND UTS:

If CV is 1 and less than 0.5, then there is no consistency with respect to regional dispersal of industries. CV= $\sigma/\bar{x}$ is a coefficient of variation and inverse of consistency. If CV is >1–1.5 then there is dispersal and if CV is <1–1.5 there is concentration. Then what is desired for dispersal is CV>1 or = 1wherein it provides a case for consistency and dispersal but no concentration.

However HH is $\Sigma x_i^2 - (\Sigma x_i)^2$ where x_i is deviation about mean. So if HH is zero (0) then there is no dispersal and no concentration. If HH is >0-0.5, then there is dispersal. If HH is < 0-0.5, then there is concentration.

CV Results for 12 Smaller States (that Include Union Territories)

The States and Union Territories taken in this category are Delhi, Chandigarh, Pondicherry, Goa-Daman-Diu, Tripura, Mizoram, Meghalaya, Nagaland, Manipur, Andaman & Nicobar Islands, Dadra & Nagar Haveli, Sikkim (though data could not be consistently available).

Table 5.1 Coefficient of Variation (CV) and Herfindahl Index (HI) of Industry Groups in Small States and UTs of India during 1959-65

		I.Nm. Co	CV Results of Variables or Structural Ratios					HH results of Variables or Structural Ratios				
Sl.No.	Range	Code	Units	PK	Emp	NVA	K/L	Units	PK	Emp	NVA	K/L
1	h	Food (IN21)	3.433	6.994	6.685	7.475	6.994	0.501	0.840	0.810	0.888	0.937
	l		1.404	5.266	3.132	5.892	4.492	0.336	0.719	0.266	0.816	0.369
	m		2.413	6.280	4.421	6.814	6.032	0.446	0.787	0.621	0.850	0.860
2	h	Textile (IN25)	4.949	7.279	7.284	7.844	0.384	0.585	0.901	0.868	0.927	0.689
	l		2.546	2.779	4.603	5.069	0.002	0.545	0.554	0.573	0.667	0.500
	m		3.586	5.815	5.077	6.884	0.166	0.572	0.730	0.656	0.745	0.549
3	h	M Prd. (IN34)	4.342	4.765	5.478	6.523	4.532	0.830	0.849	0.919	0.932	0.849
	l		1.211	1.551	2.322	2.354	1.255	0.755	0.835	0.835	0.869	0.500
	m		1.542	2.859	3.798	3.895	2.658	0.800	0.841	0.889	0.892	0.639
4	h	Tr. Eq. (IN37)	3.211	3.424	4.563	4.585	4.241	0.659	0.619	0.652	0.816	0.504
	l		1.513	1.621	2.211	2.578	1.254	0.409	0.408	0.610	0.746	0.303
	m		2.334	2.354	3.514	3.981	2.754	0.559	0.519	0.631	0.781	0.404

Note: h-highest, l-lowest, m-mean value.

In the period 1959-65, there is sparse results, suggesting that either industry was inadequately and inequitably distributed or data was not consistently available. However, results show that in Food Products Industry (IN20+21), coefficients of variation of Units, employment, productive capital, NVA and K/L are highly dispersed. This means that bulk investments in the form of fixed capital flowing from the state in the form of fixed capital or investment could be easily changed into malleable or working or productive capital by the entrepreneur-farmer-industrialists in this early phase of planned industrialisation. The mean values of units being nearer the higher CV figures also supports our above inference. The CV of K/L however shows that capital intensity in this industry was highly dispersed. The HH of all the 5 variables suggests similar inferences, though the results of HH units are not very much different from HH of other variables.

Textiles (IN23+IN24+IN25) comprising cotton, wool, silk, jute are highly dispersed in both CV and HH results, except in CV of capital intensity that shows a value less than 1.

Table 5.2. Coefficient of Variation (C.V.) and Herfindahl Index (H.I.) of Industry Groups in Small States and UTs of India during 1966-75

Sl.No.	Range	I.Nm. Co	CV Results of Variables or Structural Ratios					HH results of Variables or Structural Ratios				
			Units	PK	Emp	NVA	K/L	Units	PK	Emp	NVA	K/L
1.	h	21	3.264	7.537	6.669	8.003	6.216	0.574	0.894	0.719	0.914	0.870
	l	Food	1.697	2.955	2.174	3.930	0.694	0.422	0.507	0.420	0.703	0.163
	m		2.494	5.024	3.658	6.556	3.148	0.501	0.674	0.580	0.847	0.540
3.	h	25	6.839	7.516	6.669	5.431	2.785	0.839	0.722	0.589	0.977	0.744
	l	Textiles	1.943	1.217	2.174	2.103	1.003	0.568	0.510	0.174	0.657	0.500
	m		3.604	3.083	3.235	3.336	1.914	0.632	0.590	0.501	0.738	0.563
4.	h	27	4.714	7.090	5.737	6.810	2.837	0.654	0.892	0.809	0.822	0.567
	l	Wood	2.771	1.075	1.044	1.195	0.325	0.504	0.428	0.432	0.510	0.161
	m		3.782	2.940	2.431	3.675	1.027	0.590	0.613	0.575	0.610	0.479
5.	h	28	2.121	4.928	3.060	4.800	1.227	0.531	0.583	0.514	0.730	0.500
	l	Paper	2.033	1.066	1.058	1.677	1.120	0.315	0.500	0.500	0.520	0.242
	m		2.007	3.236	1.139	2.159	1.170	0.423	0.542	0.507	0.625	0.371
6.	h	30	5.142	4.352	5.564	3.321	4.252	0.771	0.592	0.808	0.501	0.486
	l	Chem	2.224	2.542	1.568	1.551	1.325	0.362	0.302	0.513	0.231	0.210
	m		3.542	3.655	2.689	2.15	2.756	0.424	0.364	0.636	0.334	0.329
7.	h	31	4.492	8.402	7.264	8.101	7.264	0.640	0.990	0.866	0.956	0.888
	l	Ru,P-C	2.660	4.026	3.894	1.994	3.958	0.381	0.526	0.508	0.389	0.514
	m		3.488	4.143	4.418	5.047	4.418	0.503	0.588	0.657	0.448	0.654
8.	h	32	5.010	6.672	6.249	6.506	2.444	0.682	0.952	0.876	0.921	0.523
	l	NmMP	4.243	3.002	1.298	2.697	1.801	0.625	0.563	0.512	0.551	0.416
	m		4.626	4.837	3.774	4.601	2.122	0.436	0.505	0.462	0.491	0.313
9.	h	34	6.894	7.308	6.347	7.173	2.700	0.830	0.871	0.800	0.855	0.800
	l	MetPrd	4.075	4.863	4.444	5.389	1.096	0.661	0.800	0.749	0.800	0.255
	m		5.336	6.042	5.461	6.246	1.690	0.768	0.822	0.785	0.825	0.622
10.	h	36	7.425	6.660	7.501	8.018	4.933	0.883	0.949	0.939	0.946	0.800
	l	MotTr	5.231	2.083	5.564	1.833	1.122	0.564	0.694	0.564	0.679	0.351
	m		6.407	4.675	6.556	4.975	3.401	0.766	0.811	0.799	0.808	0.672
11.	h	37	6.364	5.007	5.690	6.000	3.554	0.705	0.842	0.820	0.899	0.653
	l	Tr.Eq.	3.677	1.478	2.239	1.441	0.422	0.364	0.511	0.535	0.558	0.257
	m		4.820	3.292	4.133	4.576	1.476	0.465	0.641	0.742	0.765	0.432
12.	h	41	3.394	8.468	8.183	8.442	7.603	0.580	0.998	0.965	0.995	0.901
	l	EGS	1.697	1.210	5.128	3.675	5.835	0.520	0.510	0.683	0.594	0.736
	m		2.263	3.962	6.241	6.816	6.658	0.540	0.681	0.784	0.857	0.811

There are HH and CV results for Metal Products (IN 34) and Transport Equipment (IN 37). HH results show that they were highly dispersed over smaller states, though Metal Products (IN34) are the least dispersed among them.

1966 to 1975: (For category of Smaller states).

A maximum dispersal in Food Industry (IN21) is noticed in NVA both in CV and HH measures, though all other variables show high dispersal too. However, the mean values show a tendency to be nearer to the lowest values of CV and HH in their corresponding variables that shows that higher values are jump and not in line with the trend movement of dispersal results. But in case of Machinery other than Transport (IN36=35+36) and Other Manufacturing Industries (IN38) the mean values are nearer the higher values. So in this decade, electrical and non-electrical machinery (IN35 and IN36) and OMI did show high dispersal. This could be an offshoot of earlier growth impulses as OMI consists of pharmaceuticals, sports, jewellery related, stationery articles, feather, brooms and badges. The users of products of OMI are often those who could have lags in demonstration affect and manifest of late release of pent-up demands. Even electrical and non-electrical industry spread could be an outcome of two factors. First, it is an outcome of radio communication that reached smaller and rural areas later and so it is no wonder that electrical industry could spread there. The other is more futuristic in character. It was a sort of preparation for the electronic boom that was to spread across in the later decades. There need be little newer explanation for other elements of this industry like agricultural implements, sewing machines, etc. So industrial retrogression has not affected dispersal though Chemical Industry, still to achieve 'sunrise status' of 1970s, did show the lowest dispersal, at least in NVA values. This being a capital intensive and heavy industry, it can be said recession did not allow this industry to spread itself regionally, at least the smaller states. However, textiles, wood, rubber petroleum coal, EGS does show less dispersal as mean values are nearer lowest figure. In small states, despite low spread of industry, these industries, both capital intensive and labour intensive could have had a wider role to play, had recession not taken place. In other words, except Electrical and non-electrical machinery, which could be a fringe industry, other industries have been affected by recessionary economic environment.

1976 to 1985 (For Smaller States)

NVA and PK show higher dispersal in this decade in Food Products (IN21) both by CV and HH measures. In Beverages (IN22), employment and NVA show greater relative dispersal. Productive Capital shows maximum relative dispersal in case of Textiles (IN25), Wood (IN27) and Electricity, Gas and Steam (IN41) and Leather (IN29).

Units have maximum relative dispersal in Transport Equipment (IN37), Rubber, Petroleum and Coal (IN31), Basic Metals and Alloys (IN33) NVA in Transport Equipment and Parts (IN37) show lesser dispersal than other variables. In Metal Products (IN34), NVA showed the maximum relative dispersal.

In Textile Products (IN26) and Chemicals (IN30) the mean values of all variables are nearer the lowest values of the variables, implying relative dispersal is low in this industry. In Basic Metals and Alloys (IN33), Paper (IN28) and Electricity, Gas and Steam (IN41) opposite is the case.

Since Transport Industry show high Units dispersal but low NVA dispersal, it is obvious that setting up number of units is not bringing in either a highly productive work culture

Table 5.3. Coefficient of Variation (C.V.) and Herfindahl Index (H.I.) of Industry Groups in Small states and UTs of India during 1976-85

Sl. No.	Ind Name	Range	CV Results of Variables or Structural Ratios					HH results of Variables or Structural Ratios				
			Units	PK	Emp	NVA	K/L	Units	PK	Emp	NVA	K/L
1.	Food	h	2.379	3.863	2.622	4.294	2.703	0.379	0.671	0.456	0.746	0.447
	(IN21)	l	1.758	2.948	2.015	2.023	0.870	0.272	0.505	0.312	0.314	0.174
		m	1.975	3.314	2.296	3.148	1.241	0.307	0.587	0.362	0.551	0.223
2.	Bev'ge	h	3.361	3.715	4.033	5.896	3.207	0.538	0.538	0.589	0.816	0.476
	(IN22)	l	1.334	1.232	2.125	2.393	1.120	0.277	0.277	0.323	0.359	0.269
		m	2.473	2.183	3.033	3.426	2.284	0.398	0.357	0.446	0.506	0.358
3.	Textile	h	4.840	5.433	4.728	4.312	4.166	0.669	0.628	0.668	0.765	0.545
	(IN25)	l	2.099	1.489	2.781	1.012	2.236	0.487	0.405	0.472	0.388	0.319
		m	3.097	3.993	3.268	2.363	2.886	0.582	0.517	0.550	0.555	0.437
4.	Tex Prd	h	8.256	8.416	8.380	8.439	4.814	0.973	0.992	0.988	0.995	0.661
	(IN26)	l	5.402	1.682	3.529	5.773	1.038	0.806	0.520	0.587	0.790	0.401
		m	6.799	6.295	6.480	6.961	2.848	0.916	0.891	0.895	0.946	0.498
5.	Wood	h	2.022	3.599	3.450	3.541	1.274	0.313	0.644	0.639	0.639	0.212
	(IN27)	l	1.281	2.070	2.058	2.569	0.672	0.189	0.321	0.331	0.396	0.147
		m	1.580	2.897	2.692	2.993	0.979	0.250	0.498	0.448	0.507	0.185
6.	Paper	h	3.677	3.547	3.311	4.012	1.564	0.706	0.667	0.600	0.670	0.268
	(IN28)	l	3.006	2.848	2.752	3.009	0.855	0.451	0.425	0.409	0.520	0.182
		m	3.311	3.203	2.977	3.395	1.161	0.593	0.566	0.509	0.608	0.203
7.	Leather	h	7.460	8.202	7.989	8.176	3.993	0.886	0.967	0.943	0.964	0.800
	(IN29)	l	3.494	5.211	4.417	5.442	0.357	0.585	0.741	0.636	0.800	0.501
		m	4.011	5.886	4.525	6.772	1.681	0.772	0.814	0.789	0.823	0.717
8.	Chem	h	5.499	4.714	4.872	3.620	4.062	0.880	0.817	0.681	0.523	0.594
	(IN30)	l	3.497	3.325	3.288	2.850	2.139	0.505	0.480	0.475	0.419	0.345
		m	4.216	3.859	3.889	3.282	3.149	0.628	0.571	0.568	0.477	0.469
9.	RPC	h	5.050	5.073	5.063	5.218	6.351	0.792	0.801	0.689	0.817	0.894
	(IN31)	l	3.368	3.077	3.319	3.383	1.454	0.486	0.472	0.496	0.495	0.265
		m	4.601	3.961	4.041	3.887	3.273	0.711	0.586	0.591	0.586	0.505
10.	NmMP	h	4.427	3.628	5.063	6.304	3.337	0.744	0.566	0.793	0.776	0.553
	(IN32)	l	2.370	1.707	3.319	1.765	1.967	0.363	0.268	0.367	0.266	0.301
		m	2.984	2.585	3.537	2.897	2.705	0.471	0.396	0.546	0.412	0.432
11.	BM&A	h	5.067	4.12	6.171	5.659	3.716	0.834	0.845	0.855	0.917	0.938
	(IN33)	l	4.122	1.707	2.401	2.861	1.967	0.577	0.463	0.576	0.421	0.279
		m	4.665	3.62	4.528	4.178	3.313	0.715	0.640	0.710	0.638	0.647

Sl. No.	Ind Name	Range	CV Results of Variables or Structural Ratios					HH results of Variables or Structural Ratios				
			Units	PK	Emp	NVA	K/L	Units	PK	Emp	NVA	K/L
12.	MetPrd (IN34)	h	4.519	4.795	4.323	4.991	2.962	0.909	0.839	0.706	0.831	0.444
		l	3.376	3.717	3.528	3.641	0.498	0.451	0.559	0.509	0.738	0.199
		m	3.944	4.187	3.977	4.315	1.323	0.655	0.691	0.642	0.714	0.268
13.	MotTr (IN36)	h	6.450	6.294	6.420	6.266	1.951	0.911	0.884	0.959	0.886	0.307
		l	3.255	3.411	3.941	3.871	0.395	0.471	0.492	0.574	0.542	0.225
		m	5.059	4.994	5.107	4.938	1.221	0.796	0.782	0.805	0.768	0.287
14.	Tr. Eq. (IN37)	h	5.887	4.382	4.137	4.653	2.549	0.815	0.733	0.675	0.722	0.424
		l	3.333	2.654	2.970	2.936	0.515	0.509	0.396	0.477	0.439	0.200
		m	4.501	3.282	3.447	3.642	1.277	0.754	0.510	0.527	0.563	0.254
15.	OMI (IN38)	h	6.347	6.334	5.965	8.400	3.941	0.893	0.714	0.818	0.831	0.818
		l	2.117	2.051	1.687	1.915	1.224	0.493	0.345	0.269	0.315	0.269
		m	4.237	4.079	3.623	4.527	2.616	0.751	0.572	0.535	0.595	0.490
16.	EGS (IN41)	h	3.025	4.902	6.531	6.487	4.684	0.396	0.990	0.926	0.918	0.706
		l	1.023	2.051	1.031	2.348	0.916	0.190	0.339	0.204	0.358	0.214
		m	1.709	4.720	4.162	4.355	2.591	0.309	0.835	0.675	0.702	0.438

or any great profitability, due to lack of forward and backward linkages. Similarly, the quality of roads in smaller and rural areas must be leaving a lot to be desired.

Secondly, Textile Products (IN26) can be activated and region specific marketing and design centres can be established. Thirdly, Chemicals Industry (IN30), in this decade was a sunrise industry but in the Small States case, it is not dispersed, given the capital intensive nature of this industry and its need for forward linkages across space. But its potential can be seen in the fact that small states are agriculture intensive as also disease intensive. So fertilizer and medicines being prerequisites in smaller states, chemical industry will have a bigger role to perform than has been visualised and assigned so far.

1986 to 1995 (For Smaller States)

In this decade, Textile Products (IN26) dispersed well implying that smaller regions must have found a robust and vibrant market that enabled its spread. EGS did well in employment dispersal implying that urge for power reforms brought in greater local employment, though actual decentralisation still has a long way to go. Machinery other than Transport (IN36) and Metal Products (IN34) also dispersed well in smaller regions in this decade. So these above stated industries are the gains of industrialisation that have helped in bringing about regional spread, that is, whatever spread it could, to smaller, rural, hilly, coastal and island isolated and remote areas.

Table 5.4. Coefficient of Variation (C.V.) and Herfindahl Index (H.I.) of Industry Groups in Small states and UT of India during 1986-95.

Sl. No.	InN & Cd	Range	CV Results of Variables or Structural Ratios					HH results of Variables or Structural Ratios				
			Units	PK	Emp	NVA	K/L	Units	PK	Emp	K/L	NVA
1	Food	h	2.023	3.607	2.864	3.180	1.470	0.324	0.618	0.451	0.231	0.623
	(IN21)	l	1.506	2.160	1.956	1.500	0.714	0.200	0.370	0.324	0.151	0.237
		m	1.703	2.747	2.253	2.515	1.101	0.268	0.491	0.371	0.189	0.431
2	Bev'g	h	5.103	4.507	4.293	4.456	2.806	0.792	0.673	0.634	0.414	0.609
	(IN22)	l	1.936	1.693	2.040	2.113	1.056	0.304	0.310	0.391	0.265	0.343
		m	3.901	2.984	3.616	3.228	1.784	0.584	0.453	0.540	0.324	0.472
3	Textile	h	5.076	7.730	4.091	5.669	7.291	0.656	0.915	0.575	0.869	0.738
	(IN25)	l	2.580	3.398	2.074	2.590	2.864	0.459	0.523	0.469	0.451	0.520
		m	2.902	5.068	2.943	4.335	4.548	0.514	0.673	0.539	0.635	0.632
4	TexPr	h	6.538	6.821	6.707	6.901	3.038	0.927	0.980	0.958	0.462	0.995
	(IN26)	l	3.702	3.821	3.666	5.144	1.060	0.524	0.536	0.520	0.266	0.935
		m	4.801	5.113	4.861	6.501	2.009	0.689	0.733	0.699	0.378	0.963
5	Wood	h	1.878	3.074	2.951	3.227	1.262	0.296	0.536	0.508	0.209	0.489
	(IN27)	l	1.222	2.306	2.015	1.429	0.690	0.198	0.425	0.322	0.148	0.228
		m	1.405	2.706	2.496	2.440	0.903	0.224	0.468	0.419	0.170	0.397
6	Paper	h	3.877	4.283	3.778	4.436	2.128	0.618	0.709	0.290	0.345	0.823
	(IN28)	l	2.237	2.232	2.379	2.691	0.718	0.389	0.367	0.202	0.190	0.477
		m	2.898	3.044	2.731	3.469	1.385	0.506	0.546	0.464	0.234	0.642
7	29	h	5.201	7.586	6.883	7.453	7.989	0.688	0.900	0.829	0.943	0.886
	Leath	l	2.354	1.151	1.047	1.168	1.008	0.501	0.500	0.452	0.452	0.500
		m	3.392	3.526	2.080	4.937	3.792	0.590	0.614	0.544	0.631	0.706
8	30	h	3.993	5.059	4.125	4.602	2.902	0.666	0.911	0.683	0.425	0.788
	Chem	l	2.315	1.950	1.857	2.182	1.094	0.349	0.306	0.296	0.207	0.332
		m	3.385	3.642	3.291	3.012	1.782	0.545	0.623	0.537	0.290	0.466
9	31	h	4.238	5.059	3.812	3.418	3.518	0.701	0.911	0.604	0.352	0.525
	Ru,PC	l	2.566	2.353	2.523	1.017	0.798	0.494	0.442	0.452	0.191	0.427
		m	3.463	3.913	3.358	2.898	1.702	0.580	0.635	0.544	0.264	0.477
10	32	h	3.673	3.258	3.843	3.584	3.584	0.702	0.535	0.709	0.613	0.534
	NmMP	l	2.135	1.672	1.261	1.800	1.263	0.198	0.264	0.199	0.203	0.190
		m	2.666	2.387	2.760	2.247	2.389	0.463	0.396	0.484	0.389	0.359
11	33	h	4.625	4.668	4.229	4.090	4.572	0.742	0.805	0.697	0.781	0.971
	BM&A	l	3.022	1.453	2.258	1.623	1.430	0.454	0.240	0.344	0.273	0.273
		m	3.903	2.978	3.646	2.521	2.589	0.632	0.467	0.571	0.443	0.457

Sl. No.	I.Nm. Co	Range	CV Results of Variables or Structural Ratios					HH results of Variables or Structural Ratios				
			Units	PK	Emp	NVA	K/L	Units	PK	Emp	K/L	NVA
12	34	h	3.743	4.488	3.990	4.346	2.562	0.720	0.774	0.642	0.900	0.822
	MetPr	l	2.720	2.364	2.987	2.266	1.014	0.427	0.361	0.476	0.202	0.345
		m	3.272	3.681	3.499	3.640	1.609	0.546	0.642	0.578	0.340	0.630
13.	36	h	5.031	5.158	5.211	4.445	2.438	0.836	0.821	0.871	0.836	0.909
	MotTr	l	2.943	2.767	3.777	3.090	1.333	0.467	0.590	0.615	0.249	0.646
		m	4.045	4.115	4.287	4.358	1.624	0.710	0.727	0.764	0.373	0.789
14.	37	h	5.297	4.594	4.416	4.445	3.693	0.871	0.914	0.983	0.878	0.720
	Tr.Eq.	l	2.940	3.036	3.472	3.090	1.878	0.487	0.456	0.501	0.264	0.414
		m	3.994	3.598	3.912	3.854	2.256	0.662	0.623	0.677	0.428	0.557
15.	38	h	3.025	3.101	1.986	2.360	2.800	0.974	0.856	0.986	0.823	0.685
		l	2.097	1.744	1.204	1.454	1.082	0.172	0.280	0.191	0.182	0.229
16	OMI	m	2.365	2.383	1.669	1.861	1.594	0.471	0.591	0.453	0.362	0.384
	EGS	h	4.649	5.284	4.742	4.338	4.675	0.800	0.976	0.880	0.807	0.950
	(IN41)	l	1.889	1.994	1.189	1.485	1.114	0.203	0.087	0.239	0.235	0.243
		m	2.646	3.888	3.117	2.589	2.234	0.401	0.639	0.614	0.413	0.548

However the failures are many. The many labour intensive and capital intensive industries showed mean values both in CV and HH, nearer to lowest CV and HH values, implying that dispersal has a long winding goal to achieve.

Some Brief Inferences

This section dealt with regional spread of industries in smaller regions that comprised north-eastern hilly and inaccessible areas, coastal and islands, union territories, often with distinct administrative and population and distinct cultures that has tendency to resist homogeneity and integration with what it considers the mainstream socio-economic cultural life. While dispersal is noticed, it may often be with lesser magnitude of industries that establish themselves in these areas. So while with the limited opportunities, smaller regions can be said to have done well for themselves, a deeper and relative study of industries reveals that most HH and CV results, especially when mean values of CV and HH measures are found, it shows nearer in magnitude to the lowest values of those variables tabulated. This brought out the fact that dispersal is not so widespread and is relegated to few pockets.

Indeed there is vast scope for industries to make their presence felt in these areas and a large number of region specific measures and incentives along with market development measures can give a boost to industrialisation in these areas.

In the next paragraph, we study regional spread of industries in larger regions and see how it differs from results of smaller regions.

Table 5.5 Coefficient of Variation (C.V.) and Herfindahl Index (H.I.) of Industry Groups in Large States of India during 1959-65

Sl. No.	N.Code	Range	CV Results of Variables or Structural Ratios					HH results of Variables or Structural Ratios				
			Units	PK	Emp	NVA	K/L	Units	PK	Emp	NVA	K/L
1	Food (IN21)	h	1.078	4.228	1.157	1.287	2.706	0.501	0.840	0.810	0.888	0.937
		l	0.913	1.053	1.043	0.856	0.525	0.336	0.719	0.266	0.816	0.369
		m	1.008	1.636	1.090	1.055	0.927	0.446	0.787	0.621	0.850	0.860
2	Bev' (IN22)	h	3.848	2.361	4.762	4.668	4.657	0.425	0.546	0.568	0.551	0.741
		l	1.914	1.472	2.702	1.488	1.014	0.126	0.119	0.212	0.174	0.256
		m	2.469	1.803	3.568	2.130	2.317	0.324	0.385	0.358	0.366	0.421
3	Textiles (IN25)	h	1.407	1.720	1.760	1.792	1.668	0.585	0.901	0.868	0.927	0.689
		l	1.182	1.457	1.469	1.564	0.420	0.545	0.554	0.573	0.667	0.500
		m	1.305	1.590	1.629	1.664	0.682	0.572	0.730	0.656	0.745	0.549
4	Tex'Prds) (IN26	h	1.546	1.736	1.745	4.313	0.735	0.215	0.451	0.242	0.511	0.547
		l	1.340	1.307	1.350	1.314	0.441	0.122	0.121	0.113	0.132	0.212
		m	1.456	1.498	1.578	2.038	0.646	0.174	0.326	0.314	0.345	0.326
5	Wood (IN27)	h	1.868	2.446	1.463	3.942	3.956	0.800	0.800	0.800	0.800	0.800
		l	1.014	1.625	1.270	2.007	0.555	0.500	0.533	0.507	0.607	0.500
		m	1.402	1.941	1.424	2.465	0.925	0.726	0.739	0.718	0.745	0.724
6	Paper (IN28)	h	1.632	1.419	1.463	4.630	1.781	0.324	0.352	0.321	0.362	0.187
		l	1.458	1.040	1.270	1.430	1.161	0.121	0.212	0.212	0.177	0.141
		m	1.509	1.217	1.364	1.509	1.288	0.321	0.289	0.259	0.231	0.164
7.	Leath (IN29)	h	4.630	8.988	4.785	5.616	5.025	0.351	0.454	0.657	0.452	0.560
		l	3.155	4.061	4.081	2.486	1.578	0.121	0.231	0.241	0.126	0.211
		m	3.773	5.540	4.412	3.846	2.284	0.234	0.335	0.365	0.324	0.385
8.	ChemPr (IN30)	h	2.836	4.919	4.120	4.249	4.348	0.365	0.422	0.421	0.425	0.458
		l	2.031	2.960	2.638	2.909	1.533	0.124	0.285	0.184	0.169	0.264
		m	2.232	3.916	3.405	3.686	2.693	0.354	0.352	0.324	0.328	0.368
9.	Ru,Pe,C (IN31)	h	1.804	1.811	2.953	4.076	2.824	0.389	0.342	0.354	0.358	0.325
		l	1.285	1.467	1.425	2.148	1.195	0.211	0.16	0.124	0.158	0.124
		m	1.659	1.655	1.801	2.492	1.612	0.355	0.254	0.320	0.263	0.321
10.	NmMP (IN32)	h	1.961	3.251	2.003	3.463	2.246	0.546	0.285	0.464	0.415	0.453
		l	1.822	1.251	1.719	1.788	1.776	0.101	0.121	0.201	0.131	0.212
		m	1.893	1.983	1.891	0.986	1.970	0.366	0.241	0.321	0.321	0.276
11.	Bmet&A (IN33)	h	2.058	3.113	2.424	2.766	4.262	0.324	0.521	0.357	0.358	0.498
		l	1.585	1.835	1.663	1.860	1.081	0.145	0.187	0.161	0.125	1.56
		m	1.781	2.278	1.970	2.329	2.043	0.301	0.356	0.295	0.320	0.288

Sl. No.	I.Nm. Co	Range	CV Results of Variables or Structural Ratios					HH results of Variables or Structural Ratios				
			Units	PK	Emp	NVA	K/L	Units	PK	Emp	NVA	K/L
12	MetPrd	h	1.951	3.135	2.204	2.447	3.246	0.830	0.850	0.919	0.931	0.800
	(IN34)	l	1.680	2.337	2.008	2.002	0.502	0.755	0.500	0.800	0.800	0.570
		m	1.801	2.732	2.118	2.322	0.990	0.800	0.775	0.838	0.848	0.731
13.	MotTr	h	1.461	1.751	1.605	3.937	0.781	0.321	0.333	0.541	0.527	0.522
	(IN36)	l	1.352	1.272	1.382	1.614	0.539	0.198	0.181	0.101	0.129	0.169
		m	1.401	1.547	1.523	2.265	1.124	0.211	0.234	0.324	0.363	0.411
14	TrnEq&P	h	1.818	2.217	1.874	3.527	4.547	0.800	0.850	0.919	0.932	0.850
	(IN37)	l	1.452	1.611	1.703	1.605	0.827	0.660	0.500	0.800	0.800	0.800
		m	1.625	1.923	1.791	2.091	1.457	0.706	0.676	0.701	0.787	0.602
15	OMI	h	2.299	2.921	4.042	4.738	1.566	0.154	0.254	0.458	0.354	0.563
	(IN38)	l	1.608	1.963	1.895	2.269	0.705	0.111	0.124	0.211	0.211	0.211
		m	1.898	2.401	2.496	3.045	1.074	0.35	0.322	0.356	0.311	0.354
16	EGS	h	1.341	1.991	1.720	2.760	2.193	0.321	0.366	0.354	0.421	0.271
	(IN41)	l	0.980	0.899	0.908	1.110	0.632	0.124	0.181	0.121	0.121	0.101
		m	1.176	1.475	1.331	1.656	1.260	0.289	0.259	0.268	0.295	0.23

1959-65 A Decadal Analysis of Hhand CV Measure of Dispersal of Industries of Large States

In case of Wood (IN27), Metal Products (IN34) and Transport Equipment (IN37), high dispersal is noticed Along with mean values being nearer to highest values of the variables. While productive capital was highly dispersed in case of Food Products as found by CV and HH, in other industries it was less so.

Food (IN21), Beverages (IN22), Chemicals (IN30), Non Metallic Mineral Product (IN32), Basic Metals And Alloys (IN33) showed dispersal Mean Values near to the lowest values. So this showed that all these industries showed more concentration than dispersal in most of the years of this decade.

CV and HH Results of Industry Groups in Large States and UTs during 1966-75

While Textiles, Leather, Textile Products showed high dispersal with mean values being nearer to the highest values recorded both in CV and HH, Metal Products (IN34) also showed dispersal on the higher side with mean values being nearer to the highest values.

Beverages (IN22), Leather (IN29), show higher dispersal both in terms of higher values and in terms of mean values being nearer to higher values.

But in OMI, EGS, Chemicals, Rubber, Petroleum, Coal, Non metallic Mineral products showed mean values being near to lowest values. Thus relatively, capital intensive industries did not disperse well in the recession hit 1966-75 period. Thus recession did dampen the prospects of regional dispersal of Indian industries.

Table 5.6. Coefficient of Variation (C.V.) and Herfindahl Index (H.I.) of Industry Groups in Large States of India during 1966-75

Sl. No.	Inm & Co	Range	CV Results of Variables or Structural Ratios					HH results of Variables or Structural Ratios				
			Units	PK	Emp	NVA	K/L	Units	PK	Emp	NVA	K/L
1	Food	h	1.092	1.324	1.880	1.100	0.591	0.114	0.152	0.246	0.133	0.084
	(IN21)	l	1.002	0.869	0.868	0.825	0.417	0.098	0.102	0.101	0.097	0.072
		m	1.060	1.091	1.132	1.023	0.519	0.107	0.125	0.134	0.117	0.078
2	Bev'es	h	3.304	3.479	4.265	2.258	4.567	0.416	0.616	0.600	0.364	0.630
	(IN22)	l	1.944	1.449	2.621	1.805	0.700	0.250	0.164	0.399	0.212	0.090
		m	2.867	2.252	3.592	2.139	2.011	0.356	0.296	0.503	0.253	0.247
3	Textiles	h	1.246	1.565	1.601	4.118	3.025	0.142	0.185	0.191	0.888	0.168
	(IN25)	l	1.114	1.308	1.375	1.570	0.365	0.131	0.154	0.161	0.191	0.510
		m	1.197	1.412	1.459	2.018	0.931	0.137	0.165	0.172	0.303	0.148
4	Tex.Prd	h	1.776	2.415	2.006	4.102	3.626	0.208	0.319	0.244	0.775	0.623
	(IN26)	l	1.036	1.304	1.220	1.426	0.444	0.118	0.161	0.140	0.168	0.073
		m	1.457	1.745	1.712	2.299	1.103	0.166	0.210	0.201	0.339	0.170
5	Wood	h	3.157	4.650	1.395	4.425	4.029	0.520	0.975	0.159	0.890	0.906
	(IN27)	l	0.867	1.264	0.888	1.110	0.606	0.101	0.144	0.103	0.127	0.088
		m	1.537	2.201	1.245	2.154	2.162	0.212	0.338	0.142	0.317	0.396
6	Paper	h	1.583	4.111	2.602	3.610	3.893	0.197	0.940	0.395	0.739	0.801
	(IN28)	l	1.290	0.917	1.046	0.959	0.611	0.148	0.105	0.119	0.110	0.080
		m	1.362	1.584	1.505	1.596	1.803	0.159	0.251	0.199	0.230	0.309
7	Leather	h	4.413	4.325	3.820	5.718	3.545	0.452	0.444	0.401	0.724	0.459
	(IN29)	l	1.880	2.228	2.295	2.988	0.371	0.209	0.255	0.287	0.376	0.113
		m	3.215	3.141	3.254	3.980	1.412	0.344	0.358	0.351	0.470	0.241
8	Chem	h	2.091	5.116	3.147	3.226	5.694	0.231	0.408	0.408	0.399	0.493
	(IN30)	l	1.261	1.381	1.438	1.520	0.709	0.144	0.167	0.167	0.175	0.091
		m	1.682	2.579	2.351	2.245	2.299	0.188	0.342	0.275	0.262	0.313
9	R,P,C	h	3.655	1.811	1.667	2.246	1.412	0.756	0.213	0.189	0.324	0.160
	(IN31)	l	1.136	1.265	0.991	1.748	0.574	0.130	0.147	0.116	0.204	0.078
		m	1.847	1.618	1.448	1.971	0.894	0.261	0.194	0.167	0.248	0.112
10	NmMP	h	2.022	4.031	3.720	2.214	3.503	0.117	0.803	0.694	0.330	0.623
	(IN32)	l	1.041	1.032	1.007	1.080	0.658	0.100	0.089	0.092	0.092	0.091
		m	1.511	1.596	1.609	1.568	1.460	0.107	0.209	0.183	0.132	0.219
11	BM&A	h	1.436	1.694	1.511	2.748	1.103	0.167	0.211	0.177	0.477	0.129
	(IN33)	l	0.902	1.141	1.183	1.315	0.745	0.104	0.131	0.136	0.155	0.091
		m	1.185	1.490	1.385	1.667	0.955	0.136	0.180	0.162	0.220	0.111

Sl. No.	I.Nm. Co	Range	CV Results of Variables or Structural Ratios					HH results of Variables or Structural Ratios				
			Units	PK	Emp	NVA	K/L	Units	PK	Emp	NVA	K/L
12	MetPrd (IN34)	h	1.729	2.128	1.922	2.505	2.457	0.206	0.297	0.246	0.354	0.376
		l	0.992	1.466	1.325	1.876	0.336	0.113	0.178	0.156	0.254	0.065
		m	1.512	1.907	1.753	2.121	0.931	0.180	0.248	0.218	0.289	0.130
13	Mot Tr (IN36)	h	1.245	1.192	2.040	1.554	0.989	0.144	0.136	0.279	0.188	0.113
		l	1.017	1.008	1.096	1.196	0.498	0.116	0.115	0.125	0.138	0.074
		m	1.197	1.115	1.322	1.417	0.639	0.137	0.127	0.158	0.168	0.084
14	TrnEq (IN37)	h	1.620	1.647	2.896	1.675	4.088	0.189	0.203	0.449	0.193	0.823
		l	1.035	1.452	1.393	1.151	0.681	0.118	0.176	0.163	0.131	0.092
		m	1.283	1.562	1.750	1.394	1.396	0.147	0.186	0.221	0.160	0.218
15	OMI (IN38)	h	2.179	2.186	2.040	4.556	1.845	0.264	0.588	0.264	0.939	0.162
		l	1.665	1.008	1.096	1.605	0.464	0.148	0.187	0.158	0.192	0.074
		m	1.860	1.192	1.927	2.927	1.088	0.218	0.305	0.228	0.447	0.133
16	EGS (IN41)	h	1.405	1.813	1.841	3.995	4.140	0.160	0.104	0.108	0.891	0.640
		l	1.108	1.048	1.051	1.019	0.515	0.126	0.087	0.087	0.109	0.076
		m	1.278	1.284	1.687	1.563	1.677	0.145	0.096	0.101	0.233	0.290

1976-85 (Large States- results for all Variables)

In this decade when recession is said to have lost its sting and recovery is supposed to have begun, Capital intensive industries did well to revive dispersality.

But the hold of recession, or the lagging effect of infrastructure, especially, transport Industry, could be easily identified as the type of industries that needed to be boosted up for a more pace of industrialisation.

But while Textiles showed high dispersal, the lack of dispersal in textile products (IN26) showed lacunae in Indian Planning as far as meticulous input-output planning exercises needed to be undertaken.

Table 5.7. Coefficient of Variation (C.V.) and Herfindahl Index (H.I.) of Industry Groups in Large States of India during 1976-85

Sl. No.	Inm Co	Range	CV Results of Variables or Structural Ratios					HH results of Variables or Structural Ratios				
			Units	PK	Emp	NVA	K/L	Units	PK	Emp	NVA	K/L
1	Food (IN21)	h	1.900	3.886	1.078	1.296	0.782	0.109	0.115	0.107	0.115	0.093
		l	0.966	1.011	0.863	0.916	0.358	0.091	0.094	0.096	0.097	0.063
		m	1.374	1.038	1.003	1.067	0.508	0.098	0.108	0.101	0.103	0.074
2	Bev'ge (IN22)	h	2.358	1.404	2.635	1.988	1.226	0.365	0.168	0.423	0.258	0.142
		l	2.075	1.023	2.167	1.272	0.526	0.185	0.108	0.319	0.144	0.077
		m	2.114	1.160	2.413	1.447	0.697	0.307	0.133	0.376	0.175	0.089
3	Textile (IN25)	h	2.957	4.806	5.606	4.824	2.784	0.224	0.513	0.409	0.405	0.950
		l	2.215	2.173	4.081	3.882	1.025	0.183	0.230	0.323	0.337	0.148
		m	2.527	3.260	4.691	4.619	1.642	0.198	0.325	0.359	0.375	0.295
4	TexPrd (IN26)	h	1.669	1.406	1.560	1.701	0.837	0.207	0.168	0.194	0.219	0.099
		l	1.230	1.118	1.205	1.160	0.601	0.143	0.127	0.136	0.132	0.080
		m	1.377	1.239	1.302	1.373	0.685	0.166	0.144	0.152	0.165	0.087
5	Wood (IN27)	h	1.094	1.087	1.826	1.457	0.759	0.101	0.124	0.243	0.176	0.091
		l	0.866	0.918	1.010	1.006	0.305	0.091	0.106	0.108	0.115	0.065
		m	1.046	1.009	1.128	1.135	0.424	0.096	0.113	0.125	0.134	0.071
6	Paper (IN28)	h	1.219	2.377	1.238	1.363	3.326	0.141	0.115	0.108	0.162	0.671
		l	1.083	1.721	1.025	0.945	0.509	0.124	0.094	0.102	0.109	0.073
		m	1.130	1.293	1.041	1.126	1.025	0.130	0.103	0.106	0.130	0.155
7	Leath (IN29)	h	2.346	2.377	2.185	2.396	2.248	0.306	0.275	0.275	0.302	0.266
		l	1.892	1.721	1.895	1.889	0.701	0.215	0.233	0.233	0.232	0.097
		m	2.127	1.987	2.019	2.141	1.189	0.271	0.250	0.251	0.268	0.142
8	Chem (IN30)	h	1.380	1.682	1.542	2.095	1.311	0.923	0.968	0.930	0.931	0.927
		l	1.033	1.015	1.034	1.311	0.453	0.119	0.116	0.118	0.158	0.070
		m	1.110	1.325	1.219	1.632	0.841	0.214	0.235	0.228	0.293	0.190
9	Ru,eC (31)	h	1.277	2.105	1.860	3.739	1.573	0.902	0.921	0.928	0.952	0.742
		l	1.001	0.930	0.973	1.121	0.604	0.114	0.107	0.111	0.127	0.079
		m	1.116	1.269	1.248	1.973	0.847	0.217	0.261	0.235	0.326	0.184
10	NmMP (IN32)	h	1.093	1.877	1.098	1.501	2.130	0.999	0.643	0.795	0.743	0.310
		l	0.844	0.753	0.691	0.734	0.941	0.098	0.084	0.085	0.085	0.108
		m	0.936	1.594	1.305	1.089	1.171	0.206	0.155	0.167	0.173	0.248
11	BM&A (IN33)	h	1.246	1.801	1.163	1.381	0.976	0.807	0.980	0.912	0.915	0.802
		l	0.806	1.466	0.999	1.018	0.713	0.090	0.178	0.114	0.116	0.087
		m	1.053	1.590	1.057	1.195	0.832	0.175	0.283	0.209	0.227	0.176

Sl. No.	Inm Co	Range	CV Results of Variables or Structural Ratios					HH results of Variables or Structural Ratios				
			Units	PK	Emp	NVA	K/L	Units	PK	Emp	NVA	K/L
12	MetPrd	h	1.094	1.616	1.356	1.894	1.217	0.411	0.458	0.436	0.480	0.362
	(IN34)	l	0.986	1.197	0.838	1.722	0.219	0.106	0.138	0.098	0.223	0.062
		m	1.028	1.423	1.258	1.777	0.487	0.198	0.258	0.230	0.318	0.152
13	Mot Tr	h	1.150	1.106	1.207	1.299	1.849	0.404	0.448	0.405	0.448	0.467
	(IN36)	l	1.036	0.095	0.963	0.273	0.290	0.118	0.108	0.110	0.101	0.063
		m	1.083	0.980	1.042	1.123	0.535	0.212	0.205	0.207	0.221	0.131
14	TrnEq	h	1.291	1.742	1.398	1.638	1.589	0.490	0.422	0.428	0.414	0.458
	(IN37)	l	1.115	1.214	1.085	1.314	0.951	0.127	0.139	0.124	0.153	0.109
		m	1.175	1.517	1.247	1.454	1.345	0.229	0.270	0.230	0.258	0.245
15	OMI	h	1.915	1.880	1.356	2.561	1.786	0.915	0.436	0.427	0.444	0.329
	(IN38)	l	1.351	1.039	1.175	1.356	0.603	0.157	0.119	0.134	0.158	0.081
		m	1.606	1.308	1.279	1.745	0.912	0.277	0.240	0.234	0.313	0.183
16	EGS	h	1.386	2.102	2.547	4.039	3.217	0.571	0.540	0.852	0.772	0.438
	(IN41)	l	0.803	1.327	1.098	1.484	0.669	0.108	0.110	0.108	0.133	0.095
		m	1.113	1.714	1.694	1.943	1.602	0.231	0.251	0.243	0.332	0.269

Note: h-highest; l-lowest; m-mean value

1986-1995 (Large States-CV and HH Results for all Variables)

NVA shows less dispersal in Beverages (IN22) than Units or PK showing scope and need for policy and implementation improvement. Leather (IN29) showed maximum dispersal while Other Manufacturing Industries (IN38) showed mean values nearer the highest values though lowest values were above 1 in case of CV.

Non-Metallic Mineral Products (IN32) also shows mean values of CV and HH near to the lowest values.

In Metal Products (IN34), employment dispersal in HH show mean value near to the highest, whereas in other measures of variables, mean values are near to the lowest values. So there has been much entrepreneurial initiative in creating employment in this decade, despite the industry getting concentrated or showing low dispersal in PK, NVA and Units. This being an intermediate industry, the sooner the planners realise this trend and work for housing, education and institutional reforms along with working out of forward linkages and reducing transport costs by establishing industries that uses products of Metal Products as inputs, the sooner will be the multiplier effects get manifested with Metal Products as the leading sector.

Table 5.8. Coefficient of Variation (C.V.) and Herfindahl Index (H.I.) of Industry Groups in Large States of India during 1986-95

Sl. No.	Inm & Co	Range	CV Results of Variables or Structural Ratios					HH results of Variables or Structural Ratios				
			Units	PK	Emp	NVA	K/L	Units	PK	Emp	NVA	K/L
1	21	h	1.129	1.796	1.078	2.725	0.944	0.129	0.237	0.102	0.117	0.108
	Food	l	1.006	1.013	1.008	0.758	0.354	0.109	0.096	0.096	0.091	0.066
		m	1.052	1.134	1.045	1.120	0.524	0.119	0.118	0.099	0.105	0.076
2	22	h	2.854	2.497	2.611	1.487	1.376	0.522	0.142	0.436	0.157	0.164
	Bev'	l	1.052	1.033	1.019	1.068	0.599	0.290	0.107	0.355	0.130	0.080
		m	2.894	1.333	2.524	1.296	0.636	0.446	0.118	0.387	0.139	0.095
3	25	h	1.936	2.424	2.438	2.625	1.683	0.249	0.319	0.368	0.383	0.261
	Textiles	l	1.487	1.636	2.169	1.990	1.030	0.169	0.194	0.320	0.247	0.121
		m	1.670	2.047	2.300	2.398	1.289	0.196	0.262	0.337	0.347	0.162
4	26	h	1.705	1.380	1.923	1.765	0.872	0.220	0.164	0.227	0.231	0.112
	TexPrds	l	1.385	1.251	1.281	1.369	0.563	0.166	0.137	0.142	0.161	0.076
		m	1.511	1.314	1.542	1.512	0.736	0.184	0.154	0.179	0.184	0.090
5	27	h	1.088	1.206	1.923	1.701	0.976	0.107	0.200	0.119	0.219	0.112
	Wood	l	0.877	0.963	1.290	0.993	0.347	0.097	0.110	0.101	0.107	0.066
		m	1.027	1.175	1.305	1.254	0.636	0.102	0.137	0.108	0.149	0.083
6	28	h	1.150	2.666	1.680	1.274	1.625	0.132	0.452	0.108	0.149	0.205
	Paper	l	1.083	0.786	0.815	0.899	0.978	0.123	0.092	0.096	0.101	0.071
		m	1.123	1.131	1.341	1.036	1.173	0.129	0.146	0.100	0.119	0.109
7	29	h	3.686	2.506	2.564	2.738	1.448	0.683	0.338	0.367	0.409	0.141
	Leath	l	2.395	1.960	2.083	1.948	0.486	0.329	0.244	0.267	0.235	0.082
		m	2.706	2.200	2.340	2.218	0.976	0.404	0.289	0.317	0.292	0.119
8	30	h	1.174	1.703	1.280	1.863	0.743	0.135	0.219	0.149	0.251	0.089
	Chem	l	1.042	1.237	1.151	1.232	0.444	0.119	0.144	0.132	0.143	0.074
		m	1.102	1.449	1.216	1.637	0.611	0.126	0.176	0.141	0.209	0.080
9	31	h	1.093	1.163	1.503	1.496	1.595	0.121	0.134	0.113	0.183	0.189
	Ru,Pe,C	l	0.934	0.772	0.823	1.048	0.910	0.103	0.099	0.093	0.120	0.073
		m	1.006	1.025	1.134	1.295	1.175	0.112	0.115	0.100	0.153	0.100
10	32	h	1.811	1.071	1.166	1.072	1.084	0.097	0.122	0.084	0.101	0.124
	NmMP	l	0.815	0.955	0.668	0.869	0.659	0.093	0.105	0.082	0.087	0.083
		m	1.182	1.016	1.028	1.026	0.811	0.095	0.113	0.083	0.096	0.096
11	33	h	1.766	1.509	1.099	1.416	1.022	0.097	0.185	0.117	0.170	0.117
	BM&A	l	0.756	0.982	0.993	1.149	0.591	0.093	0.112	0.102	0.132	0.078
		m	1.079	1.284	1.021	1.254	0.776	0.092	0.152	0.111	0.146	0.093

Sl. No.	I.Nm. Co	Range	CV Results of Variables or Structural Ratios					HH results of Variables or Structural Ratios				
			Units	PK	Emp	NVA	K/L	Units	PK	Emp	NVA	K/L
12	34	h	1.800	1.792	1.148	1.883	0.894	0.114	0.237	0.125	0.255	0.094
	MetPrd	l	1.001	1.150	0.905	1.226	0.340	0.103	0.132	0.105	0.142	0.064
		m	1.127	1.381	1.063	1.518	0.496	0.109	0.167	0.122	0.189	0.074
13	36	h	1.100	1.245	1.093	1.372	1.143	0.126	0.145	0.125	0.163	0.094
	MotTr	l	1.005	0.968	0.946	1.051	0.293	0.115	0.112	0.105	0.120	0.064
		m	1.039	1.064	1.030	1.184	0.639	0.119	0.121	0.111	0.137	0.070
14	37	h	1.171	1.547	1.119	1.795	1.021	0.133	0.183	0.129	0.223	0.117
	TrEq	l	1.094	1.278	0.983	1.117	0.632	0.125	0.147	0.113	0.127	0.082
		m	1.136	1.371	1.042	1.428	0.749	0.129	0.159	0.119	0.168	0.094
15	38	h	1.530	1.418	1.241	1.545	0.504	0.184	0.167	0.139	0.220	0.126
	OMI	l	1.094	1.050	1.001	1.230	0.500	0.144	0.110	0.119	0.131	0.073
		m	1.426	1.394	1.153	1.183	1.098	0.160	0.141	0.129	0.171	0.083
16	41	h	2.921	1.989	2.631	2.562	2.255	0.468	0.243	0.430	0.336	0.266
	EGS	l	0.995	1.043	1.021	1.260	1.020	0.119	0.133	0.118	0.145	0.114
		m	1.363	1.416	1.135	1.690	1.163	0.177	0.177	0.152	0.205	0.150

Analysis of Dispersal Measures through HH and CV Analysis of all the States and Union Territories taken Together for a 40-Year Time Period

In Food Products (IN21), only productive capital (PK) shows high dispersal in both CV and HH but not so of other variables. This shows that though sufficient capital was injected into this sector, it did not result in the requisite levels of development and dispersal, presumably due to high elite consumption of entrepreneurs and rentier class of this industry, demonstration effect of luxury consumption of all sections of population together eating away the productive potential of capital. The backwardness of agriculture sector and increasing base level of population and its growth and high base level of L/O and Gini Ratio of poverty are also other factors to explain the relatively low dispersal of Food industry in other 4 variables.

In Beverages (IN22), mean value of HH measure of employment is nearer to the highest value but all the other variables' mean values are nearer to the lowest HH and CV values of the variables. So while there has been employment dispersal in Beverages Industry (IN22), it might result in underemployment and unemployment that seems to be high due to decentralised dispersal.

Table 5.9. Regional Dispersal of HH and CV, 40-year HH and CV for all 5 variable and Structural Ratios for 2-digit Industries for 1956-95.

Sl.No.	Range	IN	HHunit	HHPK	HHemp	HHnva	HH K/L	CVunit	CVPk	CVemp	CVnva	CV K/L
1.	h	21	0.127	0.874	0.242	0.125	0.682	1.796	6.747	2.972	2.147	5.725
	l		0.089	0.093	0.093	0.087	0.047	0.336	0.242	0.419	0.221	0.204
	m		0.108	0.356	0.112	0.106	0.128	1.463	1.835	1.593	1.538	1.423
2.	h	22	0.517	0.616	0.614	0.595	0.924	5.324	5.935	8.124	7.963	3.802
	l		0.120	0.100	0.113	0.116	0.063	2.466	1.495	3.189	1.699	0.804
	m		0.318	0.177	0.414	0.193	0.211	3.923	2.437	4.684	2.714	1.997
3.	h	25	0.517	0.365	0.205	0.885	2.720	2.313	3.629	2.775	6.407	1.889
	l		0.147	0.111	0.115	0.108	0.067	1.579	1.624	1.547	1.571	0.583
	m		0.183	0.185	0.148	0.221	0.725	1.889	2.394	2.087	2.377	1.116
4.	h	26	0.157	0.319	0.240	0.347	0.423	2.946	4.120	3.302	4.085	3.185
	l		0.116	0.115	0.116	0.118	0.067	1.732	1.713	1.699	1.799	0.775
	m		0.154	0.157	0.162	0.102	0.258	2.242	2.282	2.265	2.827	1.244
5.	h	27	0.508	0.972	0.176	0.889	0.786	4.998	7.376	2.630	7.030	4.046
	l		0.086	0.101	0.087	0.092	0.048	1.264	1.381	1.278	1.351	0.490
	m		0.135	0.191	0.123	0.216	0.147	1.848	2.417	1.954	3.101	1.499
6.	h	28	0.193	0.938	0.381	0.737	0.794	0.737	6.798	4.225	5.805	6.487
	l		0.099	0.077	0.079	0.089	0.054	0.089	1.141	1.168	1.316	0.669
	m		0.135	0.143	0.129	0.152	0.185	0.152	1.908	1.809	2.021	1.987
7.	h	29	0.677	0.892	0.576	0.724	0.966	7.898	15.332	8.162	9.754	8.572
	l		0.206	0.199	0.211	0.219	0.083	2.953	2.770	2.942	3.018	0.691
	m		0.354	0.359	0.340	0.360	0.237	4.881	5.340	4.996	3.193	2.452
8.	h	30	0.367	0.915	0.495	0.516	0.909	4.838	8.325	7.028	6.987	9.161
	l		0.102	0.111	0.103	0.057	0.052	1.509	1.653	1.528	1.851	0.581
	m		0.167	0.288	0.232	0.266	0.195	2.696	3.781	3.316	3.638	2.607
9.	h	31	0.752	0.230	0.388	0.829	0.183	5.871	3.032	4.823	6.654	2.758
	l		0.088	0.090	0.080	0.115	0.060	1.309	1.352	1.183	1.665	0.850
	m		0.162	0.162	0.144	0.238	0.108	2.202	2.299	2.144	2.963	1.542
10.	h	32	0.120	0.801	0.692	0.314	0.616	1.761	6.641	6.129	3.419	5.742
	l		0.082	0.075	0.107	0.084	0.067	1.211	1.124	1.092	1.171	0.267
	m		0.100	0.131	0.113	0.111	0.133	1.456	1.721	1.482	1.553	1.659

Sl.No.	Range	IN	HHunit	HHPK	HHemp	HHnva	HH K/L	CVunit	CVPk	CVemp	CVnva	CV K/L
11.	h	33	0.217	0.408	0.277	0.476	0.408	3.259	5.099	3.965	4.561	6.989
	l		0.077	0.109	0.095	0.114	0.109	1.145	1.593	1.405	1.374	0.765
	m		0.125	0.206	0.154	0.197	0.206	1.840	2.701	2.205	2.623	2.059
12.	h	34	0.207	0.440	0.253	0.345	0.291	3.096	6.603	3.376	4.088	4.850
	l		0.087	0.124	0.090	0.136	0.049	1.299	1.753	1.329	1.899	0.398
	m		0.137	0.235	0.174	0.241	0.130	1.988	2.907	2.399	3.020	1.119
13.	h	36	0.156	0.207	0.273	0.767	0.794	2.310	2.899	3.359	6.486	4.160
	l		0.095	0.105	0.092	0.097	0.051	1.407	1.406	1.404	1.442	0.491
	m		0.123	0.130	0.134	0.188	0.137	1.814	1.904	1.942	2.423	1.186
14.	h	37	0.193	0.275	0.445	0.551	0.789	2.809	1.790	4.634	5.762	7.081
	l		0.100	0.130	0.100	0.124	0.066	1.488	3.632	1.470	1.808	0.870
	m		0.130	0.182	0.166	0.187	0.170	1.929	2.508	2.347	5.085	1.857
15.	h	38	0.233	0.583	0.597	0.937	1.054	3.519	5.404	6.523	7.662	2.427
	l		0.108	0.096	0.097	0.116	0.054	1.528	1.560	1.289	1.634	0.711
	m		0.173	0.210	0.185	0.296	0.139	2.487	2.817	2.599	3.488	1.405
16.	h	41	0.145	0.377	0.377	0.891	0.927	2.288	3.392	4.735	6.613	9.390
	l		0.072	0.056	0.056	0.102	0.076	1.031	0.844	1.209	1.594	0.363
	m		0.107	0.116	0.116	0.173	0.417	1.554	1.623	2.143	2.691	3.688

The industries for which mean values of HH and CV recorded figures nearer to the lowest HH and CV values are Electricity, Gas and Steam (IN41), Basic Metals and Alloys (IN33), Non-Metallic Mineral Products (IN32) and Machinery other than Transport (IN36), Wood (IN27), Paper (IN28). So over the long term, in these industries, mean values being nearer to the lower values indicated that all those industries are relatively less dispersed due to high capital intensity in those investment goods and Intermediates category.

In Textiles (IN25), mean CV figures are nearer to the highest values of each variable while the mean HH figures are nearer to the lowest figures recorded that indicated it is less dispersed than others, because HH is superior to CV in respect of measuring regional dispersal.

In Paper (IN28) and in Non-Metallic Mineral Products, Units and also Employment show less dispersal than other three variables.

The highest dispersed industries have been Other Manufacturing Industries (IN38).

HH and CV Results of Industry Groups of All States and Union Territories of India during 1959-65

Table 5.10. Coefficient of Variation (C.V.) and Herfindahl Index (H.I.) of Industry Groups in All States and UTs of India during 1959-65

Range	IN &	CV Results of Variables or Structural Ratios					HH results of Variables or Structural Ratios				
	Code	Units	PK	Emp	NVA	K/L	Units	PK	Emp	NVA	K/L
h	21	1.823	6.747	1.947	2.147	5.725	0.121	0.874	0.130	0.143	0.682
l	Food	1.579	1.774	1.774	1.511	1.199	0.106	0.119	0.119	0.102	0.076
m		1.715	2.685	1.846	1.785	3.058	0.11	0.223	0.123	0.119	0.176
h	22	6.564	4.028	8.124	7.963	7.944	0.450	0.167	0.614	0.595	0.796
l	Bev'rag	3.270	2.511	4.610	2.625	1.729	0.229	0.259	0.376	0.174	0.132
m		4.212	3.076	6.087	3.633	3.952	0.289	0.201	0.491	0.249	0.335
h	25	1.199	2.748	2.775	2.889	1.250	0.154	0.193	0.205	0.199	1.052
l	Textiles	1.171	2.330	2.499	2.489	0.675	0.124	0.162	0.163	0.172	0.896
m		1.186	2.578	2.608	2.656	0.926	0.145	0.179	0.182	0.186	0.979
h	26	2.637	2.894	2.935	7.080	1.237	0.174	0.196	0.194	0.847	0.108
l	Tex.Prd	2.270	2.193	2.290	2.234	0.880	0.151	0.146	0.152	0.149	0.098
m		2.464	2.510	2.630	3.338	1.062	0.163	0.177	0.176	0.279	0.094
h	27	2.991	3.548	2.630	6.200	2.423	0.204	0.257	0.176	0.625	0.160
l	Wood	1.658	2.668	1.947	2.987	1.064	0.112	0.178	0.144	0.190	0.078
m		2.258	3.122	2.320	3.922	1.385	0.152	0.218	0.154	0.312	0.105
h	28	2.608	2.369	2.290	2.760	6.490	0.179	0.159	0.153	0.189	0.767
l	Paper	2.351	1.670	2.081	1.820	1.210	0.153	0.113	0.134	0.122	0.095
m		2.420	1.992	2.176	2.395	2.426	0.165	0.133	0.146	0.163	0.206
h	29	7.898	15.330	8.160	9.580	8.570	0.548	0.892	0.576	0.552	0.544
l	Leather	5.380	6.930	6.960	4.240	1.010	0.353	0.427	0.423	0.356	0.253
m		6.432	9.450	7.530	6.560	3.890	0.423	0.554	0.468	0.442	0.350
h	30	4.838	8.177	7.028	6.987	6.884	0.310	0.682	0.495	0.516	0.519
l	Chem	3.372	4.897	4.355	4.819	2.720	0.220	0.325	0.283	0.318	0.187
m		3.652	6.799	5.633	6.092	4.533	0.237	0.514	0.389	0.434	0.316
h	31	2.955	3.032	4.823	6.654	2.758	0.202	0.208	0.388	0.663	0.183
l	R-P-C	2.098	2.460	2.359	3.520	1.218	0.139	0.164	0.156	0.249	0.098
m		2.718	2.738	2.961	4.068	1.767	0.181	0.183	0.207	0.319	0.124
h	32	1.632	2.121	1.687	2.450	1.940	0.113	0.141	0.115	0.117	0.130
l	NmMP	1.400	1.124	1.232	1.367	1.300	0.101	0.091	0.094	0.100	0.096
m		1.505	1.670	1.504	1.670	1.580	0.107	0.116	0.107	0.117	0.111

Range	IN & Code	CV Results of Variables or Structural Ratios					HH results of Variables or Structural Ratios				
		Units	PK	Emp	NVA	K/L	Units	PK	Emp	NVA	K/L
h	33	3.259	5.099	3.965	4.524	6.989	0.217	0.408	0.278	0.346	0.836
l	BM&A	2.592	2.994	2.769	3.096	1.786	0.175	0.218	0.189	0.220	0.137
m		2.862	3.821	3.250	3.824	3.356	0.195	0.301	0.231	0.291	0.298
h	34	3.100	6.600	3.625	3.900	4.850	0.207	0.840	0.253	0.308	0.482
l	MetPrd	2.618	3.795	3.191	3.200	0.856	0.180	0.294	0.236	0.245	0.084
m		2.793	4.400	3.376	3.522	1.153	0.191	0.390	0.246	0.264	0.145
h	36	2.310	2.899	2.632	6.486	4.160	0.155	0.206	0.182	0.766	0.794
l	MotTr	2.157	2.124	2.264	2.669	0.879	0.141	0.144	0.520	0.186	0.080
m		2.221	2.566	2.497	3.737	2.252	0.149	0.178	0.171	0.334	0.236
h	37	2.800	3.630	3.095	5.762	7.080	0.193	0.276	0.218	0.551	0.847
l	Tr. Eq.	2.263	2.633	2.763	2.633	1.12	0.151	0.182	0.194	0.179	0.068
m		2.521	3.151	2.940	3.428	2.315	0.169	0.224	0.204	0.262	0.208
h	38	3.519	4.666	6.523	7.662	2.427	0.233	0.368	0.597	0.788	0.158
l	OMI	2.513	3.504	3.017	3.011	1.083	0.164	0.244	0.202	0.253	0.099
m		2.963	3.906	3.940	4.821	1.628	0.197	0.278	0.291	0.339	0.123
h	41	2.288	3.396	2.934	4.533	3.742	0.167	0.228	0.197	0.352	0.250
l	EGS	1.673	1.534	1.549	1.894	1.078	0.115	0.111	0.111	0.128	0.094
m		2.004	2.518	2.339	2.790	2.109	0.139	0.174	0.151	0.195	0.150

Note: h- highest value, l—lowest value, m—mean value.

The highest dispersed industries the period of 1959-65 were Beverages (IN22), Leather (IN29), Chemicals (IN30) and Basic Metals and Alloys (IN33).

In Metal Products (IN34), Transport Equipment (IN37) mean values are much nearer to the lowest values of the decade for each of the variables. NVA dispersal in Metal Products is more concentrated than dispersed.

Table 5.11. CV and HH results for All Industries of all States and UT for the period 1966-75

Sl. No.	Ind. Gr. Code	Range	CV Results of Variables or Structural Ratios					HH results of Variables or Structural Ratios				
			Units	PK	Emp	NVA	K/L	Units	PK	Emp	NVA	K/L
1.	21	h	1.5310	1.5880	1.5190	1.5230	1.5500	0.1160	0.1490	0.2450	0.1230	0.4040
	Food	l	1.3160	1.3200	1.3810	1.3520	0.5700	0.0900	0.0980	0.0980	0.0940	0.0500
		m	1.340	1.580	1.675	1.440	1.145	0.104	0.123	0.132	0.114	0.116
2.	22	h	5.636	5.935	7.275	4.707	3.501	0.410	0.616	0.592	0.414	0.630
	Bev	l	2.99	2.318	3.981	3.307	1.040	0.245	0.158	0.392	0.216	0.072
		m	4.250	3.337	5.259	3.565	1.793	0.316	0.263	0.440	0.224	0.211

Sl. No.	Ind. Gr. Code	Range	CV Results of Variables or Structural Ratios					HH results of Variables or Structural Ratios				
			Units	PK	Emp	NVA	K/L	Units	PK	Emp	NVA	K/L
3.	25	h	2.038	2.3	2.62	5.406	0.966	0.138	0.159	0.199	0.785	0.633
	Textile	l	1.578	1.933	2.163	2.038	0.587	0.114	0.148	0.153	0.165	0.206
		m	1.19	2.01	2.28	3.049	0.766	0.131	0.153	0.166	0.287	0.216
4.	26	h	2.946	4.11	3.3	6.149	6.185	0.205	0.319	0.239	0.617	0.623
	Tex.Prd	l	1.731	2.117	2.013	2.581	0.775	0.116	0.146	0.137	0.163	0.067
		m	2.42	2.89	2.833	3.665	1.833	0.163	0.206	0.197	0.184	0.165
5.	27	h	4.998	2.376	2.32	7.03	7.645	0.508	0.572	0.154	0.689	0.786
	Wood	l	1.35	2.628	1.361	1.737	1.116	0.092	0.137	0.092	0.121	0.079
		m	3.43	2.405	1.954	3.319	3.23	0.202	0.326	0.132	0.307	0.368
6.	28	h	2.43	6.808	4.225	5.804	6.41	0.193	0.938	0.381	0.737	0.795
	Paper	l	2.11	1.47	1.64	1.523	1.02	0.138	0.099	0.111	0.103	0.0643
		m	2.146	2.607	2.42	2.545	2.954	0.149	0.247	0.1901	0.221	0.2997
7.	29	h	7.528	7.378	7.526	9.754	6.047	0.452	0.444	0.402	0.725	0.966
	Leather	l	3.028	3.802	3.914	5.098	1.096	0.209	0.255	0.264	0.376	0.113
		m	5.485	5.358	5.55	6.789	2.556	0.394	0.358	0.352	0.47	0.355
8.	30	h	3.428	4.225	5.134	5.281	5.161	0.205	0.915	0.404	0.399	0.316
	Chem	l	2.008	2.224	2.179	2.244	1.086	0.137	0.145	0.151	0.157	0.079
		m	2.705	2.603	3.837	3.659	3.694	0.179	0.339	0.271	0.256	0.305
9.	31	h	5.871	3.005	2.73	3.61	2.284	0.752	0.211	0.183	0.319	0.152
	R-P-C	l	1.793	1.947	1.647	2.85	1.058	0.124	0.138	0.112	0.197	0.087
		m	2.986	2.697	2.363	3.199	1.593	0.254	0.191	0.162	0.242	0.119
10.	32	h	1.69	6.64	6.13	3.42	5.74	0.113	0.801	0.6923	0.314	0.616
	NmMP	l	1.38	1.28	1.17	1.17	0.266	0.097	0.088	0.089	0.089	0.086
		m	1.48	2.29	2.01	1.665	2.1502	0.1029	0.206	0.179	0.128	0.215
11.	33	h	2.337	2.883	2.518	4.561	1.851	0.1609	0.2107	0.1756	0.211	0.903
	BM&A	l	1.49	1.835	1.876	2.1	1.266	0.101	0.1278	0.131	0.145	0.089
		m	1.945	2.5	2.296	2.739	1.562	0.132	0.179	0.16	0.216	0.217
12.	34	h	2.69	3.459	3.119	4.08	3.97	0.187	0.289	0.236	0.345	0.991
	MetPrd	l	1.515	2.15	1.96	2.79	0.554	0.102	0.161	0.1418	0.232	0.05
		m	2.326	3.055	2.785	3.384	1.482	0.163	0.24	0.208	0.278	0.253
13.	36	h	1.962	1.990	3.359	2.521	1.619	0.132	0.134	0.273	0.184	0.872
	MotTr	l	1.637	1.598	1.731	1.876	0.776	0.111	0.108	0.118	0.128	0.064
		m	1.885	1.849	2.158	2.322	1.000	0.127	0.124	0.153	0.164	0.192

Sl. No.	Ind. Gr. Code	Range	CV Results of Variables or Structural Ratios					HH results of Variables or Structural Ratios				
			Units	PK	Emp	NVA	K/L	Units	PK	Emp	NVA	K/L
14.	37	h	2.417	2.67	4.633	2.717	6.381	0.667	0.201	0.445	0.19	0.451
	Tr.Eq.	l	1.624	2.29	2.25	1.918	1.01	0.109	0.168	0.161	0.13	0.081
		m	1.92	2.53	2.8	2.268	2.32	0.129	0.182	0.216	0.156	0.027
15.	38	h	3.337	5.404	3.42	7.484	3.008	0.236	0.583	0.243	0.937	0.211
	OMI	l	2.116	2.544	2.213	2.628	0.735	0.142	0.182	0.194	0.289	0.069
		m	2.885	3.63	2.488	4.722	1.647	0.198	0.298	0.216	0.433	0.259
16.	41	h	2.178	1.389	3.229	7.581	6.589	0.1447	0.101	0.217	0.891	0.973
	EGS	l	1.045	1.223	1.432	1.594	0.9	0.084	0.087	0.099	0.089	0.2384
		m	1.903	1.341	1.707	3.357	3.115	0.129	0.095	0.118	0.335	0.429

The highest dispersed industries are Beverages (IN22), Leather (IN29), Other Manufacturing Industries (IN38) where not only the highest values of each of the variables in CV measure are very high, relative to other industries but also that the mean values of CV and HH are nearer to the highest values as in Electricity, Gas and Steam (IN41) during the decade 1966-75, the period of industrial recession or retrogression, recovery and growth of post Third Five year Plan and Fourth Five Year Plan up to middle of Fifth Five Year Plan periods.

Table 5.12. CV and HH measures of variables in All States and UT of India during 1976-85 : Coefficient of Variation (C.V.) and Herfindahl Index (H.I.) of Industry Groups in All states and UTs of India during 1976-85

Range	I.Nm & Code	CV Results of Variables or Structural Ratios					HH results of Variables or Structural Ratios				
		Units	PK	Emp	NVA	K/L	Units	PK	Emp	NVA	K/L
h	21	1.531	1.588	1.520	1.522	1.550	0.106	0.110	0.105	0.110	0.107
l	Food	1.316	1.455	1.370	1.351	0.570	0.089	0.089	0.094	0.092	0.051
m		1.390	1.500	1.440	1.440	0.764	0.095	0.103	0.098	0.099	0.060
h	22	3.527	2.158	3.879	2.94	1.75	0.356	0.101	0.405	0.246	0.099
l	Bev	2.509	1.497	3.189	1.91	1.1	0.182	0.158	0.309	0.136	0.067
m		3.214	1.755	3.643	2.194	1.094	0.3	0.125	0.369	0.167	0.08
h	25	1.184	3.629	2.018	2.22	1.889	0.13	0.365	0.137	0.169	2.72
l	Textiles	1.611	1.977	1.654	1.882	1.467	0.117	0.143	0.115	0.135	1.71
m		1.711	2.919	1.841	2.046	1.585	0.119	0.268	0.131	0.149	2.025
h	26	2.315	2.11	2.31	2.06	1.252	0.171	0.148	0.166	0.184	0.086
l	TexPrd	1.83	1.71	1.75	1.799	1.03	0.124	0.115	0.119	0.118	0.069
m		1.83	1.84	1.891	2.03	1.07	0.141	0.124	0.131	1.839	0.076

Range	IN & Code	CV Results of Variables or Structural Ratios					HH results of Variables or Structural Ratios				
		Units	PK	Emp	NVA	K/L	Units	PK	Emp	NVA	K/L
h	27	1.416	1.53	2.51	2	0.955	0.096	0.108	0.218	0.129	0.067
l	Wood	1.264	1.381	1.384	1.492	0.49	0.085	0.094	0.091	0.99	0.048
m		1.316	1.468	1.55	1.705	0.627	0.089	0.101	0.111	0.101	0.054
h	28	1.753	1.55	1.42	1.889	4.67	0.12	0.107	0.096	0.741	0.639
l	Paper	1.522	1.23	1.27	1.478	0.769	0.111	0.084	0.086	0.099	0.058
m		1.621	1.41	1.38	1.619	1.426	0.115	0.096	0.094	0.117	0.135
h	29	3.709	3.904	3.413	3.87	2.036	0.296	0.307	0.268	0.294	0.245
l	Leather	3.062	2.77	2.941	3.136	1.038	0.212	0.196	0.211	0.232	0.085
m		3.367	3.215	3.276	3.454	1.859	0.258	0.242	0.242	0.258	0.132
h	30	2.039	2.603	2.419	3.197	2.037	0.139	0.206	0.178	0.127	0.141
l	Chem	1.524	1.786	1.528	2.067	0.793	0.103	0.111	0.125	0.144	0.062
m		1.719	2.029	1.931	2.537	1.265	0.117	0.144	0.134	0.196	0.089
h	31	1.858	3.203	2.086	5.731	1.988	0.132	0.302	0.226	0.828	0.18
l	R-P-C	1.519	1.548	1.536	1.738	1.211	0.103	0.104	0.104	0.12	0.079
m		1.687	2.202	1.936	2.598	1.639	0.106	0.168	0.14	0.243	0.112
h	32	1.76	1.731	1.348	2.01	2.77	0.12	0.099	0.091	1.76	0.245
l	NmMP	1.378	1.086	1.184	1.22	1.29	0.093	0.075	0.08	1.378	0.087
m		1.516	1.305	1.232	1.422	1.68	0.102	0.089	0.084	0.98	0.122
h	33	1.359	2.82	1.877	2.169	3.729	0.092	0.201	0.125	0.161	0.378
l	BM&A	1.216	2.31	1.6	1.676	1.452	0.084	0.174	0.111	0.114	0.08
m		1.321	2.47	1.714	1.947	2.042	0.089	0.196	0.118	0.138	0.168
h	34	1.522	3.055	2.785	2.789	1.572	0.103	0.185	0.148	0.233	0.107
l	MetPrd	1.398	2.366	2.022	2.565	0.398	0.087	0.13	0.09	0.196	0.051
m		1.417	1.843	1.329	2.696	0.691	0.964	0.16	0.131	0.226	0.061
h	36	1.725	1.663	1.883	1.925	2.638	0.118	0.11	0.213	0.146	0.213
l	MotTr	1.5	1.406	1.513	1.442	0.538	0.106	0.095	0.05	0.126	0.053
m		1.62	1.576	1.57	1.793	0.817	0.115	0.101	0.074	0.097	0.737
h	37	1.713	2.656	2.104	2.495	2.08	0.126	0.215	0.156	0.196	0.51
l	Tr.Eq.	1.541	1.9	1.75	2.002	1.384	0.104	0.133	0.118	0.143	0.097
m		1.675	2.308	1.9	2.246	1.721	0.115	0.177	0.135	0.166	0.126
h	38	2.956	2.955	2.142	4.72	2.4	0.225	0.237	0.146	0.386	0.18
l	OMI	1.785	1.799	1.586	2.62	1.07	0.132	0.115	0.118	0.143	0.062
m		2.37	2.048	1.887	2.117	1.314	0.17	0.144	123	0.211	0.096
h	41	1.357	3.89	3.089	3.001	8.452	0.092	0.377	0.383	0.667	0.886
l	EGS	1.091	0.735	1.209	1.629	0.363	0.074	0.057	0.082	0.109	0.147
m		1.355	1.267	2.278	2.179	3.336	0.082	0.106	0.185	0.161	0.444

Industries whose mean values of five variables were nearer to the highest values are Electricity, Gas and Steam (IN41) and Beverages (IN 22) while Chemicals (IN30), Rubber, Petroleum and Coal (IN31) also showed CV and HH measures of NVA higher than most other industries.

CV and HH Results of Industry Groups for all States and UTs of All India during 1986-95

Leather (IN29) and Electricity, Gas and Steam (IN41) were the most dispersed industries in this decade of 1986-95, both in terms of CV and HH and also in terms of their mean values being nearer to the highest values of the variables for both industries. Since Leather is more rural decentralised industry, it augurs well for this industry capable of being an engine of industrial growth in rural areas. EGS is an industry that is being focussed for reforms in power and water reforms for regeneration of the Indian agricultural and industrial economy. However, Units are not so well dispersed in Case of Electricity, Gas and Steam (IN41) and there is greater scope for further and greater decentralisation of this industry.

Table 5.13. CV and HH of Industry Groups of All States and UTs during 1986-95

Sl. No.	I.Nm & C	Range	CV Results of Variables or Structural Ratios					HH results of Variables or Structural Ratios				
			Units	PK	Emp	NVA	K/L	Units	PK	Emp	NVA	K/L
1.	21	h	1.743	2.597	1.440	1.605	1.059	0.127	0.233	0.099	0.112	0.072
	Food	l	1.58	1.352	1.361	1.295	0.513	0.106	0.092	0.093	0.087	0.048
		m	1.633	1.573	1.401	1.456	0.726	0.116	0.114	0.096	0.100	0.056
2.	22	h	4.546	1.933	4.003	2.337	1.588	0.517	0.169	0.409	0.173	1.492
	Bev	l	3.101	1.495	3.569	1.699	1.01	0.121	0.101	0.113	0.116	0.063
		m	4.016	1.638	3.748	1.866	1.048	0.399	0.118	0.355	0.132	0.218
3.	25	h	1.99	2.3	1.649	1.973	1.536	0.144	0.182	0.115	0.145	0.58
	Textile	l	1.588	1.62	1.547	1.571	1.039	0.119	0.111	0.108	0.108	0.199
		m	1.178	1.92	1.609	1.756	1.194	0.126	0.142	0.1	0.122	0.286
4.	26	h	2.34	1.983	2.428	2.88	1.283	0.156	0.137	0.178	0.237	0.237
	TexPr	!	1.853	1.796	1.699	2.03	0.791	0.128	0.117	0.116	0.139	0.139
		m	2.074	1.889	2.043	2.276	1.01	0.147	0.131	0.145	0.167	0.167
5.	27	h	1.46	2.26	1.459	2.25	1.159	0.099	0.186	0.099	1.489	0.78
	Wood	l	1.31	1.432	1.278	1.351	0.635	0.089	0.098	0.087	0.968	0.05
		m	1.39	1.672	1.371	1.724	0.809	0.095	0.121	0.093	0.125	0.06
6.	28	h	1.708	3.14	1.72	1.81	2.263	0.119	0.441	0.698	0.133	0.182
	Paper	l	1.496	1.21	1.168	1.365	0.718	0.099	0.077	0.079	0.089	0.054
		m	1.57	1.637	1.259	1.526	1.179	0.109	0.131	0.085	0.011	0.087

Sl. No.	I.Nm & C	Range	CV Results of Variables or Structural Ratios					HH results of Variables or Structural Ratios				
			Units	PK	Emp	NVA	K/L	Units	PK	Emp	NVA	K/L
7.	29	h	5.871	3.854	3.887	4.024	3.057	0.677	0.314	0.346	0.367	0.266
	Leathe	l	3.367	2.877	3.276	3.019	0.691	0.32	0.216	0.242	0.23	0.071
		m	4.24	3.337	3.633	3.408	1.493	0.389	0.261	0.299	0.27	0.111
8.	30	h	4.024	2.573	2.189	2.599	1.737	0.366	0.302	0.169	0.219	0.07
	Chem	l	1.509	1.619	1.712	1.02	0.581	0.102	0.104	0.119	0.057	0.052
		m	1.874	2.07	1.862	2.263	0.935	0.138	0.168	0.133	0.178	0.069
9.	31	h	1.577	1.731	1.544	2.282	2.129	0.108	0.122	0.105	0.175	0.162
	R-P-C	l	1.309	1.327	1.216	1.665	0.85	0.088	0.089	0.08	0.116	0.059
		m	1.416	1.559	1.315	1.986	1.66	0.096	0.106	0.088	0.145	0.083
10.	32	h	1.340	2.010	1.867	2.298	1.59	0.093	0.149	0.105	0.97	0.114
	NmMP	l	1.240	1.470	1.091	1.278	0.097	0.082	0.097	0.077	0.083	0.066
		m	1.318	1.612	1.170	1.456	1.218	0.089	0.113	0.081	0.301	0.083
11.	33	h	1.657	2.34	1.65	2.21	1.93	0.087	0.182	0.114	0.169	0.139
	BMt&A	l	1.144	1.59	1.41	1.69	0.764	0.077	0.109	0.095	0.116	0.06
		m	1.229	2.01	1.56	1.984	1.275	0.083	0.148	0.106	0.143	0.088
12.	34	h	1.514	2.448	1.739	2.77	1.382	0.103	0.199	0.217	0.244	0.075
	MetPr	l	1.299	1.752	1.433	1.899	0.507	0.088	0.123	0.098	0.148	0.05
		m	1.416	2.029	1.602	2.279	0.776	0.096	0.151	0.11	0.179	0.061
13.	36	h	1.666	1.897	1.847	2.093	0.985	0.113	0.139	0.118	0.155	0.07
	MotTr	l	1.407	1.48	1.388	1.668	0.491	0.095	0.1	0.092	0.115	0.515
		m	1.524	1.68	1.489	1.81	0.674	0.104	0.112	0.101	0.13	0.057
14.	37	h	1.694	2.35	1.792	2.352	1.488	0.115	0.175	0.123	0.217	0.1
	Tr.Eq.	l	1.488	1.789	1.478	1.81	0.94	0.1	0.124	0.098	0.124	0.065
		m	1.601	2.039	1.605	2.27	1.061	0.108	0.145	0.109	0.163	0.076
15.	38	h	1.968	1.968	1.682	2.369	2.27	0.143	0.15	0.123	0.205	0.192
	OMI	l	1.528	1.528	1.289	1.633	0.711	0.108	0.096	0.097	0.116	0.054
		m	1.732	1.732	1.48	1.967	1.029	0.128	0.123	0.104	0.153	0.076
16.	41	h	1.355	1.717	4.735	3.426	9.389	0.092	0.121	0.312	0.237	0.894
	EGS	l	1.031	1.005	1.481	1.457	3.177	0.072	0.069	0.097	0.102	0.242
		m	1.132	1.362	2.347	2.437	6.194	0.077	0.088	0.156	0.173	0.631

In terms of employment dispersal both in terms of CV and HH, Non-Metallic Mineral Products (IN32) was the least dispersed with values around1.170 in CV and 0.081 in HH in 1986-95. This was a period of New Economic Policies, Stabilisation and Economic Reforms of all sectors. Factories and PK getting dispersed but Employment getting concentrated show that in this Intermediate, employment planning did not get the requisite focus.

Wood Industry (IN27), being a agro-forestry based industry is also a cause for concern for their decentralised Units and Employment variables, HH and CV, showing high concentration.

Capital Intensity (K/L) was not so well dispersed in many industries despite other variables in those respective industries being dispersed. These industries were: Textile Products (IN26), Wood (IN27), Food (IN21), Metal Products (IN34), Manufacturing other than Transport (IN36) and Transport Equipment (IN37).

Conclusion and Policy Inferences—Period Wise

1959-65:

Metal Products (IN34) show more relative concentrated in case of Small States Group and All States in India. But this industry did disperse well in 1986-95.

1966-75:

In both large states and small states separately in each group, capital intensive industries did not show dispersal. But in case of All States and UT being taken together, Except for three Industry groups, viz; Electricity Gas and Steam (IN41), Basic Metals and Alloys (IN33) and Machinery other than transport (IN36), most other Capital Intensive industries like Chemicals (IN30), Transport Equipment (IN37), Rubber-Petroleum-Coal (IN31), Other Manufacturing Industries (IN38) showed mean values nearer to the lowest dispersal values.

While Leather, Paper, Wood, Beverages showed high dispersal, Textile, Textile Products, Food showed mean dispersal values nearer to lowest values of the variables.

1976-85:

Transport (IN37), Textile Products (IN26) in both Small and Large States and Chemicals (IN30) in Small States showed less dispersal. Textiles showed greater dispersal in both Small States and Large States but Textiles Products showed less dispersal.

1986-95:

Metal Products (IN34) showed regional dispersal in All States and Union Territories (UT).

Smaller States and UT failed in many fronts except in Textile Products, Machinery other than Transport and Transport Equipment where high dispersal is noted. But in Large States, NVA in Beverages (IN22), but Non Metallic Mineral Products (IN32) and CV of OMI (IN38) showed more concentration. In All States, Food, Wood emp, showed less dispersal. Food employment may be temporary once a long term planning of this industry comes into operation. But K/L dispersal being low in capital goods industry like Electrical and Non electrical machinery (IN36) and transport (IN37) show employment dispersal in these industries as not spreading out.

Industry Specific Policy Inferences

In the recent two decades of policy initiatives of increasing trade, macro economic stabilisation and industrial liberalisation, Food and Wood are the two exceptions being directly land based.

In All States and long term 40-year case, Beverages Industry showed higher dispersal in employment but less so in the other four variables. Improvement of labour productivity and greater marketing innovation need to be devised to help in Beverages Industry dispersal.

For the 40-year All States and Union Territories, Wood (IN27), Paper (IN28), Non-Metallic Mineral Products (IN32), Basic Metals and Alloys (IN33), Machinery other than transport, Electricity, Gas and Steam (IN41) having mean values of variables and Structural ratios nearer the lowest values, implied that these industries were relatively less dispersed over the long term.

So policy directions should enable capital goods and intermediates industries to be more decentralised/ regionally dispersed. Intermediate goods Industries must be dispersed after a careful study of linkages, both backward and forward, and institutional set up and behaviour of the Indian economy. Paper and Wood Industries, being L intensive industries, have greater potential for employment absorption. Employment planning in these industries should be based on regional resource linkages.

Wood (IN27) also did well in Small States category in the first and third decades but showed more concentration in second 'recession' decade. But Wood (IN27) showed more concentration in each of the five variables in the All States—40-year long-term category and in 1986-95 period in All States Category. This Intermediate provides inputs to Paper, Ship- Building, Housing, Transport (Trucks' body), Sports Goods, etc. and so market demand surveys, developing marketing channels for its products, intensive agroforestry programmes, reduction of illegal felling of trees with a greater role for decentralised political authority, etc will help make this industry getting more dispersed and raising its value addition potential and make greater contribution to national income.

Food Products (IN21), a key industry linking agriculture and industry, showed less dispersal in most variables (except PK in 1959-95 in All States category) in the long term. This was supported by Food Industry (IN21) getting concentrated in 1959-95 for Large States Category. More regional Planning in an Input-Output Frame outlining its Intermediate Input Coefficient for regional skill based Industries will cause for greater dispersal in Food Industry.

Non-Metallic Mineral Products, EGS, Basic Metals and Alloys, Machinery other than Transport, being the industries that showed more relative concentration over long term in All States and UT Category implied that Greater Regional Planning in these in an Input-Output frame will bring out their growth potential that will cause for dispersal. EGS can revitalise and enhance power availability and provide much needed lateral boost to industrialisation, Machinery other than transport (IN36) must be made amenable to decentralisation, this being a key capital goods industry. Probably greater R&D will enable MotTr (IN36) industry to be more dispersed over the regions in the future.

Chapter 6

Regional Dispersal Analysis of Indian Industries—A Diagrammatic Presentation of Long Term Trends of Dispersal Measures of Variables and Structural Ratios

INTRODUCTION

This Chapter 6 deals with Graphical Presentation of Long Term Trends of Dispersal Measures (HH and CV) of Five Size Variables and Structural Ratios of two-digit Indian Industries for the time period 1956-95. The Chapter comprises 4 Sections. Each Section deals with Groups of two-digit industries identified and grouped on the basis of similar characteristics. Group 1(Consumer Non-Durables—CND) clubs Food Products Industry (IN21 = IN20 + IN21), Beverages Industry (IN22) and the Textile Group of Industries (IN25 = IN23 + IN24 + IN25). All these above industries are Consumer Goods Non-Durable (CND). Group 2 comprises Intermediate and L-Intensive (ILI) Goods like Textile Products (IN26), Wood and Wood Products Industry (IN27), Paper (IN28) and Leather (IN29). Group 3 comprises Intermediate Goods with higher Capital Intensity (IKI), viz. Chemical Industry (IN30), Rubber, Petroleum and Coal (IN31), Non-Metallic Mineral Products (IN32), Basic Metals and Alloys (IN33), Metal Products (IN34). Group 4 comprises Capital Goods Industry (CGI) like Electrical and Electronic Machinery other than Transports (IN36=IN35+IN36), Transport Equipment Industry (IN37), Other Manufacturing Industry (IN38) and Electricity, Gas and Steam (IN41 = IN40 + IN41).

This Section deals with Consumer (Durable and Non-Durable) Goods like Food (IN21), Beverages (IN22) and Textiles (IN25). HH and CV Trends of each Size Variable for this Group1 is presented separately to facilitate comparable analysis to enable drawing more appropriate policy measures.

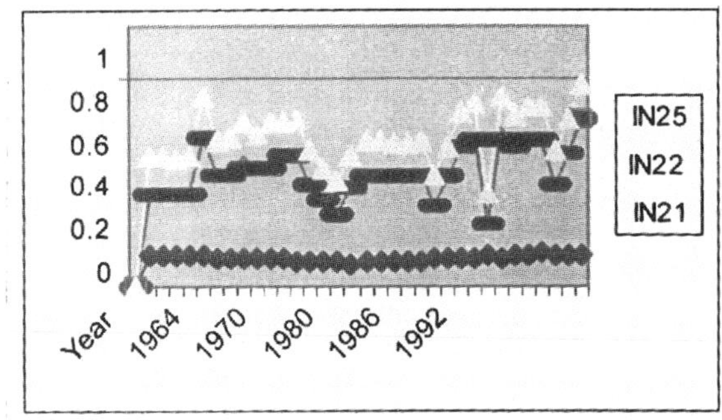

Fig. 6.1a. Dispersal (HH) Trend in Factories of CND Industries for 1956-95

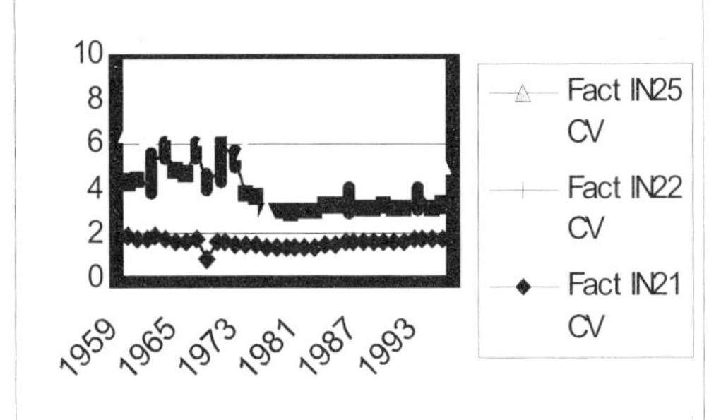

Fig. 6.1b. Dispersal (CV) Trend in Factories of CND Industries for 1956-95

While HH and CV measures of Food Industry (IN21) show concentration of Factories over the long period, Beverages (IN22) and Textiles (IN25) show a rising trend. The latter two are more dispersed, though marked by severe fluctuations. However, CV shows less rising trend though HH is clearly on an upward mode. Notwithstanding this, there was a fall in factories' dispersal in 1980s and again in 1992 in both HH and CV that goes on to show liberalisation moves in both these times did not account for this crucial agro Industry. The planners probably hoped that trickle-down effects of prosperity and entrepreneurship in industrial and trade sectors will filter down to the agricultural and agro-industrial sectors.

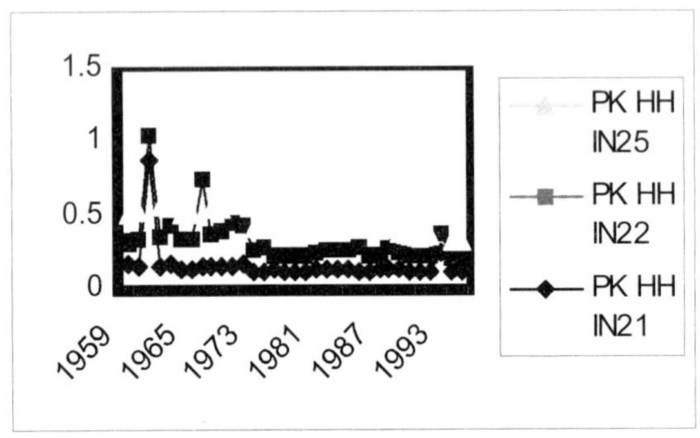

Fig. 6.2a. Dispersal (HH) Trend in PK in CND Industries for 1956-95

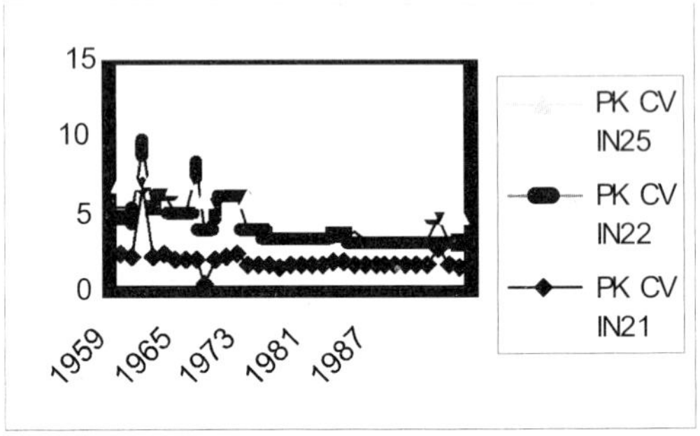

Fig. 6.2b. Dispersal (CV) Trend in CND Industries for 1956-95

Similar trends noticed in both measures of HH and CV for Productive Capital in Food Industry with all the three Consumer Non-Durable showing marked signs of more concentration from 1980 onwards. The increasing tendencies towards greater dispersal was marked both in the Pre-Retrogression and the Recovery Phases, then greater concentration (more marked in HH) in late 1970s depression when oil prices shot up and there was political instability at the Centre.

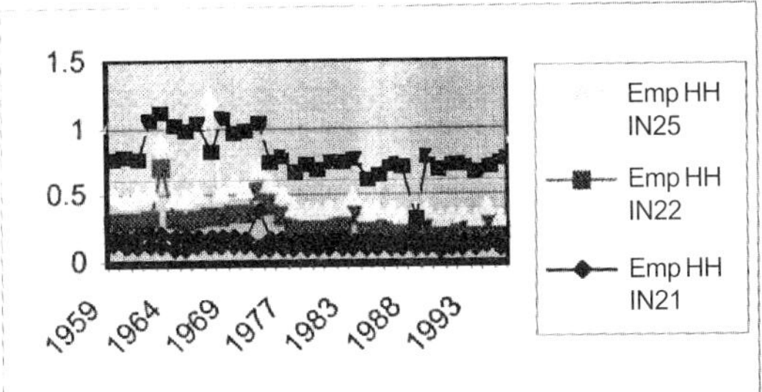

Fig. 6.3a. Dispersal (HH) Trend in CND Industries for 1956-95

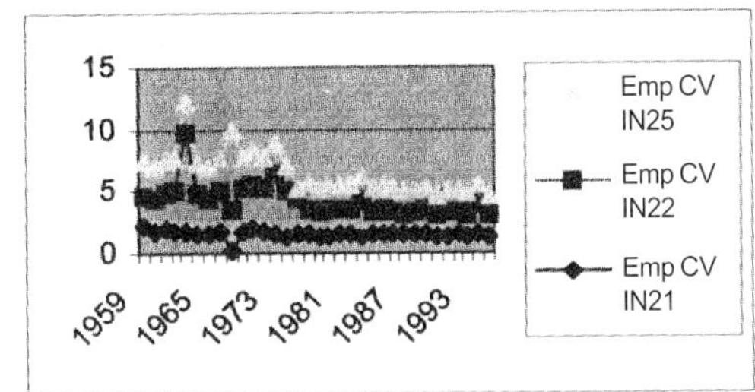

Fig. 6.3b. Dispersal (CV) Trend in CND Industries for 1956-95

Employment is concentrated in Food Industry for all of the 40years, except of high in mid1970s during 4th and 5th Plan period when special attention was being given to Small Scale Industries and Backward Area Development.

Employment in Beverages and Textiles however show higher dispersal, though marked by great fluctuations. Both started low when they were concentrated and then dispersed. Dispersal marked downward trend during retrogression and again in mid 1980s when Rajiv Gandhi Government laid much focus on imports of machine goods and luxury items.

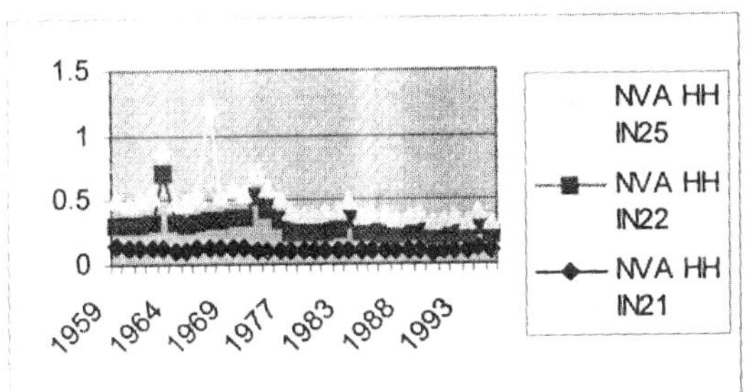

Fig. 6.4a. Dispersal (HH) Trends in NVA in CND Industries for 1956-95

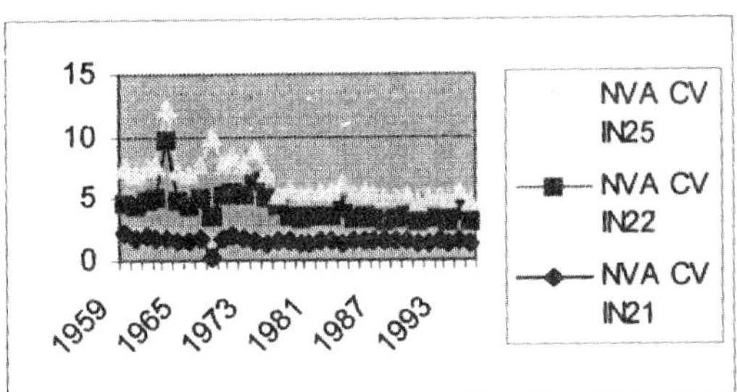

Fig. 6.4b. Dispersal (CV) Trend in NVA in CND Industries for 1956-95

NVA Dispersal in Food Industry followed similar pattern to its Inputs Dispersal pattern. However, the sharp spurts in dispersal got manifested a little earlier in 1968-9 since gestation period in this industry is much less. Yet, a small spurts noticed during Rajiv Gandhi liberalisation measures of mid 1980s and Narasimha Rao-Manmohan Singh reforms of 1992-3 showed that liberalisation impulses quickly impacted the output growth and dispersal than inputs.

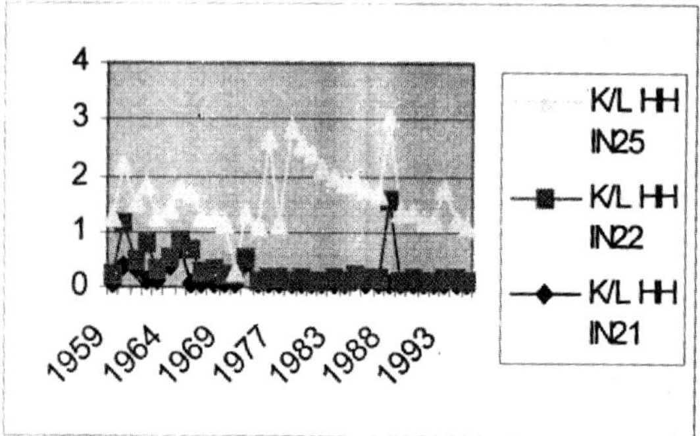

Fig. 6.5a. Dispersal (HH) Trend in K/L in CND Industry for 1956-95

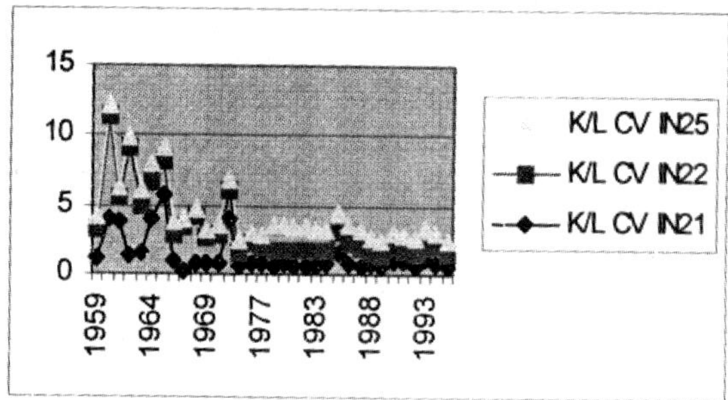

Fig. 6.5b. Dispersal (CV) Trend in CND Industry for 1956-95

While Food Industry showed less fluctuations due to low technological diffusion and so lesser increases in capital intensity in this industry which has followed not very radically innovative methods to boost production. Beverages also showing similar culture of technological diffusion, did increase very high in mid 1980s, largely due to import led growth and demonstration effect in consumption patterns led by the urban rich. Textiles however followed large jumps and falls in dispersal due to the unsustainable nature of liberalisation processes that did not matched high capital injections in spurts with less capacity for labour entry or exit.

Section 6.2

This Section shows trend of the Size Variables and Structural Ratio of K/L in Group 2 Industries of Intermediates that are more Labour Intensive in character comprising Textile Products (IN26), Wood (IN27), Paper (IN28) and Leather (IN29).

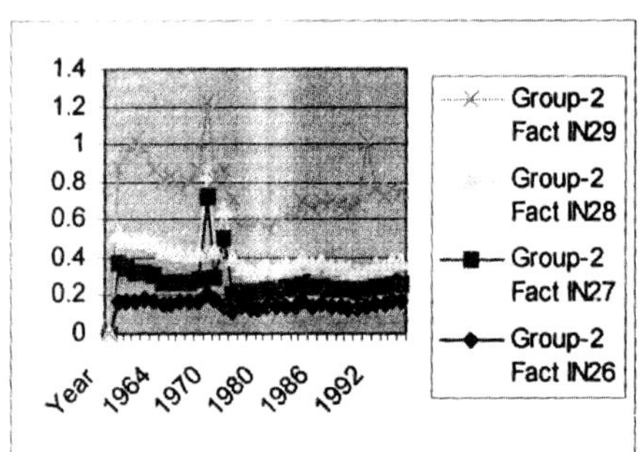

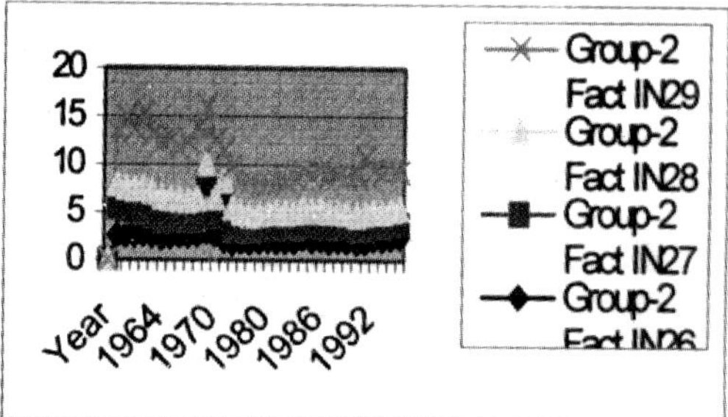

Fig. 6.6a. Dispersal (HH) Trend in Factories in ICI Industries for 1956-95

Fig. 6.6b. Dispersal (CV) Trend in Factories in ILI Industry for 1956-95

This group of industries show severe fluctuations, more prominently in HH. Textile Products show more of concentration. Leather shows high dispersal in both HH and CV. The mid-seventies and mid eighties show relatively more movement towards dispersal, due to growth inducing policies undertaken in those periods. The advent of the 4th Plan in

1970s that laid stress on removal of regional disparities effected more dispersal in industry. The post 1990s spurt in Leather could be due to liberalisation and reform measures of the government that brought about much optimism for industrial progress and economic development, though our data is limited to 1995, when the impact of reforms had not made itself felt in much of the industries and the economy as a whole.

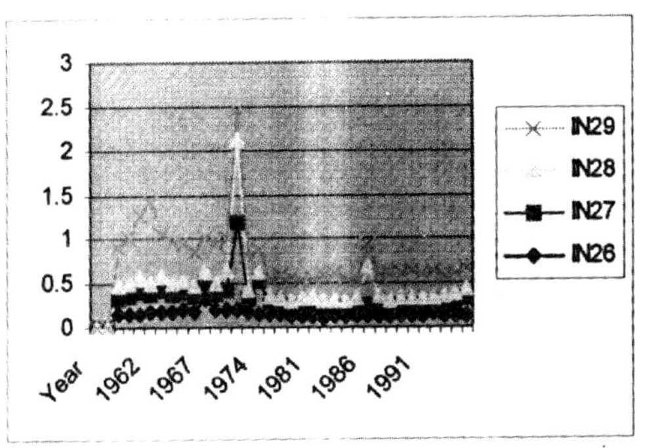

Fig. 6.7a. Dispersal (HH) Trend in PK for ILI Industries for 1956-95

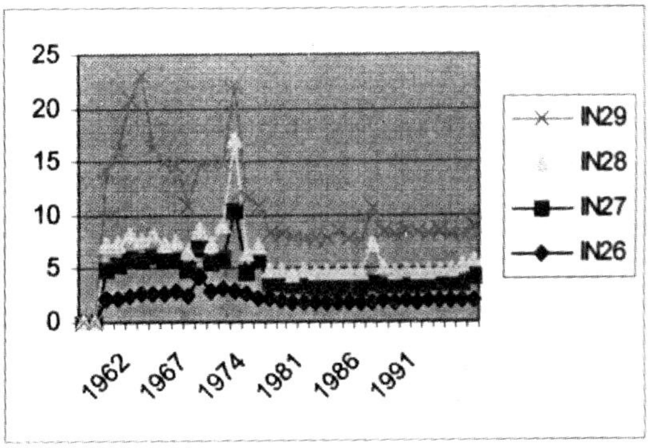

Fig. 6.7b. Dispersal (CV) Trend in PK for ILI Industries for 1956-95

High dispersal of PK noticed in mid 1970s and mid 1980s, the first due to Recovery and focus on small scale industries development and second phase as an outcome of post Indira Gandhi assassination import liberalisation drive. Wood and Paper dispersal or lack of it, move at tandem largely due to direct input-output dependency relationship in this two industries. Hence the need for planning for these two industries considering their nature of a structurally dependent relationship.

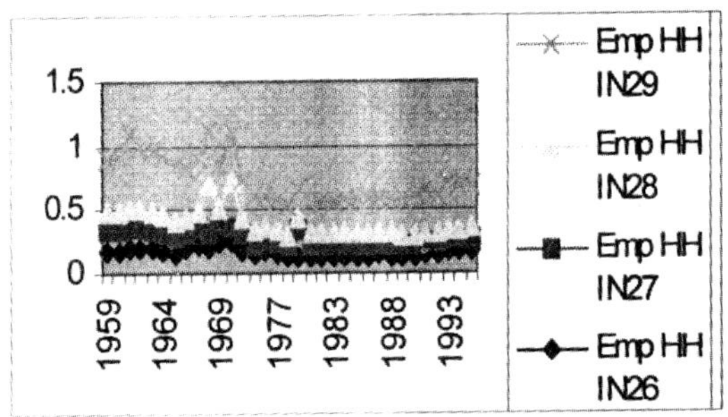

Fig. 6.8a. Dispersal (HH) Trend in Employment in ILI Industries for 1956-95

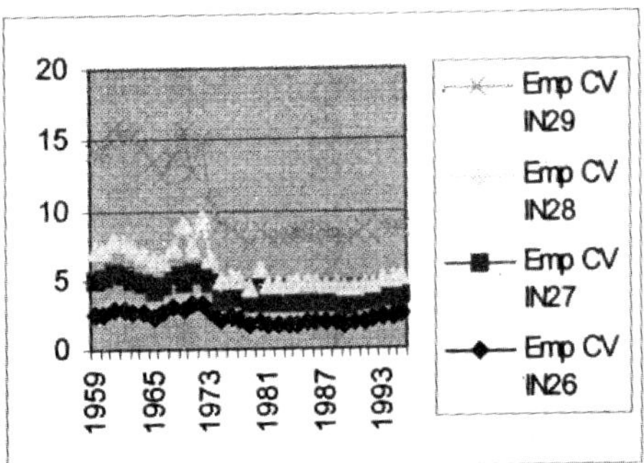

Fig. 6.8b. Dispersal (CV) Trend in Employment in ILI Industries for 1956-95

Dispersal of employment is highest in Leather but concentration noticed in Textile Products (IN26). But Paper showed more employment dispersal than Wood especially in the 4th Plan. However, Wood and Paper Industries show greater clubbing than Textile Products Industry or Leather Industry. However, despite higher Labour Intensiveness of production of these Intermediates, employment dispersal is less than expected. The Labour absorption capacity in these industries being high, a more rigorous employment planning with a period wise monitoring mechanism is needed. Productivity and wage relationships in these industries that depend so much on greater Labour Intensification is also necessary for proper employment planning in them if economy is to reap the rewards of a just industrialization leading to more equitable income distribution.

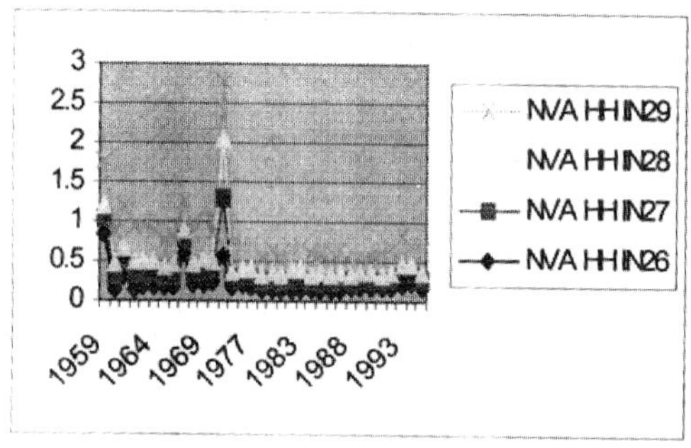

Fig. 6.9a. Dispersal (HH) in NVA in ILI Industries for 1956-95

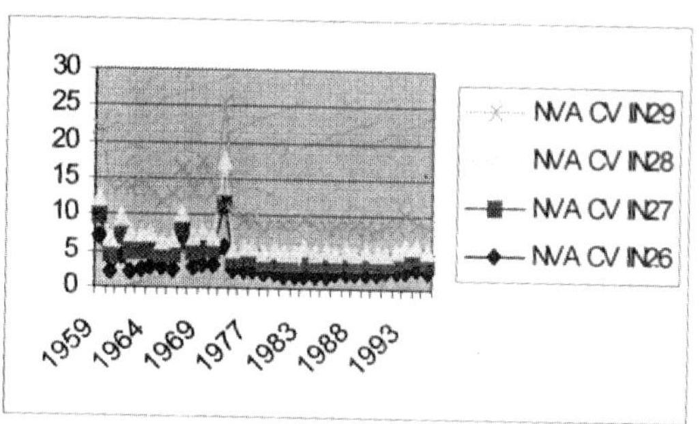

Fig. 6.9b. Dispersal (CV) Trend in NVA in ILI Industries for 1956-95

High dispersal of NVA in Leather compared to other three industries of the group in mid 1970s. But NVA more concentrated in all through the 40 years except this brief mid 1970s phase. This concentration noticed in all the 4 Intermediates showing a distinct lack of planning for Intermediates of the nature of more Labour-intensive production. NVA tending towards more concentration than dispersal is due to lack of employment planning and not treating employment planning as an addendum of growth. NVA in Textile Products is lagging as much as NVA in Textiles as seen in Sec. 6.2.

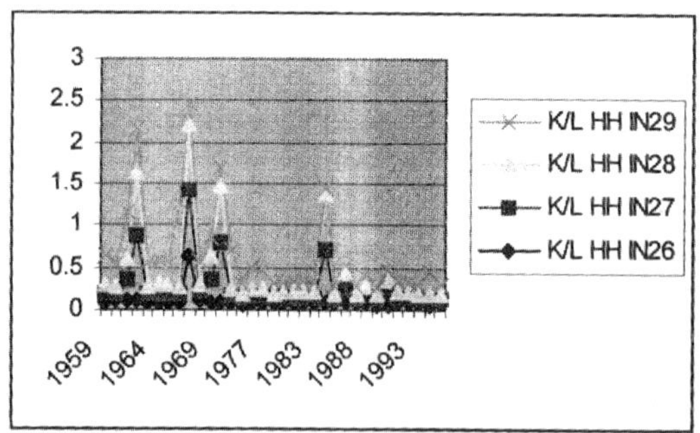

Fig. 6.10a. Dispersal (HH) of K/L in Industries for 1956-95

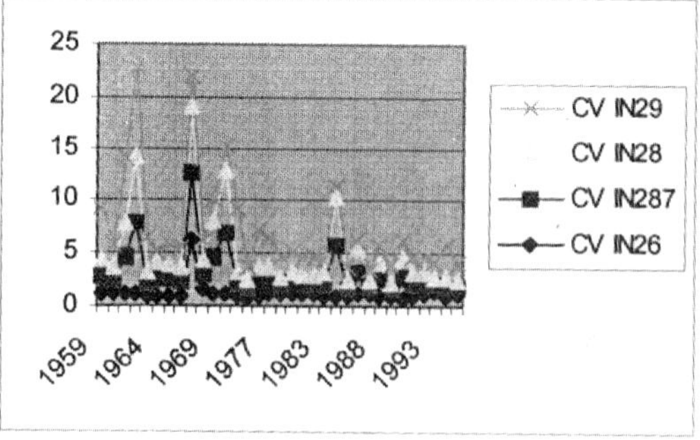

Fig. 6.10b. Dispersal (CV) of K/L in ILI Industries for 1956-95

Severe fluctuations in dispersal of Capital Intensity noticed in both HH and CV measures. There have been high phases of dispersal in Pre 1964, then 1968 when there was an infusion of more capital during recovery phase but falling in dispersal again. Thus capital infusion for expediting recovery phase must have been internal trade related or it led to conspicuous consumption feeding on pent-up demand or Labor absorption was instantaneous, leading to fall in K/L dispersal. There was a relatively stable phase in 1977-1986, but later periods marked by high fluctuations in dispersal figures. Textile Products showed more concentration in K/L and marked by absence of severe fluctuations.

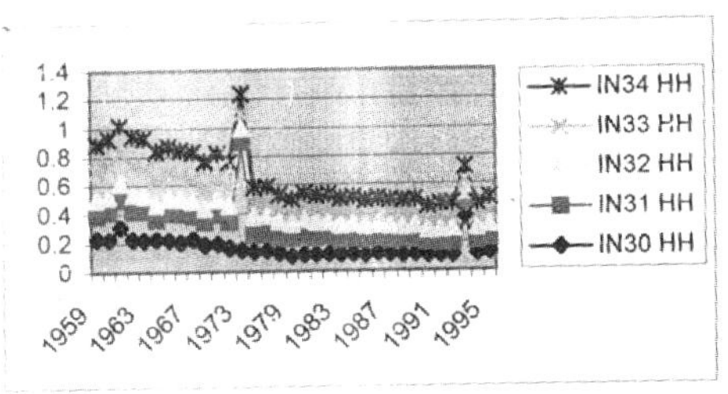

Fig. 6.11a. Dispersal (HH) Trend in Factories for IKI Industries for 1956-95

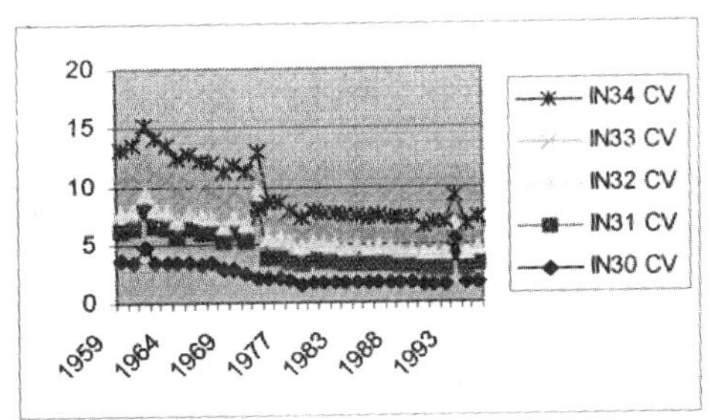

Fig. 6.12b. Dispersal (CV) Trend in Factories for IKI Industries for 1956-95

Section 6.3

This section shows long term trends in Factories for Group 3 or IKI Industries comprising Capital Good Intermediates with higher capital intensity in the nature of production. They are Chemicals (IN30), Rubber-Petroleum and Coal (IN31), Non metallic Mineral Products (IN 32), Basic Metals and Alloys (IN33), Metal Products (IN34).

While all industries show concentration in Factories, Metal Products (IN34) short term high dispersal. The Pre retrogression period marked a tendency for greater dispersal in these Capital Intensive Intermediates, that was cut short by the retrogression. While industries tended to get concentrated, the mid- 1970s was marked by a brief recovery cycle that was short lived. Then all these 5 industries concentrated, except in 1992 phase, it showed a tendency to disperse.

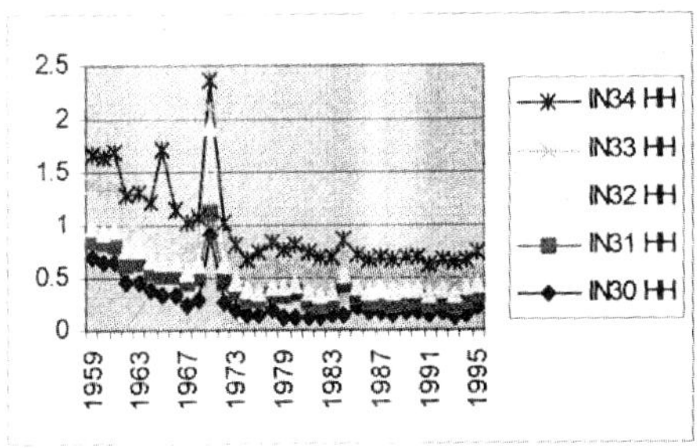

Fig. 6.12a. Dispersal (HH) Trend for PK Trend for IKI Industries for 1956-95

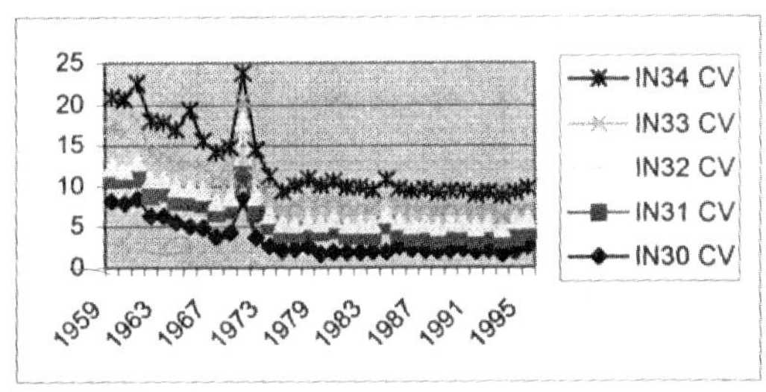

Fig. 6.12b. Dispersal (CV) Trend for PK for IKI Industries for 1956-95

Both Line Diagrams of Dispersal Trends of Productive Capital for Group 3 Industries show similar trends. Chemicals show high concentration. Metal Products show dispersal with high spurt in mid seventies. Less dispersal in IKI group is due to relative neglect of planning for dispersal of Prodcutive Capital.

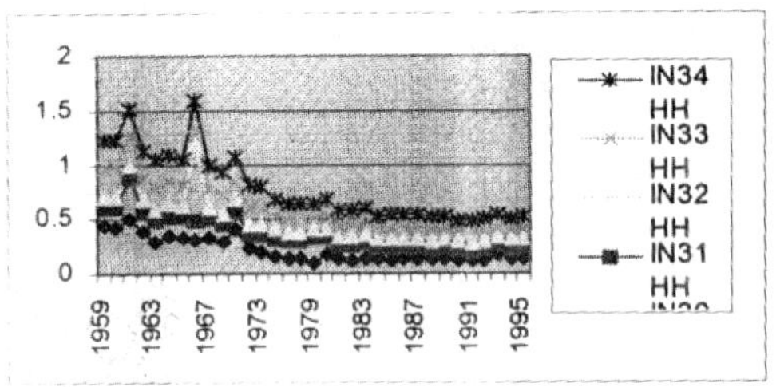

Fig. 6.13a. Dispersal (HH) Trend in Employment in IKI Industries for 1956-95

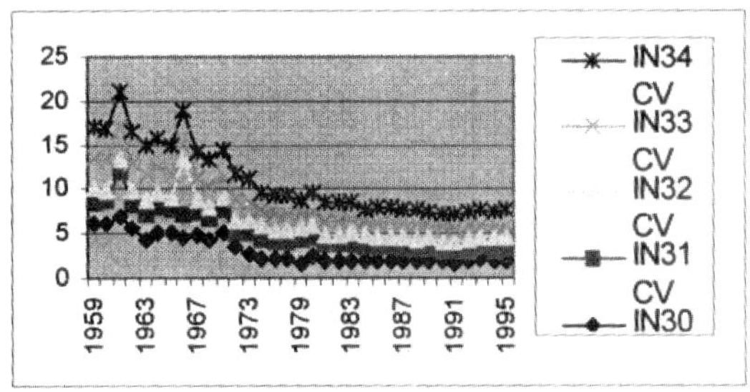

Fig. 6.13b. Dispersal (CV) Trend for Employment in IKI Industries for 1956-95

There is more of employment concentration in this group of industries though Metal Products show increases in sixties before settling down towards concentration as other metal and mineral intermediates were showing no signs of dispersal. Concentration in Intermediates in Employment shows low commitment for a comprehensive planning for Intremediate expansion and integrated with other industries, esp. K-goods Industries.

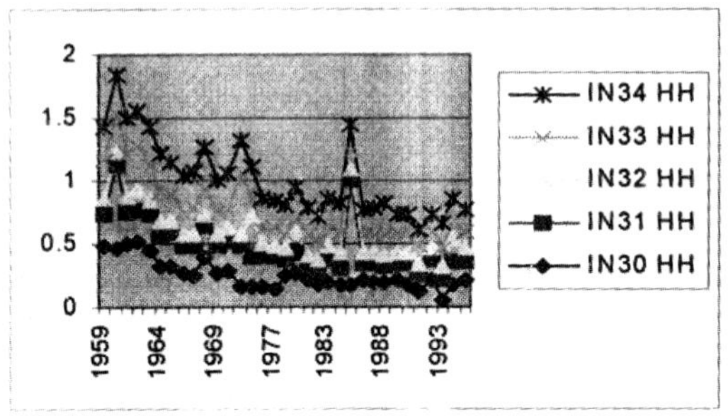

Fig. 6.14a. Dispersal (HH) Trend in NVA for IKI Industries for 1956-95

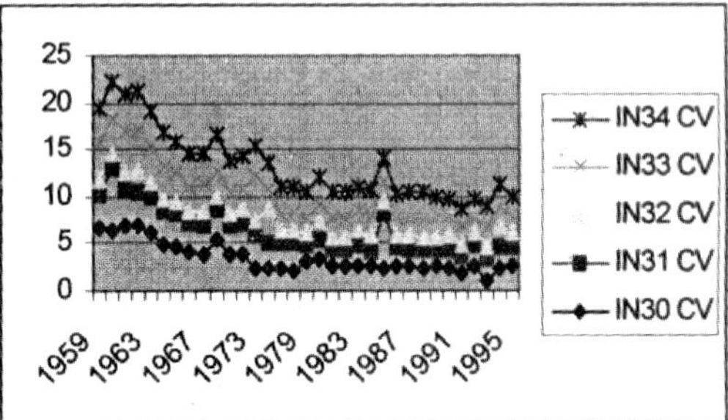

Fig. 6.14b. Dispersal (CV) in NVA for IKI Industries for 1956-95

Severe fluctuations noticed in each of these 5 intermediate industries and being K-intensive in nature, has been less amenable to dispersal. Concentration is seen in long term for IKI Industries. But Metal Products showed higher relative dispersal with Basic Metals closely following it. Chemicals are concentrated that shows the potential of this sunrise indusry of 1970s and 1980s has not been adequately tapped. RPC (IN31) seems to follow Chemcials route to concentration, both being being mutually dependent to a certain extent and also being similarly K intensive in nature.

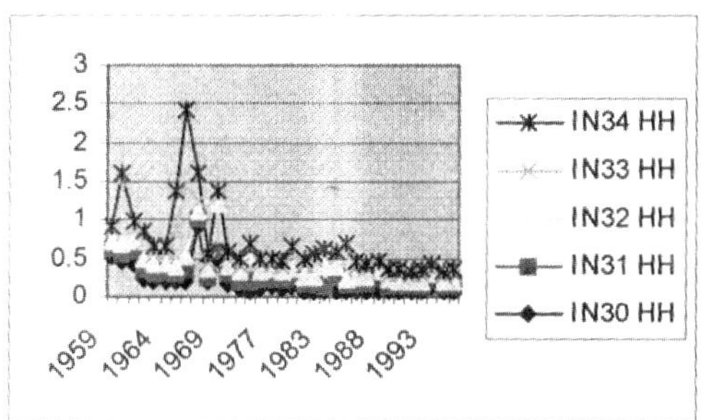

Fig. 6.15a. Dispersal (HH) Trend in K/L in IKI

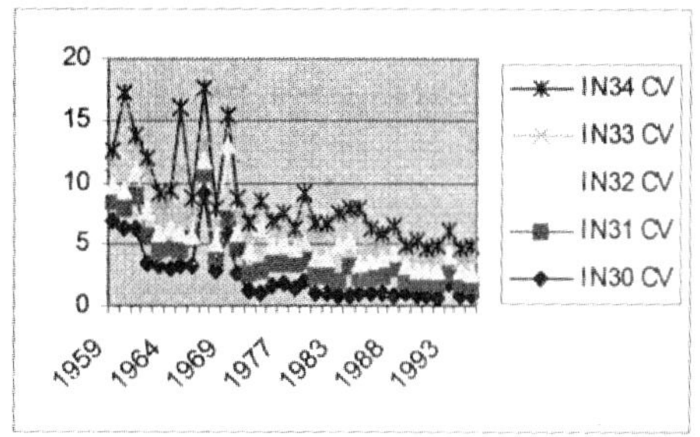

Fig. 6.15b. Dispersal (CV) Trend in K/L in IKI Industries for 1956-95

Similar patterns as above for this group of industries also noticed here. Severe fluctuations are seen in dispersal patterns with CV measure showing fluctuations in all industries more prominently. IKI Industries are concentrating in K/L in long term. Economies of Scale are not being reaped in this IKI Group as NVA and Employment showed more concetration than Factories. Over and above this, K/L is less dispersed, though regularity in spurts is evidence that capital infusion has not helped employment dispersal in these Intermediates.

Section 6. 4

This Section charts long term trends in dispersal measures of HH and CV for capital goods industries like Electrical and Electronics machinery, Transport Equipment and Parts, Other Manufacturing and Electricity, Gas and Steam (IN 41).

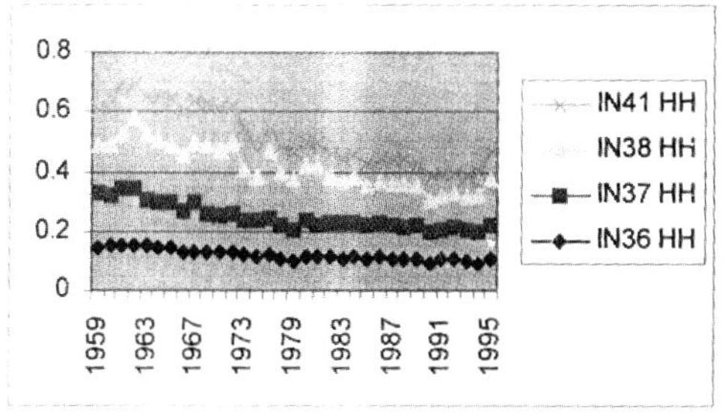

Fig. 6.16a. Dispersal (HH) Trend in Factories in K-Goods Industries for 1956-65

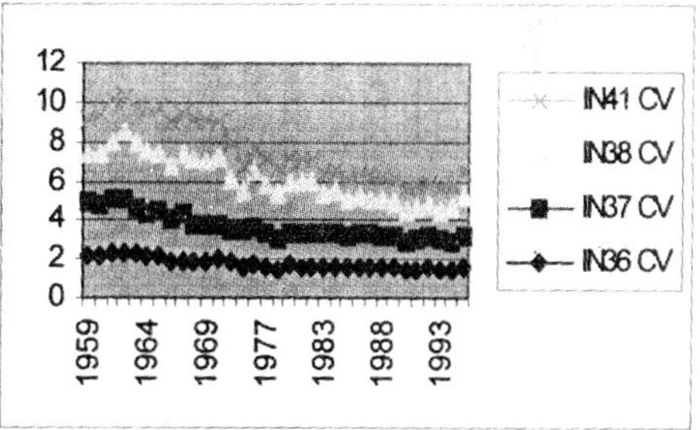

Fig. 6.16b. Dispersal (CV) in Factories in K-Goods Industries for 1956-95

Electrical and Electronics Machinery (IN36) show high concentration in both HH and CV. Electricity, Gas and Steam (IN41) start from higher dispersal but come down to concentration due to lack of dispersal in other supporting high investment industries. Of late after 1992, EGS show movement towards dispersal as an outcome of new growth impulses released due to liberalisation measures for industry, trade and the economy as a whole.

Transport showed a dip in dispersal in recession hit period of mid sixties. Other manufacturing industries due to its miscellany nature of type of industries comprising it, show a more chequered graph, though still moving towards concentration. This industry capable of high Lintensiveness needs a clear policy thrust that would enable it to act a leading sector for growth in an economy like India's.

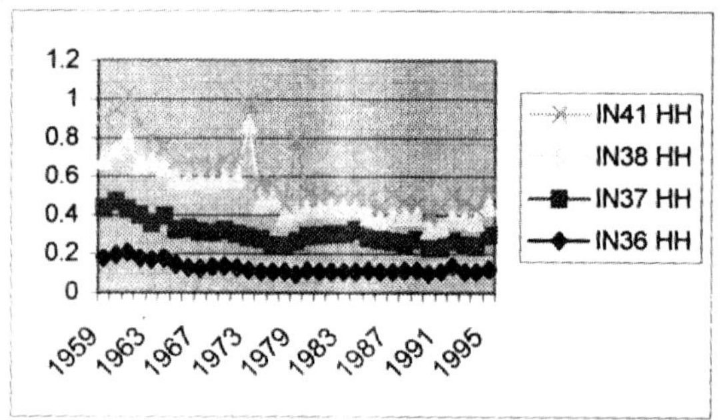

Fig. 6.17a. Dispersal (HH) in PK for K-Goods Industries for 1956-65

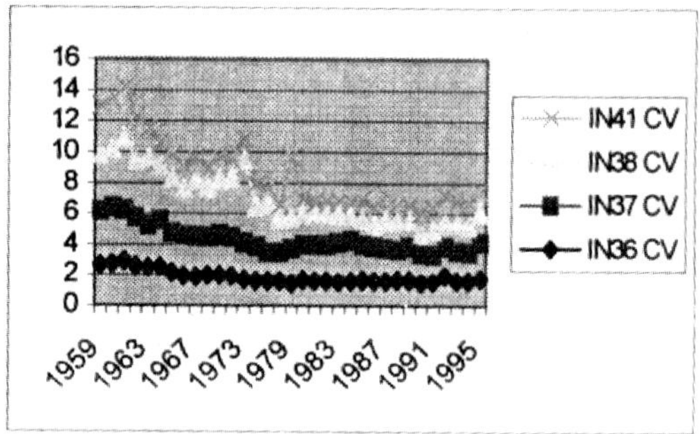

Fig. 6.17b. Dispersal (CV) in PK for K-Goods Industries for 1956-95

Electrical and Non Electrical Machinery other Than Transport (IN36) show high and uniform concentration in both HH and CV. This is an industry that is more related to the development in the knowledge based economy, akin to the software industry of latter decades. Progress, growth or dispersal in this industry IN36 is dependent on R&D development and development of the education sector, a service or tertiary sector. The recent upsurge in service originated GDP does not give much weightage to this and even then it is difficult to deduce the dispersal fortunes and potential of IN36. Transport Equipment Industry (IN37), more related to fortunes of other sectors and industries, shows greater dispersal than IN36. This being a key infrastructure industry, the relative negligence meted out to infrastructure sector is seen in the post recession or recovery phase of Indian industry, when this industry struggled to get more dispersed. But after 1979, it shows more vibrancy and spread and this phase continued till 1987-88 when imbalances in economic indicators, leading to bop crisis, fiscal crisis etc, hence leading to economic reforms, did reduce the spread of this Industry (IN37) again, till post 1992 reform phase brought in a concomitant awareness of the importance of this sector.

OMI (IN38) shows high dispersal but given to fluctuations as does the EGS (IN41). Despite high dispersal in the beginning phase, these 2 industries found it difficult to sustain its spread and grew more concentrated with post 1992-93 saw quicker and more immediate response in terms of higher dispersal, which is a good sign for Indian Industrial development and economic progress.

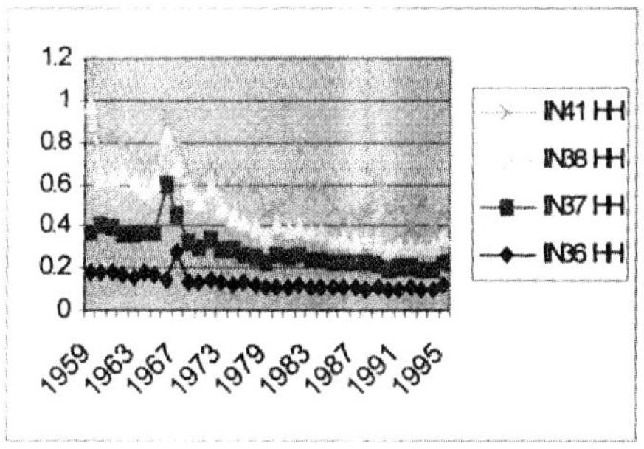

Fig. 6.18a. Dispersal (HH) Trend in Emp in K-goods for 1956-65

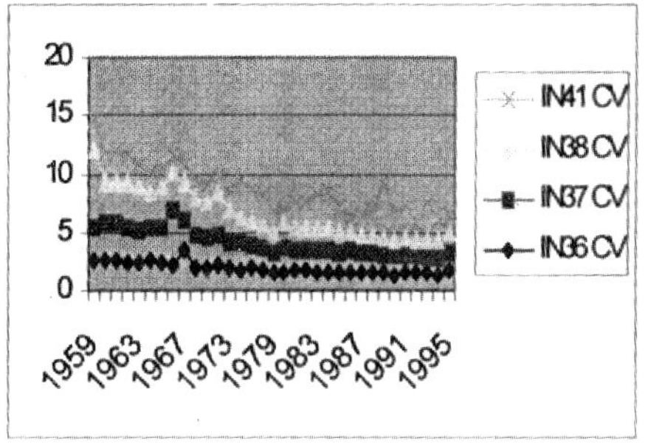

Fig. 6.18b. Dispersal (CV) Trend in Employment in K-goods Industries for 1956-95

Employment in capital goods industry is more concentrated than seen in PK or NVA. Yet maximum dispersal is noticed in EGS (IN41) which does not show smooth downward sloping line as in other three industries. OMI trying to be nearer EGS trend line, did not really follow it and showed more concentration in 1980s. That showed the nature of OMI industry, which despite being capital intensive caters to the direct consumption needs as regards the need and usage of capital goods of this type say instrumentation, surgical instruments, agricultural implements, electronics goods , etc that caters to a market segment, quite distinct from heavy machine goods or the Type for EGS that required heavier capital investment. IN37 dispersal in employment followed more towards and bunches with OMI group, especially in later 1980s, showing trade related concerns had gained prominence.

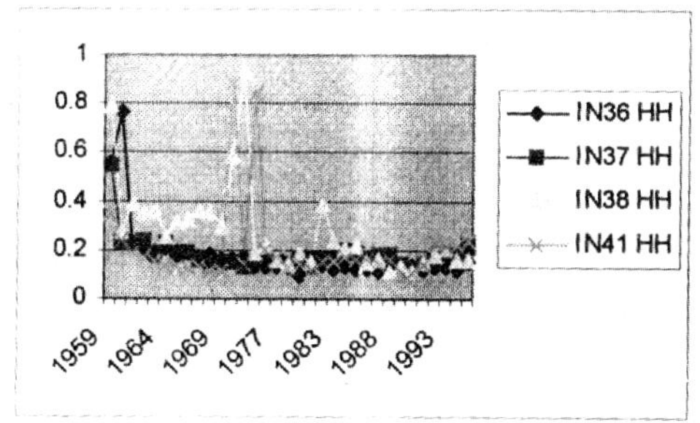

Fig. 6.19a. Dispersal (HH) Trend in NVA for K-goods for 1956-95 Industries for 1956-65

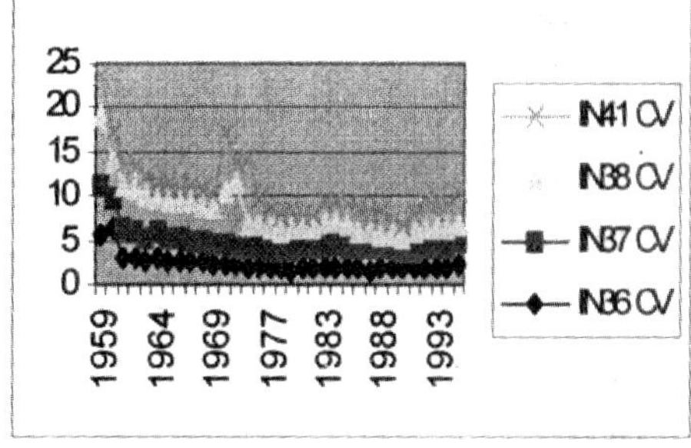

Fig. 6.19b. Dispersal (CV) Trend in NVA for K-goods Industries (1956-95)

HH dispersal in NVA show similar trends for all industries of this group with high fluctuations in mid seventies and ultimately settling down after 1980s. CV trend show concentration in all, though initial dispersal is high in EGS. OMI NVA pattern is similar to other variables and ratios for this industry. EGS follows patterns of other industries in this group, except OMI. Thus all capital goods industries show greater concentration in outputs, if not fully in inputs of K and L.

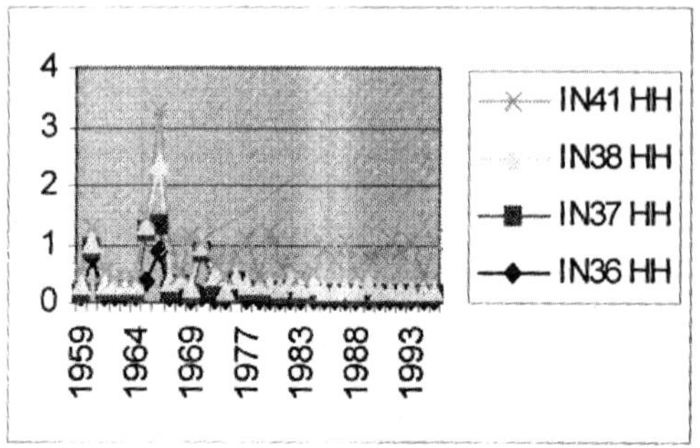

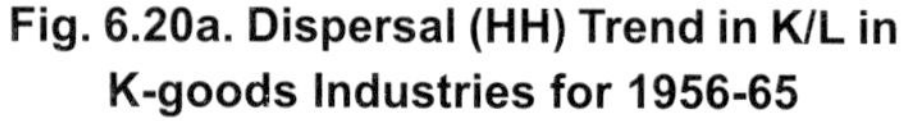
Fig. 6.20a. Dispersal (HH) Trend in K/L in K-goods Industries for 1956-65

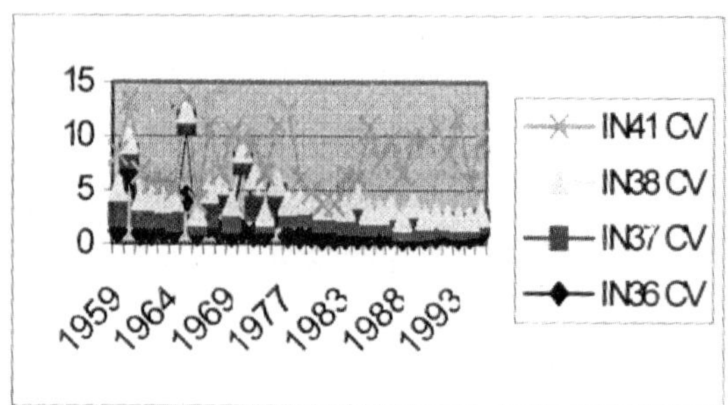

Fig. 6.20b. Dispersal (CV) Trend in K/L in K-goods Industries (1956-95)

K/L dispersal shows fluctuations in CV, though HH is more clear-cut. EGS is more dispersed in K/L which is good sign when the Indian economy is seeking more decentralisation of the power sector. Electrical and Electronic machinery is highly concentrated in K/L and is clearly in need of more clear policy inputs as to dispersal. This group showed reaping of scale economies more than IKI group.

Section 6. 5 : Summary Results and Policy Recommendations

While Consumer and User and Intermediates show greater dispersal, Capital Goods and Capital goods Intermediate are more concentrated in long term Indian Industrialisation. Beverages, Leather, Metal Products and EGS in each of the respective Groups show a contrary trend vis a vis trends in variables and structural ratios of their respective groups. More clear-cut policy formulations await Chemicals, Electrical and Non electrical Machinery, Textile Products for each of these to act as leading sectors of growth.

Williamson hypothesis of Growth leading to concentration in long run, is proved in Food Products, EGS, Textiles, Metal Products and mostly IKI group.

Wood (IN27), Textile Products (IN26), Transport equipment (IN37) and Electrical and electronic machinery (IN36) prove Self-perpetuation hypothesis. Dispersal and Self-perpetuation is noticed in K-goods Industry group. However, concentration comes about due to low growth and industry-specific and region specific policy packages to boost their key factor use to raise efficiency will help in greater dispersal of Indian Industry.

Economic Impact Analysis of Contributions of Total Factor Productivity (TFP), Partial Productivities, Capital Intensity on Regional Dispersal of Industries : 1956-95

INTRODUCTION

This Chapter 7 deals with contributions of relevant explanatory variables, viz. Total Factor productivity, Partial Productivities of Factors, Capital Intensity on regional dispersal measures of Herfindahl Index (HI) and Coefficient of Variation (CV) of Net Value Added (NVA) and Employment (NW) of two-digit industry groups of India, for 40 years period of 1956-95 and separately for each of the 10 years periods(4) covering successive five-year plans, including Plan holiday, industrial recession/retrogression, recovery and growth periods. This study is an analysis of tracing nature of and extent of causal relationships (b estimate) in the estimate of simple linear regressions of Regional dispersal on each of the explanatory variables, mentioned above separately estimated for tracing causal relationships distinctly for each of the dependent variables, as otherwise multiple regressions estimations posed problems of single multiple regressions estimation that provided very low R^2, $\bar{R}^2$, F and student t statistic and high standard errors, hence could not be pursued even stepwise multiple regressions estimations for all possible combinations as to their contributions to regional dispersal. The dependent variable was distinguished in 4 specifications estimated considering HH of Net Value Added and of Employment and CV of employment and NVA as to account for each industry's each of the regional dispersal measures regressed on each of five explanatory variables. This analysis alone brings out distinct contributions as desired for the rate of economic impact analysis. This Chapter is divided into five Sections, each for the cited time periods. For each time period, while detailed Tables are presented to point out how results of short term periods have a bearing or corresponds to long term results.

Impact Analysis of Relevant Explanatory Variables on Regional Dispersal for 1956-65

In this Section, we regress HH NVA, HH emp on TFP-S, K/L, K-productivity and L-productivity for 1956-65.

Table 7.1. Regional Dispersal (HH and CV) of Industries' output (NVA) in response to TFP by Solow (at current prices) 1956-1965

Specification: HH *nva* = *a* + *b*(*TFP-S*); CV *nva* = *a* + *b*(TFP-S)

Ind. Name	IN Code	Dispersal Measures		HH nva	HH nva	HH nva	CV nva	CV nva	CV nva
		CV nva	HH nva	Industry	$\overline{\beta}$	$(b/r)^2$	Industry	$\overline{\beta}$	$(b/r)^2$
1	2	3	4	5	6	7	8	9	10
Food	21	1.001	0.001	29	1.479	6.580	25	4.938	156.307
Bev'rage	22	3.633	0.249	26	1.057	21.080	26	1.091	85.020
Textiles	25	2.656	0.186	27	1.022	3.146	37	0.834	3.147
Tex Prd	26	3.338	0.279	32	0.807	2.238	32	0.819	2.313
Wood	27	0.312	3.922	22	0.729	8.052	34	0.813	3.843
Paper	28	2.395	0.163	25	0.727	3.858	36	0.277	1.967
Leather	29	6.560	0.442	21	0.401	6.991	33	0.183	2.576
Chemical	30	6.092	0.434	36	0.4	1.649	27	0.14	0.039
R-P-C	31	4.068	0.319	41	0.274	0.284	30	0.138	0.086
Nm MPrd	32	1.670	0.117	37	0.235	0.186	41	0.129	0.022
BM&A	33	3.824	0.291	33	0.207	2.678	28	0.099	0.029
Mel Prd	34	3.722	0.284	28	0.152	1.650	38	0.098	0.157
MotTr	36	3.737	0.334	34	0.148	0.110	22	0.058	0.259
Tr.Eq.	37	7.662	0.788	30	0.126	0.021	31	0.05	0.004
OMI	38	4.821	0.339	31	0.061	0.083	21	0.029	0.008
EGS	41	2.790	0.195	38	0.018	0.006	29	0.011	0.001

Textile Products (IN26), Non-Metallic Mineral Products (32), Textiles (25), show higher influence of TFP on NVA. Since $(b/r)^2$ is high, less dispersal/ concentration in these industries are due to TFPG.

Rubber-Petroleum-Coal (IN31), Food Products (IN21), Paper (IN28), Other Manufacturing Industries (IN38), Basic Metals and Alloys (IN33) show least influence of TFP on NVA. Food (IN21) and Basic Metals and Alloys (IN33) show concentration with high b/r meaning that non-dispersal is better influenced by TFPG, viz; in Food and an Intermediate like Basic Metals, TFPG is not influencing for dispersal. This is an interesting finding. Rubber-Petroleum-Coal (IN31), Other Manufacturing Industries (IN38) show low b/r implying that dispersal is not due to TFPG but due to some other causes.

Table 7.2. Regional dispersal of Indian Industries' employment in response to TFP by Solow for 1956-65

Specification: HH emp = a+b (TFP); CV emp = a+b (TFP)

In. Nm	Measures of Industrial Dispersal			Cvemp	Cvemp	Cvemp	HHemp	HHemp	HHemp
	IN Code	CV emp	HH emp	IN Code	$\overline{\beta}$	$(b/r)^2$	IN Code	$\overline{\beta}$	$(b/r)^2$
1	2	3	4	5	6	7	8	9	10
Food	21	1.001	0.001	32	2.442	47.317	33	2.09	7.531
Bevrges	22	6.087	0.491	22	1.588	11.675	29	1.494	5.583
Textiles	25	2.608	0.182	25	1.406	10.802	36	1.338	4.42
Tex Prd	26	2.63	0.176	26	1.133	1.422	22	1.123	7.248
Wood	27	2.32	0.154	33	1.19	1.386	27	0.666	0.713
Paper	28	2.176	0.146	28	1.119	16.966	31	0.532	1.993
Leather	29	7.53	0.468	31	1.111	2.047	25	0.428	1.124
Chemical	30	5.633	0.389	21	1.108	1.103	32	0.388	0.528
R-P-C	31	2.961	0.207	30	1.011	7.957	26	0.342	0.625
Nm MPrd	32	1.504	0.107	29	1.066	5.919	37	0.316	2.774
BM&A	33	3.25	0.231	36	0.919	1.287	41	0.286	0.135
Met Prd	34	3.376	0.246	34	0.594	1.066	28	0.265	0.062
MotTr	36	2.497	0.171	27	0.531	0.411	38	0.146	0.52
Tr.Eq.	37	6.523	0.597	37	0.308	2.018	30	0.115	0.082
OMI	38	3.94	0.291	38	0.246	0.132	34	0.035	0.012
EGS	41	2.339	0.151	41	0.217	0.192	21	0.032	0.008

Beverages (IN22), Textiles (IN25), Textile Products (IN26), Basic Metals and Alloys (IN33), Leather (IN29), NmMP (IN32), Rubber-Petroleum-Coal (IN31) showed greater response in employment dispersal to influence of TFP.

While dispersal has been good, $(b/r)^2$ has been higher. This reveals that regional dispersal of these industries has been brought by TFPG.

The least influence is seen in Food (IN21), Electricity, Gas and Steam (IN41), Other Manufacturing Industries (IN38), Transport Equipment (IN37). Here, $(b/r)^2$ is low implying that dispersal/concentration of employment in these L-intensive and/or K-intensive industries is not due to TFPG in this first decade of industrialisation.

Table 7.3. Regional Dispersal(CV) of Industries' output(NVA) in response to Capital intensity (at current prices) 1956-65: Specification:

CV nva = $a + b$(K/L); HH nva = $a + b$(K/L)

Ind. Name	IN Code	Dispersal Measures		CV nva	CV nva	CV nva	HH nva	HH nva	HH nva
		HHNVA	CVNVA	Industry	$\bar{\beta}$	$(b/r)^2$	Industry	$\bar{\beta}$	$(b/r)^2$
1	2	3	4	5	6	7	8	9	10
Food	21	0.001	5.376	29	2.595	30.333	21	2.717	15.875
Bev'	22	0.249	3.633	21	1.828	7.296	30	1.649	7.118
Textiles	25	0.186	2.656	37	1.558	2.911	34	1.297	6.571
Tex Prd	26	0.279	3.338	33	1.546	6.908	33	0.913	3.688
Wood	27	0.312	3.922	32	1.417	10.404	25	0.57	1.633
Paper	28	0.163	2.395	30	1.358	5.657	38	0.567	1.546
Leather	29	0.442	6.56	36	1.098	2.208	37	0.499	2.075
Chemic	30	0.434	6.092	34	1.064	1.791	26	0.475	1.465
R-P-C	31	0.319	4.068	25	1.013	2.133	36	0.452	0.376
NM MP	32	0.117	1.67	31	0.419	0.554	29	0.448	1.761
BM&A	33	0.291	3.824	26	0.312	0.338	41	0.276	0.134
M. Prd	34	0.284	3.722	38	0.275	0.204	32	0.107	0.032
MotTr	36	0.334	3.737	28	0.231	0.087	27	0.087	0.023
Tr.Eq.	37	0.788	7.662	22	0.071	0.022	28	0.078	0.006
OMI	38	0.339	4.821	41	0.07	0.008	31	0.045	0.018
EGS	41	0.195	2.79	27	0.025	0.002	22	0.005	0.002

The industries' with higher influences are Textiles (IN25), Metal Products (IN34), Chemicals (IN30), Food Products (IN21), Basic Metals and Alloys (IN33) and Non-Metallic Mineral Products (IN32). $(b/r)^2$ being high, dispersal of NVA occurs through influence of K/L in the long run.

The least influence of K/L on NVA is found in Beverages (IN22), EGS (IN41), Wood (IN27), Paper (IN28). $(b/r)^2$ being low in all industries, it follows concentration is due to low K/L in long run.

Table 7.4. Regional Dispersal(CV) of Industries' employment in response to Capital intensity (at current prices) 1956-1965

Specification: CV emp = a+b(K/L); HH emp= a+b(K/L)

In. Nm	Dispersal Measures			CV emp	CV emp	CV emp	HH emp	HH emp	HH emp
	IN Code	CV emp	HH emp	Industry	$\bar{\beta}$	$(b/r)^2$	IN Code	$\bar{\beta}$	$(b/r)^2$
1	9	7	8	1	2	3	4	5	6
Food	21	1.001	0.001	25	1.857	31.637	37	2.616	6.983
Bev'	22	6.087	0.491	38	1.815	7.538	21	1.974	6.812
Textiles	25	2.608	0.182	37	1.373	1.914	33	0.731	1.713
Tex Prd	26	2.630	0.176	26	1.366	4.923	27	0.625	1.289
Wood	27	2.320	0.154	21	1.125	2.213	38	0.523	0.613
Paper	28	2.176	0.146	33	0.998	3.172	32	0.516	1.325
Leather	29	7.530	0.468	27	0.79	2.364	25	0.505	0.802
Chemical	30	5.633	0.389	29	0.604	0.518	34	0.375	11.719
R-P-C	31	2.961	0.207	32	0.601	3.969	28	0.36	1.641
Nm MPrd	32	1.504	0.107	30	0.246	0.747	41	0.356	0.524
BM&A	33	3.250	0.231	36	0.229	0.243	22	0.351	0.147
Met. Prd	34	3.376	0.246	41	0.169	0.155	30	0.25	0.710
MotTr	36	2.497	0.171	34	0.16	0.088	26	0.194	0.352
Tr.Eq.	37	6.523	0.597	28	0.072	0.028	36	0.145	0.121
OMI	38	3.940	0.291	31	0.068	0.033	29	0.078	0.047
EGS	41	2.339	0.151	22	0.034	0.006	31	0.061	0.031

Textile (IN25), Other Manufacturing Industries (IN38), Wood (IN27), Basic Metals and Alloys (IN33), Non-Metallic Mineral Products (IN32), show higher K/L influence. In Textiles (IN25), Other Manufacturing Industries (IN38), Non-Metallic Mineral Products (IN32), Basic Metals and Alloys (IN33) and Wood (IN27), high $(b/r)^2$ implies that in each of these industries influence of K/L did not affect dispersal in any discernible way.

The Least K/L influence is in Beverages (IN22), Rubber, Petroleum and Coal (IN31), Machinery other than Transport (IN36), Leather (IN29), Electricity, and Steam (IN41), Metal Products (IN34), Paper (IN28). In Beverages (IN22) and Paper (IN28), dispersal in Beverage is not due to K/L as b/r is low, whereas in Paper, concentration in this period is due to K/L influence. Thus in Paper, K/L influence did not bring about dispersal in this first period of industrialisation. In Leather (IN29), dispersal has not been due to influence of K/L.

Table 7.5. Regional Dispersal(HH) of Industries' output(NVA) in response to Capital productivity (at current prices) 1956-1965;

Specification: HH nva = *a*+ *b*(K-productivity); CV *nva* = *a* + *b*(K-productivity)

Ind. Name	IN Code	Dispersal Measures		HH nva	HH nva	HH nva	CV nva	CV nva	CV nva
		HHNVA	CVNVA	Industry	$\hat{\beta}$	$(b/r)^2$	Industry	$\hat{\beta}$	$(b/r)^2$
1	2	3	4	5	6	7	8	9	10
Food	21	0.328	2.000	31	0.453	0.946	38	1.931	11.580
Bev'	22	0.249	3.633	30	0.452	1.353	25	1.786	10.776
Textiles	25	0.186	2.656	38	0.428	0.496	41	1.374	11.654
Tex Prd	26	0.279	3.338	22	0.335	0.249	31	1.255	8.036
Wood	27	0.312	3.922	25	0.263	0.238	29	1.232	18.739
Paper	28	0.163	2.395	41	0.206	0.276	28	1.152	3.206
Leather	29	0.442	6.560	29	0.105	0.054	34	0.814	1.140
Chemical	30	0.434	6.092	28	0.081	0.656	36	0.733	1.613
R-P-C	31	0.319	4.068	37	0.075	0.029	21	0.351	0.520
Nm MPrd	32	0.117	1.670	36	0.074	0.014	30	0.328	0.681
BM&A	33	0.291	3.824	26	0.074	0.015	27	0.214	0.175
Met. Prd	34	0.284	3.722	34	0.06	0.009	22	0.158	1.248
MotTr	36	0.334	3.737	32	0.033	0.009	26	0.11	0.032
Tr.Eq.	37	0.788	7.662	21	0.023	0.002	33	0.031	0.003
OMI	38	0.339	4.821	33	0.022	0.002	32	0.016	0.001
EGS	41	0.195	2.790	27	0.021	0.001	37	0.015	0.002

High influence of Capital Productivity on NVA is noticed in Rubber, Petroleum and Coal (IN31), Other Manufacturing Industries (IN38), Textiles (IN25), Electricity, Gas and Steam (IN41), Leather (IN29). In all these industries, dispersal in these industries was due to influence of capital productivity on NVA.

Least influence of capital productivity on NVA dispersal is in Wood (IN27), Transport (IN37), Non-Metallic Mineral Products (IN32), Basic Metals and Alloys (IN33), Textile Products (IN26). High dispersal in these industries was not due to capital productivity influence.

Table 7.6. Regional Dispersal of Industries' employment in response to Capital productivity (at current prices) 1956-1965

Specification: CV emp = *a* + *b*(K-productivity); HH emp = *a* + *b* (K-productivity)

In. Nm	Measures of Industrial Dispersal			CV emp	CV emp	CV emp	HH emp	HH emp	HH emp
	IN Code	CV emp	HH emp	Industry	$\hat{\beta}$	$(b/r)^2$	Industry	$\hat{\beta}$	$(b/r)^2$
1	2	3	4	5	6	7	8	9	10
Food Pro	21	1.001	0.001	28	1.953	11.318	25	1.654	6.943
Beverages	22	6.087	0.491	25	1.591	6.750	22	0.643	0.458
Textiles	25	2.608	0.182	30	1.571	2.840	30	0.521	0.703
Textile Prd	26	2.630	0.176	22	1.207	6.253	21	0.482	0.362
Wood	27	2.320	0.154	41	1.035	5.822	28	0.438	0.702
Paper	28	2.176	0.146	29	0.776	2.641	31	0.189	0.812
Leather	29	7.530	0.468	32	0.531	0.540	26	0.074	0.021
Chemical	30	5.633	0.389	26	0.4	0.300	27	0.073	0.013
Ru-Pet-Co	31	2.961	0.207	38	0.369	0.605	29	0.067	0.018
Nm MPrd	32	1.504	0.107	27	0.314	0.253	34	0.064	0.216
BM&A	33	3.250	0.231	21	0.247	0.310	41	0.058	0.017
Metal Prd	34	3.376	0.246	33	0.236	0.066	32	0.041	0.003
MotTr	36	2.497	0.171	37	0.205	0.271	37	0.036	0.007
Tr.Eq.	37	6.523	0.597	31	0.15	0.388	38	0.032	0.003
OMI	38	3.940	0.291	34	0.142	0.133	36	0.023	0.002
EGS	41	2.339	0.151	36	0.039	0.005	33	0.017	0.000

Capital Productivity's influence on dispersal of employment is higher in Paper (IN28), Beverages (IN22), Textiles (IN25), Chemicals (IN30). $(b/r)^2$ is high in all of the above industries except in Chemicals (IN30). So dispersal in Chemicals came about not due to influence of capital productivity in this initial period, as the build up for this industry to be one of the sunrise industries of 1970s has not started. The rest being Labour intensive in nature, employment dispersal was aided by capital productivity growth.

The Low influence industries were in Machinery other than transport (IN36), Basic Metals and Alloys (IN33), Transport Equipment (IN37). In Basic Metals and Alloys (IN33) characterised by low $(b/r)^2$, dispersal did not accrue due to influence of Capital productivity. In others, i.e. IN36 and IN37, both being high capital intensive industries, influence of capital productivity was low on employment dispersal, especially in this first period of industrialisation.

Table 7.7. Regional Dispersal(CV) of Industries' output(NVA) in response to Labour productivity (at current prices) 1956-65;Specification: CV nva = *a* + *b* (L-productivity); HH nva = *a* + *b* (L-Productivity)

In. Nm	Measures of Industrial Dispersal			CV nva	CV nva	CV nva	HH nva	HH nva	HH nva
	IN Code	HH nva	CV nva	In Code	$\hat{\beta}$	$(b/r)^2$	IN Code	$\hat{\beta}$	$(b/r)^2$
1	2	3	4	5	6	7	8	9	10
Food Pro	21	0.454	1.332	32	3.1	65.822	38	1.978	19.760
Beverage	22	0.249	3.633	36	1.821	14.355	29	1.261	14.325
Textiles	25	0.186	2.656	34	1.636	12.391	31	0.864	15.552
Text Prd	26	0.279	3.338	31	1.454	9.925	25	0.822	1.856
Wood	27	0.312	3.922	38	1.256	4.431	30	0.806	13.534
Paper	28	0.163	2.395	25	1.249	4.575	41	0.604	1.614
Leather	29	0.442	6.560	28	1.099	7.946	34	0.491	1.153
Chemical	30	0.434	6.092	26	1.064	24.087	32	0.371	0.348
Ru-Pet-C	31	0.319	4.068	41	0.969	3.504	33	0.359	0.207
Nm MPrd	32	0.117	1.670	33	0.898	1.335	28	0.212	0.202
BM&A	33	0.291	3.824	22	0.605	0.515	21	0.156	0.035
MetPrd	34	0.284	3.722	37	0.579	3.020	27	0.086	0.045
MotTr	36	0.334	3.737	30	0.454	7.361	36	0.064	0.019
Tr.Eq.	37	0.788	7.662	21	0.439	0.272	26	0.058	0.105
OMI	38	0.339	4.821	27	0.161	0.220	22	0.045	0.003
EGS	41	0.195	2.790	29	0.013	0.004	37	0.041	0.010

The Higher influences of Labour productivity on NVA dispersal are seen in Metal Products (IN34), Rubber, Petroleum and Coal (IN31), Other Manufacturing Industries (IN38), Textiles (IN25). With high b/r, dispersal in IN31, 34, 38/concentration in textiles is on account of Labour productivity influence.

The lower influences of labor productivity on NVA in this first decade of planned industrialisation are in Transport Equipment (IN37), Beverages (IN22), Wood (IN27), Food Products (IN21). In Food and Beverages, $(b/r)^2$ low, Concentration in Food and Dispersal in Beverages was not due to influence of labour productivity on NVA dispersal. Thus labour intensive firms as Food and Beverages did not respond to labour productivity influence. But in Wood and Transport, $(b/r)^2$ being low, dispersal was not affected by labour productivity influence.

Table 7.8. Regional Dispersal(HH) of Industries' employment in response to Labor productivity (at current prices) 1956-1965

Specification: HH emp = *a* + *b*(L-productivity); CV emp = *a* + *b*(L- productivity)

In. Nm	Measures of Industrial Dispersal			HH emp	HH emp	HH emp	CV emp	CV emp	CV emp
	IN Code	CV emp	HH emp	Industry	$\hat{\beta}$	$(b/r)^2$	Industry	$\hat{\beta}$	$(b/r)^2$
1	2	3	4	5	6	7	8	9	10
Food Pro	21	1.001	0.001	26	2.327	9.055	38	1.987	6.591
Beverages	22	6.087	0.491	29	1.732	5.976	36	1.954	6.538
Textiles	25	2.608	0.182	28	1.588	**105.073**	22	1.905	9.402
Tex. Prd	26	2.630	0.176	32	1.479	4.215	34	1.339	5.050
Wood	27	2.320	0.154	36	1.366	3.168	28	1.321	91.844
Paper	28	2.176	0.146	33	1.136	14.665	41	1.311	3.201
Leather	29	7.530	0.468	21	1.095	3.172	37	1.308	4.054
Chemical	30	5.633	0.389	41	1.042	1.625	30	1.297	3.298
Ru-P -Co	31	2.961	0.207	37	0.92	2.187	32	1.266	2.888
Nm MPrd	32	1.504	0.107	25	0.8	1.139	29	1.237	2.767
BM&A	33	3.250	0.231	34	0.551	3.943	31	1.06	6.208
Met Prd	34	3.376	0.246	38	0.544	0.435	25	1.017	1.569
MotTr	36	2.497	0.171	31	0.196	0.198	27	0.514	0.751
Tr.Eq.	37	6.523	0.597	30	0.148	0.040	26	0.501	20.917
OMI	38	3.940	0.291	22	0.074	0.008	21	0.451	0.503
EGS	41	2.339	0.151	27	0.021	0.001	33	0.013	0.003

Higher influences of Labour Productivity on employment dispersal in this decade are in Paper (IN28), Non-Metallic Mineral Products (IN32), Machinery other than transport (IN36), Electricity, Gas and Steam (IN41). With high *b*/*r*, dispersal is due to L-productivity influence on employment dispersal.

Lower influences of Labour productivity on employment dispersal are in Wood (IN27), Rubber, Petroleum and Coal (IN31). But the process of dispersal in the early phase of industrialisation was not due to influence of L-productivity.

Summary (1956-65)

While TFPG influence did not bring about NVA dispersal, TFPG did influence dispersal of employment in both labour intensive and capital intensive industries. Employment dispersal or non-dispersal thereof has not shown yielding to K/L influence, though NVA dispersal has been noticed to be affected by growth of K/L. Capital productivity influence affected both NVA and employment dispersal, though in Chemicals (IN30) employment showed more concentration despite influence of capital productivity.

Labour intensive industries like Textiles got concentrated due to influence of L-productivity, but in EGS (IN41) and MotTr (IN36), both capital-intensive, Labour productivity did influence employment dispersal. This was an encouraging sign for Indian industries' to move towards greater equity in dispersal process, through setting up capital goods and capital-intensive industries. The policy recommendation being Labour productivity needs to be enhanced even in capital goods industries for objective of equitable regional distribution of industries to be achieved thus serving the cause of regional equity and balanced regional development.

Table 7.9. Regional Dispersal (HH & CV) of Industries' output(NVA)in response to TFP by Solow (at current prices) 1966-1975

Specification: HH nva = $a + b$(TFP-S): CV nva = $a + b$(TFP-S)

Ind. Name	IN Code	Dispersal Measures		HH nva	HH nva	HH nva	CV nva	Cv nva	CV nva
		CV nva	HH nva	Industry	$\hat{\beta}$	$(b/r)^2$	Industry	$\hat{\beta}$	$(b/r)^2$
1	2	3	4	5	6	7	8	9	10
Food	21	1.440	0.114	28	2.911	32.220	31	1.54	28.922
Bev'rage	22	3.565	0.224	30	1.915	7.819	29	1.234	1.993
Textiles	25	3.049	0.287	41	1.539	24.169	25	1.134	53.582
Tex Prd	26	3.665	0.184	26	1.392	6.568	21	1.009	2.767
Wood	27	3.319	0.307	31	1.37	12.513	34	0.917	3.036
Paper	28	2.545	0.221	25	1.307	51.765	30	0.841	1.016
Leather	29	6.789	0.47	33	1.164	4.413	41	0.536	1.122
Chemical	30	3.659	0.256	34	0.941	3.232	32	0.165	0.036
R-P-C	31	3.199	0.242	29	0.425	1.212	26	0.162	0.106
Nm MPrd	32	1.665	0.128	21	0.274	1.831	28	0.146	0.110
BM&A	33	2.739	0.216	38	0.235	0.321	38	0.124	0.025
Metal Prd	34	3.384	0.278	37	0.111	0.051	22	0.08	0.037
MotTr	36	2.322	0.164	22	0.074	0.017	27	0.065	0.004
Tr.Eq.	37	2.268	0.156	27	0.065	0.004	33	0.049	0.013
OMI	38	2.521	0.184	36	0.042	0.007	36	0.02	0.001
EGS	41	1.876	0.128	32	0.025	0.007	37	0.019	0.001

IMPACT ANALYSIS OF RELEVANT EXPLANATORY VARIABLES ON REGIONAL DISPERSAL MEASURES FOR THE PERIOD 1966-75

This Section presents regression results showing the response of each of the various explanatory variables on HH and CV Measures of NVA and of Employment for Indian Industries for the period 1966-75.

Chemicals (IN30), Rubber-Petroleum (IN31), Textiles (IN25), Electricity, Gas and Steam (IN41), show higher influence of TFP on dispersal of NVA. $(b/r)^2$ is high and so TFPG influence is established as a cause for NVA dispersal in Capital goods, Intermediate and Consumer Industries even in the recessionary period.

The least influence of TFP on NVA dispersal is seen in Machinery other than Transport (IN36), Non-Metallic Mineral Products (IN32), Transport (IN37), Wood (IN27), Beverages (IN22), Other Manufacturing Industries (IN38). $(b/r)^2$ is low implied dispersal was due to TFPG in Wood, Beverages, MotTr, NmMP, Transport.

Table 7.10. Regional Dispersal of Industries' Employment in response to TFP by Solow for (at current prices) 1966-75

Specification: HH emp = *a* + *b*(TFPS), CV emp = *a* + *b* (TFP-S).

Ind. Name	IN Code	Dispersal Measures		CV emp	CV emp	CV emp	HH emp	HH emp	HH emp
		CV Emp	HH Emp	Industry	$\hat{\beta}$	$(b/r)^2$	Industry	$\hat{\beta}$	$(b/r)^2$
1	9	7	8	1	2	3	4	5	6
Food Pro	21	1.675	0.132	21	2.749	38.167	30	0.929	2.936
Beverage	22	5.259	0.440	29	2.668	203.378	41	0.788	1.651
Textiles	25	2.28	0.166	31	2.623	33.562	22	0.786	3.510
TextPrd	26	2.833	0.197	28	2.285	39.555	31	0.75	2.961
Wood	27	1.954	0.132	33	1.912	15.964	21	0.651	0.609
Paper	28	2.42	0.1901	27	1.862	3.767	25	0.493	0.135
Leather	29	5.55	0.352	25	1.049	1.769	36	0.456	7.557
Chemical	30	3.837	0.271	30	0.845	5.805	37	0.451	1.937
R-P-C	31	2.363	0.162	38	0.634	1.905	32	0.241	1.056
Nm MPrd	32	2.01	0.179	41	0.613	2.147	28	0.214	0.314
BM&A	33	2.296	0.16	22	0.586	5.203	26	0.212	0.175
MetPrd	34	2.785	0.208	34	0.505	2.298	29	0.141	0.173
MotTr	36	2.158	0.153	36	0.251	0.863	33	0.082	5.057
Tr.Eq.	37	2.8	0.216	32	0.217	0.230	38	0.053	0.009
OMI	38	3.359	0.273	37	0.047	0.071	27	0.05	0.045
EGS	41	1.93	0.117	26	0.013	0.001	34	0.029	0.208

Food Products (IN21), Textiles (IN25), Chemicals (IN30), Rubber-Petroleum-Coal (IN31), Electricity, Gas and Steam (IN41) show higher influence of TFP on employment dispersal. In case of Food (IN21), Chemicals, (IN30) Rubber-Petroleum-Coal (IN31) and Electricity, Gas and Steam (IN41), high *b*/*r* implied TFPG caused for employment dispersal.

The least influence of TFP on employment dispersal is noticed in case of Textile Products (IN26), Wood (IN27), Non-Metallic Mineral Products (IN32), Basic Metals and Alloys (IN33), Metal Products (IN34), Manufacturing other than Transport (IN36), Transport Equipment (IN37). In Textile Products (IN26), Wood (IN27) and Transport Equipment (IN37), $(b/r)^2$ is lower implying dispersal not influenced by TFPG in this period.

In Non-Metallic Mineral Products (IN32), Basic Metals and Alloys (IN33), Metal Products (IN34), Machinery other than Transport (IN36) $(b/r)^2$ higher implying even in capital goods industry and intermediates with higher capital intensive-ness, recession was a cause for low TFPG influence and not so high dispersal.

Table 7.11. Regional Dispersal of Industries' Output (NVA) in Response to TFP by Solow for 1966-75 (at Current Prices)

Specification: CV nva = a+b(K/L); HH nva = a+ b(K/L)

Ind. Name	IN Code	Dispersal Measures		CV nva	CV nva	CV nva	HH nva	HH nva	HH nva
		HH nva	CV nva	Industry	$\hat{\beta}$	$(b/r)^2$	Industry	$\hat{\beta}$	$(b/r)^2$
1	2	3	4	5	6	7	8	9	10
Food	21	0.114	1.440	22	1.804	18.921	21	3.367	12.513
Bev'	22	0.224	3.565	29	1.521	21.421	34	1.474	38.798
Textiles	25	0.287	3.049	33	1.51	4.079	33	1.198	2.540
Tex Prd	26	0.184	3.665	21	1.14	1.859	26	0.842	2.541
Wood	27	0.307	3.319	26	0.883	5.268	22	0.708	1.223
Paper	28	0.221	2.545	41	0.869	4.468	29	0.297	0.152
Leather	29	0.47	6.789	27	0.491	2.172	32	0.202	0.358
Chemical	30	0.256	3.659	37	0.411	0.329	27	0.17	0.172
R-P-C	31	0.242	3.199	34	0.311	0.624	30	0.131	0.111
Nm MPrd	32	0.128	1.665	28	0.114	0.083	28	0.114	0.117
BM&A	33	0.216	2.739	31	0.093	0.786	37	0.105	0.029
Met. Prd	34	0.278	3.384	36	0.051	0.010	38	0.097	0.013
MotTr	36	0.164	2.322	38	0.033	0.002	25	0.029	0.007
Tr.Eq.	37	0.156	2.268	25	0.019	0.001	31	0.018	0.003
OMI	38	0.184	2.521	32	0.016	0.002	36	0.018	0.001
EGS	41	0.128	1.876	30	0.011	0.002	41	0.024	0.004

Higher influences of K/L on dispersal of NVA are in Beverages (IN22), Food Products (IN21), Metal Products (IN34), Basic Metals and Alloys (IN33), Textile Products (IN26). Basic Metals and Alloys (IN33) show higher $(b/r)^2$ implying that in this decade of recession, User and Intermediate goods Industries did show K/L being cause for NVA dispersal. Food was more concentrated and so high K/L influence could not bring about dispersal of Food Industry.

Least influences are in Chemicals (IN30), Other Manufacturing Industries (IN38), Textiles (IN25), Machinery other than Transport (IN36), Rubber, Petroleum and Coal (IN31), Transport Equipment (IN37). In Rubber (IN31), despite being a Capital Intensive industry, showed dispersal but not due to K/L.

Low $(b/r)^2$ in Chemicals, but dispersal being higher in Chemicals, this must been a prelude to this industry becoming a sunshine industry in 1970s and 1980s, despite K/L's minimal influence on dispersal per se. Textiles (IN25) showed more dispersal than Textile Products or MotTr (IN36); thus recession did not directly impact this Consumer Non Durable Industry and NVA dispersal was not due to contribution of K/L.

Table 7.12. Regional Dispersal(CV) of Industries' employment in response to Capital intensity (at current prices) 1966-75

Specification: CV emp = *a* + *b*(K/L); HH emp = *a* + *b*(K/L)

Ind. Name	IN Code	Dispersal Measures		CV emp	CV emp	CV emp	HH emp	HH emp	HH emp
		CV Emp	HH Emp	Industry	$\hat{\beta}$	$(b/r)^2$	Industry	$\hat{\beta}$	$(b/r)^2$
1	9	7	8	1	2	3	4	5	6
Food	21	1.675	0.132	25	2.509	35.366	27	0.729	1.293
Bev'	22	5.259	0.440	36	1.405	22.432	31	0.633	28.621
Textiles	25	2.28	0.166	38	1.257	3.198	36	0.507	0.851
Tex Prd	26	2.833	0.197	33	1.232	2.701	41	0.361	0.582
Wood	27	1.954	0.132	32	1.011	1.129	25	0.339	0.771
Paper	28	2.42	0.1901	21	0.635	0.437	34	0.323	0.130
Leather	29	5.55	0.352	41	0.541	1.644	22	0.272	0.477
Chemical	30	3.837	0.271	22	0.47	0.321	26	0.198	0.087
R-P-C	31	2.363	0.162	27	0.469	0.565	38	0.181	0.234
Nm MPrd	32	2.01	0.179	37	0.467	1.154	29	0.18	0.309
BM&A	33	2.296	0.16	28	0.442	2.171	30	0.174	0.452
Met. Prd	34	2.785	0.208	31	0.442	0.909	33	0.129	0.130
MotTr	36	2.158	0.153	26	0.384	0.452	28	0.125	0.822
Tr.Eq.	37	2.8	0.216	30	0.322	0.447	21	0.091	0.080
OMI	38	3.359	0.273	34	0.313	0.852	37	0.068	0.029
EGS	41	1.93	0.117	29	0.144	0.026	32	0.031	0.005

The Higher K/L influence on dispersal of Employment is in this first period of planned industrialisation is seen in Textiles (IN25), Machinery other than Transport (IN36), Electricity, Gas and Steam (IN41). In the three industries dispersal due to K/L influence.

The Low K/L influence is in Leather (IN29), Chemicals (IN30), Textile Products (IN26), Paper (IN28). Paper and Chemicals got dispersed despite minimal or negligent K/L influence.

Table 7.13. Regional Dispersal (HH) of Industries' output (NVA) in response to Capital productivity (at current prices) 1966-1975

Specification: HH nva = *a* + *b*(K-productivity); CV nva = *a* + *b* (K-productivity)

Ind. Name	IN Code	Dispersal Measures		HH nva	HH nva	HH nva	CV nva	CV nva	CV nva
		HH nva	CV nva	Industry	$\hat{\beta}$	$(b/r)^2$	Industry	$\hat{\beta}$	$(b/r)^2$
1	2	3	4	5	6	7	8	9	10
Food	21	0.114	1.440	30	0.51	0.781	31	1.228	22.176
Bev'	22	0.224	3.565	29	0.509	1.234	22	1.216	22.404
Textiles	25	0.287	3.049	21	0.399	9.950	29	1.134	17.861
Tex Prd	26	0.184	3.665	28	0.334	0.907	37	0.611	0.789
Wood	27	0.307	3.319	27	0.263	0.494	26	0.87	3.674
Paper	28	0.221	2.545	31	0.259	0.919	34	0.45	0.306
Leather	29	0.47	6.789	25	0.217	0.329	21	0.238	2.575
Chemical	30	0.256	3.659	22	0.14	0.059	32	0.174	0.206
R-P-C	31	0.242	3.199	38	0.117	0.123	27	0.1	0.116
Nm MPrd	32	0.128	1.665	41	0.08	0.012	41	0.098	0.013
BM&A	33	0.216	2.739	37	0.044	0.006	33	0.084	0.014
Met. Prd	34	0.278	3.384	33	0.033	0.002	28	0.047	0.007
MotTr	36	0.164	2.322	26	0.027	0.004	25	0.037	0.008
Tr.Eq.	37	0.156	2.268	36	0.031	0.002	30	0.033	0.003
OMI	38	0.184	2.521	34	0.017	0.001	38	0.019	0.001
EGS	41	0.128	1.876	32	0.011	0.001	36	0.011	0.001

In 1966-75, influence of K-productivity on NVA dispersal was higher in Leather (IN29), Chemicals (IN30), Rubber, Petroleum and Coal (IN31). Thus despite recession, NVA of Intermediates dispersed due to capital productivity influence.

The Least influence of capital productivity is in Non-Metallic Mineral Products (IN32), Machinery other than transport (IN36), Other Manufacturing Industries (IN38), Basic Metals and Alloys (IN33) and low $(b/r)^2$ revealed low influence of capital productivity was not conducive to dispersal of these capital intensive industries.

Table 7.14. Regional Dispersal(CV) of Industries' employment in response to Capital productivity (at current prices) 1966-1975

Specification: CV emp = *a* + *b*(K-productivity); HH Emp = *a* + *b*(K- productivity)

Ind. Name	IN Code	Measures of Industrial Dispersal		CV emp	CV emp	CV emp	HH emp	HH emp	HH emp
		CV Emp	HH Emp	Industry	$\hat{\beta}$	$(b/r)^2$	Industry	$\hat{\beta}$	$(b/r)^2$
1	2	3	4	5	6	7	8	9	10
Food Pro	21	1.675	0.132	31	2.916	28.063	29	0.643	2.7563
Beverages	22	5.259	0.440	22	2.483	14.610	21	0.48	2.1943
Textiles	25	2.28	0.166	38	1.684	13.009	31	0.401	0.4030
TextilePrd	26	2.833	0.197	41	1.654	5.759	38	0.391	0.9676
Wood	27	1.954	0.132	29	0.655	10.215	30	0.361	0.8408
Paper	28	2.42	0.19	34	0.353	0.737	41	0.314	0.2809
Leather	29	5.55	0.352	30	0.322	0.405	37	0.275	0.3361
Chemical	30	3.837	0.271	27	0.305	3.322	22	0.266	0.1877
Ru-P-Co	31	2.363	0.162	37	0.243	0.492	36	0.214	0.1832
Nm MPrd	32	2.01	0.179	36	0.117	6.845	28	0.087	0.0470
BM&A	33	2.296	0.16	28	0.114	0.033	26	0.052	0.5408
Met Prd	34	2.785	0.208	25	0.105	0.055	25	0.041	0.0139
MotTr	36	2.158	0.153	32	0.105	0.068	32	0.036	0.0061
Tr.Eq.	37	2.8	0.216	26	0.032	0.341	33	0.036	0.0105
OMI	38	3.359	0.273	21	0.029	0.008	27	0.031	0.0458
EGS	41	1.93	0.117	33	0.014	0.001	34	0.019	0.0036

Higher influence of capital productivity in industries like Rubber, Petroleum and Coal (IN31), Leather (IN29), Electricity (IN41), Other Manufacturing Industries (IN38) on employment dispersal and higher $(b/r)^2$ meant dispersal in these mostly capital intensive industries was due to influence of capital productivity.

Low influence of capital productivity on employment dispersal were in Basic Metals and Alloys (IN33), Textile Products (IN26), Non-Metallic Mineral Products (IN32), Textiles (IN25), Paper (IN28), Machinery other than Manufacturing (IN36). But dispersal process in these was not affected by little influence of capital productivity.

Table: 7.15. Regional Dispersal(CV) of Industries' output(NVA) in response to Labour productivity (at current prices) 1966-75

Specification: CV nva = *a* + *b* (L-productivity); HH nva = *a* + *b* (L-Productivity)

Ind. Name	IN Code	Measures of Industrial Dispersal		CV nva	CV nva	CV nva	HV nva	HH nva	HH nva
		HH nva	CV nva	Industry	$\hat{\beta}$	$(b/r)^2$	Industry	$\hat{\beta}$	$(b/r)^2$
1	2	3	4	5	6	7	8	9	10
Food Pro	21	0.114	1.440	21	1.161	35.472	38	0.896	2.212
Beverages	22	0.224	3.565	41	0.945	1.393	21	0.454	3.889
Textiles	25	0.287	3.049	32	0.788	4.889	41	0.32	0.175
Textile Prd	26	0.184	3.665	27	0.716	1.038	27	0.186	0.186
Wood	27	0.307	3.319	37	0.59	0.744	26	0.186	0.066
Paper	28	0.221	2.545	28	0.436	1.777	25	0.113	0.073
Leather	29	0.47	6.789	38	0.134	0.020	22	0.101	0.132
Chemical	30	0.256	3.659	22	0.12	0.178	33	0.092	0.020
Ru-Pet-Co	31	0.242	3.199	34	0.078	0.011	34	0.091	0.022
Nm MPrd	32	0.128	1.665	25	0.053	0.004	37	0.09	0.023
BM&A	33	0.216	2.739	30	0.039	0.138	31	0.074	0.365
Metal Prd	34	0.278	3.384	33	0.038	0.003	30	0.06	0.008
MotTr	36	0.164	2.322	29	0.034	0.006	28	0.032	0.011
Tr.Eq.	37	0.156	2.268	31	0.031	0.007	32	0.027	0.005
OMI	38	0.184	2.521	26	0.026	0.001	36	0.011	0.000
EGS	41	0.128	1.876	36	0.012	0.013	29	0.01	0.003

Higher influences of Labour Productivity on dispersal of NVA are in Food Products (IN21), Electricity, Gas and Steam (IN41), Wood (IN27). While $(b/r)^2$ is relatively high, it did not bring about dispersal in Food. Wood being L-intensive, could be better dispersed due to Labour productivity influence, despite the climate of recession. In EGS, high b/r did not bring about higher dispersal.

The lower influences of labour productivity on NVA dispersal are in Machinery other than Transport (IN36), Leather (IN29), Rubber, Petroleum and Coal (IN31), Basic Metals and Alloys (IN33), Chemicals (IN30). While dispersal in these industries are higher, $(b/r)^2$ in HH is relatively high in Rubber-petroleum and Coal (IN31). Thus dispersal of these industries is however less due to Labour productivity except in RPC (IN31).

Table 7.16. Regional Dispersal(HH& CV) of Industries' employment in response to Labour productivity (at current prices) 1966-1975

Specification: HH emp = *a* + *b*(L-productivity); CV emp = *a* + *b*(L-productivity)

In. Nm	Measures of Industrial Dispersal			HH emp	HH emp	HH emp	CV emp	CV emp	CV emp
	IN Code	CV emp	HH emp	IN Code	$\hat{\beta}$	$(b/r)^2$	INCode	$\hat{\beta}$	$(b/r)^2$
1	2	3	4	5	6	7	8	9	10
Food Pro	21	1.675	0.132	36	1.393	22.304	21	1.985	12.275
Beverages	22	5.259	0.440	41	1.01	10.100	41	1.924	11.390
Textiles	25	2.28	0.166	28	0.666	9.437	33	0.877	7.256
Textile Prd	26	2.833	0.197	22	0.631	0.773	36	0.864	2.629
Wood	27	1.954	0.132	33	0.61	0.737	31	0.797	1.784
Paper	28	2.42	0.19	38	0.597	2.256	34	0.746	0.608
Leather	29	5.55	0.352	27	0.596	0.920	30	0.515	1.153
Chemical	30	3.837	0.271	21	0.367	0.159	29	0.364	0.679
Ru-Pet-Co	31	2.363	0.162	26	0.345	0.561	25	0.297	0.175
Nm MPrd	32	2.01	0.179	25	0.339	0.771	22	0.246	0.696
BM&A	33	2.296	0.16	32	0.333	0.331	28	0.236	0.052
Metal Prd	34	2.785	0.208	34	0.213	0.405	32	0.151	0.145
MotTr	36	2.158	0.153	29	0.178	0.308	26	0.073	0.010
Tr.Eq.	37	2.8	0.216	37	0.162	0.151	38	0.072	0.006
OMI	38	3.359	0.273	30	0.032	0.003	27	0.018	0.009
EGS	41	1.93	0.117	31	0.018	0.001	37	0.011	0.002

In this period, the Higher influences of Labour Productivity on employment dispersal are in Food (IN21), Electricity (IN41), Machinery other than transport (IN36), Basic Metals and Alloys (IN33). Food showed more of concentration, implying labour productivity influence did not bring about employment dispersal in this Consumer Non-Durable Industry.

Low influences of Labour Productivity on employment dispersal are in Transport (IN37), Leather (IN29), Textile Products (IN26) implied dispersal was independent of Labour productivity influence.

IMPACT ANALYSIS OF RELEVANT EXPLANATORY VARIABLES ON REGIONAL DISPERSAL MEASURES FOR THE PERIOD 1976-85

This Section deals with regression results showing response of various explanatory variables when regressed on dispersal measures for Indian Industries.

Specification: HH nva = *a* + *b* (TFP-S); CV nva = *a* + *b*(TFP-S)

Ind. Name	IN Code	Dispersal Measures		HHNVA	HHNVA	HHNVA	CVNVA	CVNVA	CVNVA
		CVNVA	HHNVA	Industry	$\hat{\beta}$	$(b/r)^2$	Industry	$\hat{\beta}$	$(b/r)^2$
1	2	3	4	5	6	7	8	9	10
Food	21	1.440	0.099	22	1.894	32.112	41	1.803	41.677
Bev'rage	22	2.194	0.167	32	1.362	12.706	31	1.354	57.291
Textiles	25	2.046	0.149	34	1.1	2.553	22	1.024	15.888
Tex Prd	26	2.03	0.839	38	0.83	5.467	33	0.58	3.031
Wood	27	1.705	0.101	33	0.78	0.927	37	0.393	0.398
Paper	28	1.619	0.117	29	0.708	7.265	38	0.146	0.344
Leather	29	3.454	0.258	28	0.479	0.578	26	0.107	0.012
Chemical	30	2.537	0.196	31	0.417	2.319	34	0.074	0.041
R-P-C	31	2.598	0.243	27	0.296	3.983	28	0.067	0.080
Nm MPrd	32	1.422	0.987	41	0.149	0.396	30	0.063	0.008
BM&A	33	1.947	0.138	21	0.115	0.348	21	0.049	0.009
MetPrd	34	2.696	0.226	36	0.112	0.111	25	0.047	0.004
MotTr	36	1.793	0.097	26	0.107	0.012	29	0.024	0.008
Tr.Eq.	37	2.246	0.166	25	0.103	0.096	27	0.019	0.003
OMI	38	2.117	0.211	30	0.049	0.009	32	0.018	0.001
EGS	41	2.179	0.161	37	0.04	0.005	36	0.014	0.001

In Beverage (IN22) TFP influence is higher in this period than in the previous decade. Rubber-Petroleum-Coal (IN31), Basic Metals and Alloys (IN33) also reveal higher TFP influence on NVA dispersal. NVA Dispersal occurs through high TFPG influence

Machinery other than Transport (IN36), Food (IN21), Chemicals (IN30), Textiles (IN25), show lower TFP on NVA dispersal. (*b*/*r*) was low in and IN21 and IN36 implying low TFPG was a factor for relative concentration in these two.

Table 7.17. Regional Dispersal(CV)of Industries' employment in response to TFP by Solow (at current prices) 1976-1985

Specification: CV emp = *a* +*b* (TFP-S) and HH emp = *a* + *b*(TFP-S)

Ind. Name	IN Code	Dispersal Measures		CV emp	CV emp	CV emp	HH EMP	HH Emp	HH emp
		CVemp	EVemp	Industry	$\hat{\beta}$	$(b/r)^2$	Industry	$\hat{\beta}$	$(b/r)^2$
1	2	3	4	5	6	7	8	9	10
Food Pro	21	1.440	0.098	36	2.158	12.191	22	1.11	10.904
Beverage	22	3.643	0.369	30	2.102	24.799	30	0.687	0.955
Textiles	25	1.841	0.131	26	1.73	4.988	31	0.65	0.901
TextPrd	26	1.891	0.131	21	1.598	24.320	26	0.61	2.001
Wood	27	1.55	0.111	31	1.439	98.606	36	0.494	0.311
Paper	28	1.38	0.094	28	0.965	9.220	33	0.479	1.793
Leather	29	3.276	0.242	33	0.876	1.358	41	0.454	4.793
Chemical	30	1.931	0.134	25	0.677	0.559	29	0.336	0.221
R-P-C	31	1.936	0.14	27	0.627	3.419	34	0.247	0.587
Nm MPrd	32	1.232	0.0836	29	0.336	0.221	28	0.221	0.215
BM&A	33	1.714	0.1182	37	0.384	0.400	32	0.203	0.468
MetPrd	34	1.329	0.131	41	0.12	1.029	25	0.067	0.007
MotTr	36	1.57	0.074	22	0.102	0.236	27	0.06	0.045
Tr.Eq.	37	1.9	0.135	34	0.032	0.025	21	0.057	0.155
OMI	38	1.887	123	38	0.021	0.037	38	0.049	0.023
EGS	41	2.278	0.185	32	0.02	0.002	37	0.043	0.005

Machinery other than Transport (IN36), Chemicals (IN30), Textile Products (IN26), Rubber-Petroleum-Coal (IN31) show higher TFP influence on dispersal of employment. Textile Products (26), Chemicals (IN30), Rubber-Petroleum-Coal (IN31) and Machinery other than Transport (IN36) with high *b*/*r* did not bring about high employment dispersal in this period of 1976-85.

Transport Equipment (IN37), Other manufacturing Industries (IN38), Electricity, Gas and Steam (IN41), Leather (IN29), Wood (IN27), Textiles (IN25), Metal Products (IN34) show lower influence of TFP on employment dispersal. Textiles (IN25), Leather (IN29) and Electricity, Gas and Steam (IN41) dispersal occurred despite low TFP influence. Wood (IN27), Metal Products (IN34), Transport (IN37), Other Manufacturing Industries (IN38) showed low *b*/*r* means concentration was due to low TFP influence.

Table 7.18. Regional Dispersal(CV) of Industries' output(NVA) in response to Capital intensity (at current prices)1976-1985

Specification: CV nva = a +b(K/L); HH nva = a +b(K/L)

Ind. Name	IN Code	Dispersal Measures		CVNVA	CV nva	CV nva	HH nva	HH nva	HH nva
		HHNVA	HHNVA	IN Code	$\overline{\beta}$	$(b/r)^2$	IN code	$\overline{\beta}$	$(b/r)^2$
1	2	3	4	5	6	7	8	9	10
Food	21	0.099	1.440	31	1.093	3.588	34	0.566	2.786
Bev'	22	0.167	2.194	29	0.961	6.282	21	0.404	0.581
Textiles	25	0.149	2.046	28	0.912	1.840	31	0.34	0.366
Tex Prd	26	1.839	2.03	26	0.787	5.682	28	0.076	0.009
Wood	27	0.101	1.705	27	0.751	3.398	33	0.068	0.008
Paper	28	0.117	1.619	33	0.67	0.777	37	0.061	0.005
Leather	29	0.258	3.454	41	0.649	1.337	38	0.059	0.007
Chemical	30	0.196	2.537	37	0.62	0.519	27	0.059	0.009
R-P-C	31	0.243	2.598	38	0.565	1.017	22	0.056	0.016
Nm MPrd	32	0.980	1.422	22	0.444	1.493	41	0.046	0.004
BM&A	33	0.138	1.947	34	0.423	0.503	26	0.044	0.012
Met. Prd	34	0.226	2.696	21	0.415	0.596	32	0.038	0.007
MotTr	36	0.097	1.793	25	0.411	1.482	29	0.035	0.007
Tr.Eq.	37	0.166	2.246	36	0.045	0.081	36	0.031	0.009
OMI	38	0.211	2.117	30	0.028	0.011	25	0.023	0.003
EGS	41	0.161	2.179	32	0.022	0.004	30	0.02	0.001

Higher influences of K/L on NVA are in Rubber-Petroleum-Coal (IN31), Food Products (IN21), Metal Products (IN34), Paper (IN28), Basic Metals and Alloys (IN33), Wood (IN27). Paper, Food and Textile Products did not show high b/r and so low dispersal in them is due to low K/L. In Rubber, Chemicals and Basic Metals, that are traditional highly capital intensive did show higher dispersal in this period of 1976-85 but it was again not due to influence of K/L.

Least influences of Capital Intensity on dispersal of NVA are in Textiles (IN25), Chemicals (IN30), Non-Metallic Mineral Products (IN32), Machinery other than transport (IN36), Electricity, Gas and Steam (IN41). In Non-Metallic Mineral Products (IN32), Textiles (IN25), Machinery other than transport (IN36), $(b/r)^2$ was low in this decade implying K/L's influence though low on dispersal of NVA, concentration in these industries in this period could be either due to low K/L or independent of it.

Table 7.19. Regional Dispersal of Industries' employment in response to capital intensity (at current prices) 1976-85

Specification: CVemp = *a* + *b*(K/L); HH emp = *a* + *b*(K/L)

Ind. Name	IN Code	Dispersal Measures		CV emp	CV emp	CV emp	HH emp	HH emp	HH emp
		CV Emp	HH Emp	Industry	$\hat{\beta}$	$(b/r)^2$	Industry	$\hat{\beta}$	$(b/r)^2$
1	2	3	4	5	6	7	8	9	10
Food	21	1.440	0.098	25	3.183	88.100	41	0.533	1.743
Bev'	22	3.643	0.369	29	1.481	6.667	21	0.362	0.528
Textiles	25	1.841	0.131	26	0.934	2.254	29	0.332	0.302
Tex Prd	26	1.891	0.131	41	0.587	1.914	33	0.323	1.373
Wood	27	1.55	0.111	36	0.517	0.849	27	0.273	0.731
Paper	28	1.38	0.094	33	0.462	1.503	22	0.256	0.851
Leather	29	3.276	0.242	21	0.376	0.568	32	0.154	0.659
Chemical	30	1.931	0.134	38	0.356	1.093	25	0.133	0.182
R-P-C	31	1.936	0.14	37	0.354	0.103	34	0.125	1.563
Nm MPrd	32	1.232	0.084	27	0.275	0.741	26	0.059	0.009
BM&A	33	1.714	0.118	32	0.17	0.826	30	0.047	0.197
Met. Prd	34	1.329	0.131	34	0.168	1.568	31	0.041	0.563
MotTr	36	1.57	0.074	22	0.161	0.785	36	0.028	0.006
Tr.Eq.	37	1.9	0.135	31	0.066	0.545	28	0.026	0.002
OMI	38	1.887	0.123	28	0.039	0.005	37	0.022	0.029
EGS	41	2.278	0.185	30	0.036	0.015	38	0.022	0.001

The industries that show higher influences of Capital Intensity (K/L) on dispersal of employment are Textiles (IN25), Leather (IN29), Food Products (IN21), Basic Metals and Alloys (IN33), Electricity, Gas and Steam (IN41).

The Least influences of K/L on employment dispersal are in Chemicals (IN30), Paper (IN28), Rubber, Petroleum and Coal (IN31), Beverages (IN22), Metal Products (IN34), Non- Metallic Mineral Products (IN32). With high *b*/*r* dispersal in Paper and Concentration in the rest is achieved through influence of K/L on employment dispersal.

Table 7.20. Regional Dispersal of Industries NVA in response to Capital Productivity (at current prices) 1976-1985 Specification: HH nva= *a* + *b*(K-productivity); CV nva = *a* + *b*(K-productivity)

Ind. Name	IN Code	Dispersal Measures		HH nva	HH nva	HH nva	CV nva	CV nva	CV nva
		HVNVA	CVNVA	Industry	$\hat{\beta}$	$(b/r)^2$	Industry	$\hat{\beta}$	$(b/r)^2$
1	2	3	4	5	6	7	8	9	10
Food	21	0.099	1.440	21	0.209	0.2275	38	1.345	8.614
Bev'	22	0.167	2.194	38	0.174	0.1346	29	1.332	10.366
Textiles	25	0.149	2.046	26	0.087	0.0400	26	0.889	4.676
Tex Prd	26	1.839	2.03	30	0.072	0.4320	31	0.528	8.200
Wood	27	0.101	1.705	27	0.066	0.3351	22	0.369	2.196
Paper	28	0.117	1.619	31	0.062	0.0353	28	0.331	0.234
Leather	29	0.258	3.454	29	0.051	0.0406	33	0.327	0.226
Chemical	30	0.196	2.537	33	0.029	0.0035	41	0.305	0.660
R-P-C	31	0.243	2.598	25	0.023	0.0240	21	0.191	0.529
Nm MPrd	32	0.98	3.422	28	0.022	0.0011	34	0.187	0.312
BM&A	33	0.138	1.947	22	0.02	0.0253	25	0.142	0.458
Met. Prd	34	0.226	2.696	34	0.016	0.0012	30	0.083	0.007
MotTr	36	0.097	1.793	36	0.016	0.0122	37	0.078	0.358
Tr.Eq.	37	0.166	2.246	37	0.013	0.0154	36	0.058	0.030
OMI	38	0.211	2.117	32	0.011	0.0004	27	0.025	0.007
EGS	41	0.161	2.179	41	0.011	0.0009	32	0.011	0.001

Industries that showed relatively higher influence of Capital Productivity on NVA dispersal in this period were Other Manufacturing Industries (IN38), Textile Products (IN26), Rubber, Petroleum and Coal (IN31), Basic Metals and Alloys (IN33). But b/r are uniformly low in HH in all industries and despite higher influence of Capital productivity, this was not a factor for dispersal/concentration.

Basic Metals and Textile Products being more labour intensive, despite high capital productivity's higher influence on NVA dispersal, did not really show much dispersal. Rubber-Petroleum-Coal and Other Manufacturing Industries, being capital intensive, showed greater dispersal, both in CV and HH measures, due to higher capital productivity's influence on dispersal.

Least influences is in Electricity, Gas and Steam (IN41), Non-Metallic Mineral Products (IN32), Wood (IN27), Metal Products (IN34), Transport (IN37), Machinery other than transport (IN36). Concentration was due to low *b*/*r* in these industries as most of them are capital intensive.

Table 7.21. Regional Dispersal(CV)of Industries' employment in response to Capital productivity (at current prices) 1976-85

Specification: CV emp = *a* +*b*(K-productivity); H H hemp = *a* + *b*(K-productivity)

Ind. Name	IN Code	Measures of Industrial Dispersal		CV emp	CV emp	CV emp	HH emp	HH emp	HH emp
		CV Emp	HH Emp	Industry	$\hat{\beta}$	$(b/r)^2$	Industry	$\hat{\beta}$	$(b/r)^2$
1	2	3	4	5	6	7	8	9	10
Food Pro	21	1.440	0.098	21	1.228	10.258	21	1.15	9.583
Beverages	22	3.643	0.369	41	0.725	2.628	41	0.71	2.447
Textiles	25	1.841	0.131	29	0.669	1.279	28	0.439	1.606
Textile Prd	26	1.891	0.131	36	0.559	0.542	31	0.336	5.376
Wood	27	1.55	0.111	28	0.456	1.733	27	0.244	0.783
Paper	28	1.38	0.094	37	0.438	0.909	32	0.157	0.536
Leather	29	3.276	0.242	38	0.386	0.680	33	0.147	0.831
Chemical	30	1.931	0.134	25	0.289	1.705	34	0.096	1.536
Ru-Pet-Co	31	1.936	0.14	27	0.248	0.799	25	0.057	0.009
Nm MPrd	32	1.232	0.084	32	0.171	0.665	22	0.055	1.008
BM&A	33	1.714	0.118	34	0.135	1.161	36	0.051	0.163
Metal Prd	34	1.329	0.131	33	0.12	0.465	30	0.039	0.138
MotTr	36	1.57	0.074	22	0.073	0.666	37	0.028	0.004
Tr.Eq.	37	1.9	0.135	26	0.061	0.034	38	0.023	0.002
OMI	38	1.887	0.123	30	0.043	0.132	29	0.022	0.002
EGS	41	2.278	0.185	31	0.05	2.500	26	0.012	0.004

Food (IN21), Electricity, Gas and Steam (IN41), Paper (IN28) show higher influences of Capital productivity on employment but concentration in them is despite high b/r, showing higher capital productivity influence is not bringing about dispersal.

Low influence of Capital Productivity on dispersal of employment were in industries like Chemicals (IN30), Textile Products (IN26), Beverages (IN22), Basic Metal and Alloys (IN33), Metal Products (IN34), Non-Metallic Mineral Products (IN32). While Chemicals and Metal Products showed relatively high $(b/r)^2$ implying despite high influence, dispersal was not brought about.

Table 7.22. Regional Dispersal(CV) of Industries' output(NVA) in response to Labour productivity: (at current prices) 1976-85

Specification: CV nva = *a* +*b*(L-productivity); HH nva = *a* + *b* (L-productivity)

Ind. Name	IN Code	Measures of Industrial Dispersal		CV nva	CV nva	CV nva	HV nva	HH nva	HH nva
		HH nva	CV nva	IN code	$\hat{\beta}$	$(b/r)^2$	IN code	$\hat{\beta}$	$(b/r)^2$
1	2	3	4	5	6	7	8	9	10
Food Pro	21	0.099	1.440	29	1.734	30.681	30	1.819	15.108
Beverage	22	0.167	2.194	37	0.784	0.670	37	1.353	2.134
Textiles	25	0.149	2.046	22	0.687	7.866	41	0.13	0.128
Tex Prd	26	1.839	2.03	33	0.668	0.596	31	0.108	0.084
Wood	27	0.101	1.705	38	0.607	1.746	25	0.074	0.249
Paper	28	0.117	1.619	27	0.551	4.048	38	0.071	0.024
Leather	29	0.258	3.454	32	0.519	1.522	33	0.068	0.012
Chemical	30	0.196	2.537	25	0.315	6.202	28	0.061	0.032
Ru-Pet-C	31	0.243	2.598	31	0.312	0.854	26	0.06	0.007
Nm MPrd	32	0.9797	1.422	41	0.305	0.388	22	0.059	0.048
BM&A	33	0.138	1.947	28	0.225	0.405	32	0.031	0.009
Met.Prd	34	0.226	2.696	36	0.222	0.189	29	0.026	0.008
MotTr	36	0.097	1.793	34	0.148	0.070	27	0.026	0.007
Tr.Eq.	37	0.166	2.246	30	0.122	0.103	21	0.026	0.011
OMI	38	0.211	2.117	26	0.065	0.007	34	0.013	0.001
EGS	41	0.161	2.179	21	0.05	0.078	36	0.012	0.001

The higher influence of Labour productivity on NVA dispersal are in Transport (IN37), Electricity (IN41), Rubber-Petroleum and Coal (IN31), Textiles (IN25), Chemicals (IN30). $(b/r)^2$ is not so high in all and so relatively less dispersal than in previous decades is due to low influence of labour productivity.

The Least influences are in Food (IN21), Machinery other than Transport (IN36), Metal Products (IN34). $(b/r)^2$ being low, concentration is due to low influence of labour productivity.

Table 7.23. Regional Dispersal(HH&CV) of Industries' employment in response to Labor productivity (at current prices) 1976-85

Specification: HH emp = *a* + *b*(L-productivity); CV emp= *a* + *b*(L- productivity)

In. Nm	Measures of Industrial Dispersal			HH emp	HH emp	HH emp	CV emp	CV emp	CV emp
	IN Code	CV emp	HH emp	IN Code	β	$(b/r)^2$	IN Code	β	$(b/r)^2$
1	2	3	4	5	6	7	8	9	10
Food Pro	21	1.440	0.098	30	1.079	2.854	29	1.724	8.099
Beverages	22	3.643	0.369	29	0.448	0.629	31	1.538	5.884
Textiles	25	1.841	0.131	21	0.180	0.771	41	1.200	4.299
Textile Prd	26	1.891	0.131	31	0.092	0.073	30	1.054	2.750
Wood	27	1.55	0.111	41	0.084	0.021	26	0.899	1.858
Paper	28	1.38	0.094	36	0.082	0.009	28	0.790	1.950
Leather	29	3.276	0.242	22	0.073	0.063	36	0.726	1.722
Chemical	30	1.931	0.134	26	0.058	0.009	33	0.699	1.613
Ru-Pet-Co	31	1.936	0.14	28	0.055	0.009	32	0.446	0.448
Nm MPrd	32	1.232	0.084	33	0.048	0.002	27	0.433	0.677
BM&A	33	1.714	0.118	27	0.029	0.002	38	0.347	0.380
Metal Prd	34	1.329	0.131	34	0.020	0.002	37	0.311	0.446
MotTr	36	1.57	0.074	32	0.017	0.001	34	0.224	0.252
Tr.Eq.	37	1.9	0.135	25	0.013	0.172	21	0.190	0.820
OMI	38	1.887	0.123	38	0.013	0.001	25	0.016	0.262
EGS	41	2.278	0.185	37	0.010	0.011	22	0.013	0.001

High influences of labour productivity on employment dispersal are in Chemicals (IN30), Leather (IN29), Rubber, Petroleum and Coal (IN31), Electricity, Gas and Steam (IN41). While $(b/r)^2$ is higher in these industries, less dispersal in this decade noticed in these cases too meant that higher influence of labour productivity could not help in greater dispersal.

Least influences are in Transport (IN37), Other Manufacturing Industries (IN38), Wood (IN27), Non-Metallic Mineral Products (IN32), Basic Metals and Alloys (IN33) and with low $(b/r)^2$, lower concentration could be due to low influence of labour productivity.

IMPACT ANALYSIS OF RELEVANT EXPLANATORY VARIABLES ON REGIONAL DISPERSAL MEASURES FOR THE PERIOD 1986-95

This Section deals with Regression results of HH and CV Measures of NVA and Employment of each of the 2-digit Industries for the period 1986-95 along with the Regional dispersal measures cited in the columns (3) and (4) to make an effective influence assessment through recourse to Grassacks instrument of $(b/r)^2$.

Table 7.24. Regional Dispersal of Industries Output (NVA) in Response to Capital Intensity (at Current Year Prices) for 1986-95

Specification: CV nva = *a* + *b*(K/L); HH nva = *a* + *b*(K/L)

Ind. Name	IN Code	Dispersal Measures		CV nva	CV nva	CV nva	HH nva	HH nva	HH nva
		HHNVA	CVNVA	Industry	$\hat{\beta}$	$(b/r)^2$	Industry	$\hat{\beta}$	$(b/r)^2$
1	2	3	4	5	6	7	8	9	10
Food	21	0.100	1.456	32	1.815	3.365	38	1.244	1.570
Bev'	22	0.132	1.866	38	1.244	3.286	32	1.124	1.266
Textiles	25	0.122	1.756	31	1.001	1.117	29	0.764	3.207
Tex Prd	26	0.167	2.276	27	0.546	1.017	31	0.097	0.011
Wood	27	0.125	1.724	30	0.489	2.061	22	0.091	0.025
Paper	28	0.011	1.526	41	0.423	0.394	21	0.077	0.006
Leather	29	0.27	3.408	26	0.215	0.105	27	0.073	0.018
Chemical	30	0.178	2.263	37	0.212	0.091	36	0.06	0.006
R-P-C	31	0.145	1.986	28	0.141	0.092	33	0.054	0.014
Nm MPrd	32	0.101	1.456	22	0.11	0.036	41	0.038	0.003
BM&A	33	0.143	1.984	36	0.057	0.006	34	0.034	0.002
Met. Prd	34	0.179	2.28	33	0.05	0.008	28	0.022	0.003
MotTr	36	0.13	1.81	29	0.031	0.004	37	0.015	0.000
Tr.Eq.	37	0.163	2.27	34	0.029	0.001	*30*	0.012	0.001
OMI	38	0.153	1.967	21	0.025	0.003	*26*	0.012	0.003
EGS	41	0.173	2.437	25	0.024	0.001	25	0.011	0.002

The maximum influence of Capital Intensity on dispersal of Net Value Added (NVA) is seen in Non-metallic mineral products (IN32), Other Manufacturing Industries (IN38), Rubber-Petroleum and Coal (IN31) in both CV and HH measures. Dispersal is consistently higher in these three industries. $(b/r)^2$ is high in these three industries, especially in the CV case. $(b/r)^2$ being consistently high in both HH and CV cases,. RPC, OMI and NmMP, all being capital intensive, show influence of K/L to bring about dispersal.

The lowest effect of K/L is seen in Textiles (IN25), with industries nearer this being Paper (IN28), Other Manufacturing Industries (IN38), Machinery other than Transport (IN36), Basic Metals and Alloys (IN33), Metal Products (IN34), both in CV and HH regressions. This was the nature of dispersal in this decade, as far as these industries were concerned. Excepting HH (IN28), other dispersal measures show higher relative dispersal. $(b/r)^2$, except in Other Manufacturing Industries (IN38). Dispersal in Basic Metals and

Alloys (IN33) and Paper (IN28) low $(b/r)^2$, these more concentrated did not see much influence of K/L. Thus lack of dispersal in these two industries in the fourth decade of planned industrialisation may be a pointer to recession in these two consumer-oriented industries, largely due to lack of planning for dispersal and inadequacy of regional market surveys for Paper Demand. Lack of Input-Output Planning in Basic Metals Industry, which is an Intermediate Industry also can be a cause for lack of dispersal.

Table 7.25. Regional Dispersal(CV of Industries' employment in response to Capital intensity (at current prices) 1986-95

Specification: CV emp = a + b(K/L); HH emp= a + b(K/L)

Ind. Name	IN Code	Dispersal Measures		CV emp	CV emp	CV emp	HH emp	HH emp	HH emp
		CV Emp	HH Emp	Industry	$\hat{\beta}$	$(b/r)^2$	Industry	$\hat{\beta}$	$(b/r)^2$
1	2	3	4	5	6	7	8	9	10
Food	21	1.401	0.096	22	2.22	12.445	21	1.72	4.964
Bev'	22	3.748	0.355	25	2.038	26.122	41	0.135	2.025
Textiles	25	1.609	0.1	34	0.842	4.604	30	0.058	0.012
Tex Prd	26	2.043	0.145	21	0.747	2.082	31	0.051	0.004
Wood	27	1.371	0.093	29	0.625	1.170	34	0.047	0.019
Paper	28	1.259	0.085	26	0.384	0.170	22	0.045	0.010
Leather	29	3.633	0.2989	31	0.331	0.184	33	0.041	0.019
Chemical	30	1.862	0.1332	32	0.327	0.279	38	0.034	0.002
R-P-C	31	1.315	0.088	27	0.069	0.022	36	0.033	0.020
Nm MPrd	32	1.867	0.081	41	0.046	0.014	25	0.027	0.001
BM&A	33	1.56	0.106	30	0.055	0.011	32	0.023	0.014
Met. Prd	34	1.602	0.11	33	0.052	0.027	27	0.02	0.002
MotTr	36	1.489	0.101	37	0.039	0.002	26	0.014	0.002
Tr.Eq.	37	1.605	0.109	38	0.019	0.001	28	0.014	0.001
OMI	38	1.48	0.104	28	0.012	0.001	37	0.015	0.019
EGS	41	2.347	0.156	36	0.011	0.037	29	0.011	0.002

Industries showing Higher K/L influence on employment are in Food Products (IN21), Beverages (IN22), Non-Metallic Mineral Products (IN32), Wood (IN27), Textile Products (IN26). In Wood and Textile Products, b/r is low implying that dispersal in Textile Products and concentration in Wood is due to lack of K/L influence. In Beverages $(b/r)^2$ is high in CV measure and is cause for dispersal. In Food, $(b/r)^2$ are high, but there is still concentration. In non-metallic mineral products industry and Textiles though influence of K/L was high on employment dispersal, it came about K/L influence.

Table 7.26. Regional Dispersal (HH& CV) of industries' output (NVA) in response to Capital Productivity (at current prices) 1986-1995.

Specifications: HH nva = *a* + *b* (K-productivity): CV nva = a + *b*(K-Productivity)

Ind. Name	IN Code	Dispersal Measures		HH nva	HH nva	HH nva	CV nva	CV nva	CV nva
		HHNVA	CVNVA	Industry	$\hat{\beta}$	$(b/r)^2$	Industry	$\hat{\beta}$	$(b/r)^2$
1	2	3	4	5	6	7	8	9	10
Food	21	0.100	1.456	41	0.305	0.142	29	1.468	4.685
Bev'	22	0.132	1.866	26	0.295	0.592	41	1.446	3.035
Textiles	25	0.122	1.756	38	0.201	0.111	38	0.883	2.057
Tex Prd	26	0.167	2.276	29	0.159	0.086	30	0.699	5.959
Wood	27	0.125	1.724	33	0.125	0.018	34	0.627	1.136
Paper	28	0.011	1.526	30	0.12	0.060	32	0.387	0.282
Leather	29	0.27	3.4078	27	0.094	0.028	25	0.281	0.244
Chem	30	0.178	2.263	34	0.079	0.017	26	0.275	1.454
R-P-C	31	0.145	1.986	37	0.071	0.504	21	0.146	0.140
Nm MP	32	0.101	1.456	31	0.064	0.011	36	0.118	0.121
BM&A	33	0.143	1.984	28	0.054	0.023	33	0.095	0.009
M. Prd	34	0.179	2.279	22	0.053	0.007	28	0.093	0.069
MotTr	36	0.13	1.81	25	0.026	0.002	27	0.088	0.041
Tr.Eq.	37	0.163	2.27	32	0.023	0.001	31	0.063	0.009
OMI	38	0.153	1.967	21	0.022	0.003	22	0.051	0.039
EGS	41	0.173	2.437	36	0.011	0.008	37	0.04	0.015

Industries showing higher influence of capital productivity on NVA dispersal are Electricity, Gas and Steam (IN41), Other Manufacturing Industries (IN38), Leather (IN29), Chemicals (IN30), show higher K productivity influence and is cause for dispersal. It is encouraging that Leather Industry, labour intensive industry, also showed capital productivity's influence on dispersal of output in the fourth decade of industrialisation and during the time when liberalisation was manifesting. In Leather also, dispersal finds cause in capital productivity influence.

Least influences of capital productivity are in Machinery other than transport (IN36), Rubber, Petroleum and Coal (IN31), Beverages (IN22), Paper (IN28). Petroleum and Machinery other than transport being capital intensive showed dispersal, though less due to influence of capital productivity. But the overall liberalising climate had an influence in bringing about dispersal in these two capital goods industries. Paper and Beverages, being labour intensive showed more concentration and less dispersal than the two capital-intensive industries.

Table 7.27. Regional Dispersal(CV)of Industries' employment in response to Capital productivity (at current prices) 1986-95

Specification CV emp = a + b(K-productivity); HH emp = a + b(K- productivity)

Ind. Name	IN Code	Measures of Industrial Dispersal		CV emp	CV emp	CV emp	HH emp	HH emp	HH emp
		CV Emp	HH Emp	Industry	$\hat{\beta}$	$(b/r)^2$	Industry	$\hat{\beta}$	$(b/r)^2$
1	2	3	4	5	6	7	8	9	10
Food Pro	21	1.401	0.096	37	4.033	24.794	29	0.731	1.558
Beverages	22	3.748	0.355	29	0.802	1.360	38	0.653	1.929
Textiles	25	1.609	0.1	41	0.775	1.347	41	0.53	0.424
Textile Prd	26	2.043	0.145	22	0.649	0.462	36	0.494	0.444
Wood	27	1.371	0.093	28	0.563	0.809	30	0.349	0.206
Paper	28	1.259	0.085	26	0.559	0.659	37	0.184	0.086
Leather	29	3.633	0.299	36	0.39	0.869	31	0.076	0.057
Chemical	30	1.862	0.133	25	0.125	0.028	26	0.075	0.009
Ru-Pet-Co	31	1.315	0.088	34	0.086	0.062	25	0.057	0.032
Nm MPrd	32	1.867	0.081	32	0.076	0.152	28	0.047	0.007
BM&A	33	1.56	0.106	33	0.074	0.022	21	0.032	0.007
Metal Prd	34	1.602	0.11	30	0.033	0.002	22	0.024	0.013
MotTr	36	1.489	0.101	21	0.024	0.001	27	0.022	0.002
Tr.Eq.	37	1.605	0.109	27	0.021	0.002	33	0.09	0.050
OMI	38	1.48	0.104	38	0.017	0.002	34	0.07	0.258
EGS	41	2.347	0.156	31	0.012	0.001	32	0.059	0.134

High influence of capital productivity on employment dispersal seen in Transport (IN37), Electricity, Gas and Steam (IN41), and Leather (IN29). $(b/r)^2$ being high, dispersal is brought about by the influence of capital productivity.

Low influences of capital productivity on employment dispersal were in Food (IN21), Textiles (IN25), Metal Products (IN34), Non-Metallic Mineral Products (IN32), Basic Metals and Alloys (IN33), Wood (IN27). In IN32, IN33 and IN34, the Intermediate Goods Industries, moderate dispersal is despite lack of influence of capital productivity. Food, Textiles and Wood show concentration and with little influence of capital productivity.

Table 7.28. Regional Dispersal(CV and HH) of Industries' output(NVA) in response to Labour productivity (at current prices) 1986-95

Specification: CV nva = a + b(L-productivity); HH nva = a + b(L- productivity)

Ind. Name	IN Code	Measures of Industrial Dispersal		CV nva	CV nva	CV nva	HH nva	HH nva	HH nva
		HHNVA	CVNVA	IN code	$\hat{\beta}$	$(b/r)^2$	IN code	$\hat{\beta}$	$(b/r)^2$
1	2	3	4	5	6	7	8	9	10
Food Pro	21	0.100	1.456	36	1.394	1.999	41	0.301	0.115
Beverage	22	0.132	1.866	29	1.251	20.867	28	0.248	0.293
Textiles	25	0.122	1.756	26	0.741	0.877	31	0.095	0.017
Text Prd	26	0.167	2.276	30	0.646	12.274	34	0.092	0.032
Wood	27	0.125	1.724	41	0.447	0.298	27	0.084	0.034
Paper	28	0.011	1.526	33	0.396	0.504	37	0.07	0.017
Leather	29	0.27	3.4078	38	0.208	0.084	33	0.063	0.005
Chemical	30	0.178	2.263	21	0.118	0.114	36	0.059	0.066
Ru-Pet-C	31	0.145	1.986	31	0.092	0.021	30	0.056	0.016
Nm MPrd	32	0.101	1.456	27	0.092	0.067	25	0.052	0.007
BM&A	33	0.143	1.984	37	0.074	0.027	21	0.044	0.003
Met.Prd	34	0.179	2.279	25	0.052	0.006	22	0.036	0.029
MotTr	36	0.13	1.81	32	0.044	0.004	29	0.015	0.001
Tr.Eq.	37	0.163	2.27	22	0.032	0.038	26	0.015	0.004
OMI	38	0.153	1.967	28	0.022	0.004	32	0.015	0.001
EGS	41	0.173	2.437	34	0.015	0.001	38	0.014	0.003

Higher influences of Labour productivity on NVA dispersal are in Electricity, Gas and Steam (IN41), Basic Metals and Alloys (IN33), Machinery other than Transport (IN36), Chemicals (IN30), Rubber, Petroleum and Coal (IN31), Wood (IN27). $(b/r)^2$ was been high in Rubber, Petroleum and Coal (IN31), Machinery other than Transport (IN36) and Electricity (IN41), there is more concentration, despite influence of labour productivity on dispersal process. But dispersal being higher in Chemicals, high $(b/r)^2$ shows influence of Labour Productivity on NVA dispersal in this decade. In Basic Metals, high b/r could not bring about much dispersal.

The Least influences are in Beverages (IN22), Non-Metallic Mineral Products (IN32), Textiles (IN25). While labour productivity has shown less influence in these industries' dispersal, these being labour intensive industries, concentration has manifested rather than conspicuous dispersal.

Table 7.29. Regional Dispersal (HH&CV) of Industries' employment in response to L- productivity (at current prices) 1986-95 Specification: HH emp = a + b(L-productivity); CV emp = a + b(L-productivity)

In. Nm	Measures of Industrial Dispersal			HH emp	HH emp	HH emp	CV emp	CV emp	CV emp
	IN Code	CV emp	HH emp	IN Code	$\hat{\beta}$	$(b/r)^2$	IN Code	$\hat{\beta}$	$(b/r)^2$
1	2	3	4	5	6	7	8	9	10
Food Pro	21	1.401	0.096	33	0.805	0.931	26	0.393	0.179
Beverages	22	3.748	0.355	37	0.402	1.171	22	0.304	0.889
Textiles	25	1.609	0.1	27	0.09	0.029	27	0.195	0.166
Textile Prd	26	2.043	0.145	25	0.081	0.298	41	0.172	0.035
Wood	27	1.371	0.093	41	0.062	0.116	29	0.072	0.015
Paper	28	1.259	0.085	34	0.061	0.620	28	0.072	0.008
Leather	29	3.633	0.299	38	0.028	0.002	33	0.067	0.005
Chemical	30	1.862	0.133	30	0.026	0.002	32	0.023	0.001
Ru-Pet-Co	31	1.315	0.088	22	0.021	0.003	37	0.018	0.002
Nm MPrd	32	1.867	0.081	21	0.019	0.003	25	0.017	0.003
BM&A	33	1.56	0.106	29	0.017	0.000	38	0.017	0.001
Metal Prd	34	1.602	0.11	32	0.016	0.001	36	0.016	0.002
MotTr	36	1.489	0.101	26	0.015	0.000	31	0.015	0.001
Tr.Eq.	37	1.605	0.109	31	0.013	0.000	30	0.012	0.001
OMI	38	1.48	0.104	36	0.003	0.000	21	0.012	0.002
EGS	41	2.347	0.156	28	0.001	0.000	34	0.005	0.002

In the fourth decade of industrialisation, Basic Metals and Alloys (IN33), Transport (IN37), Wood (IN27), Electricity (IN41), show higher influences of labour productivity on employment dispersal. *b*/*r* being on the lower side, lower influence of labour productivity was a determining cause for lack of dispersal.

Lower influences are in Food Products (IN21), Machinery other than transport (IN36), Chemicals (IN30) Other Manufacturing Industries (IN38), Non-Metallic Mineral Products (IN32). Dispersal in hthese industries were not due to Labour productivity influence.

Table 7.30. Regional Dispersal(CV)of Industries' employment in response to TFP by Solow (at current prices) 1986-95 Specification : CV emp = *a* + *b* (TFP-S), HH emp = *a* + *b*(TFP-S)

Ind. Name	IN Code	Dispersal Measures		CV emp	CV emp	CV emp	HH emp	HH emp	HH emp
		CV Emp	HH Emp	Industry	$\hat{\beta}$	$(b/r)^2$	Industry	$\hat{\beta}$	$(b/r)^2$
1	2	3	4	5	6	7	8	9	10
Food Pro	21	1.401	0.096	36	2.632	13.530	29	1.142	5.695
Beverage	22	3.748	0.355	32	1.838	3.617	32	0.51	0.798
Textiles	25	1.609	0.1	21	1.837	6.428	22	0.45	8.409
Text Prd	26	2.043	0.145	34	1.294	3.390	30	0.399	0.910
Wood	27	1.371	0 093	29	1.242	0.433	36	0.392	0.309
Paper	28	1.259	0.085	33	0.954	4.027	21	0.314	0.405
Leather	29	3.633	0.2989	27	0.779	2.380	34	0.31	0.169
Chemical	30	1.862	0.1332	26	0.752	3.448	41	0.191	0.304
R-P-C	31	1.315	0.088	25	0.677	1.614	38	0.178	0.062
Nm MPrd	32	1.867	0.081	41	0.442	2.147	25	0.067	0.015
BM&A	33	1.56	0.106	30	0.41	1.303	33	0.063	0.018
Met Prd	34	1.602	0.11	37	0.372	0.623	27	0.062	0.022
MotTr	36	1.489	0.101	28	0.097	0.076	26	0.058	0.120
Tr.Eq.	37	1.605	0.109	22	0.072	0.216	37	0.033	0.161
OMI	38	1.48	0.104	38	0.053	0.005	28	0.028	0.007
EGS	41	2.347	0.156	31	0.033	0.024	31	0.015	0.001

Food (IN21), Leather (IN29), Non-metallic Mineral Products (IN32), Machinery other than Transport (IN33) show higher influence of TFP on employment dispersal in 1986-95. In Basic Metals and Alloys (IN33), and Leather (IN29), concentration or less dispersal shows TFP influence. But Food still shows concentration, despite TFPG influence being high.

Rubber-Petroleum-Coal (IN31), Paper (IN28), Other Manufacturing Industries (IN38), Transport Equipment (IN37), Textile Products (IN26) showed less influence of TFP on employment dispersal. B/r is higher in IN26, IN37, dispersal/concentration in IN37 was due to TFP influence. Transport had entered a consolidation phase. In Other Manufacturing Industries (IN38) *b*/*r* is low and concentration is noticed. In Paper (IN28) and Rubber-Petroleum-Coal (IN31) concentration is seen with low $(b/r)^2$.

Table 7.31. Regional Dispersal of Industries' Output (NVA) in Response to TFP by Solow (at current prices) for 1986-95

Specification: HH nva = $a + b$ (TFP-S); CV nva = $a + b$ (TFP-S)

In. Nm	Measures of Industrial Dispersal			HH NVA	HH NVA	HH NVA	CV NVA	CV NVA	CV NVA
	IN Code	CV NVA	HH NVA	IN Code	$\hat{\beta}$	$(b/r)^2$	IN Code	$\hat{\beta}$	$(b/r)^2$
1	2	3	4	5	6	7	8	9	10
Food Pro	21	1.456	0.100	22	2.034	12.313	22	1.505	8.917
Beverage	22	1.866	0.132	41	1.21	5.567	31	1.386	2.366
Textiles	25	1.756	0.122	29	1.162	1.857	41	1.217	5.445
TextPrd	26	2.276	0.167	33	1.08	25.920	34	0.316	3.698
Wood	27	1.724	0.125	32	0.988	1.198	21	0.22	0.949
Paper	28	1.526	0.011	21	0.824	1.801	37	0.179	0.091
Leather	29	3.408	0.27	31	0.771	1.607	32	0.11	0.015
Chemical	30	2.263	0.178	30	0.569	11.991	30	0.077	0.156
Ru-Pe-Co	31	1.986	0.145	34	0.435	1.931	29	0.066	0.029
Nm MPrd	32	1.456	0.101	27	0.271	0.350	25	0.043	0.023
BM&A	33	1.984	0.143	37	0.229	0.177	27	0.031	0.004
Metal Prd	34	2.279	0.179	38	0.102	0.128	38	0.027	0.008
MotTr	36	1.81	0.13	36	0.098	0.267	33	0.02	0.003
Tr.Eq.	37	2.27	0.163	28	0.094	0.044	26	0.015	0.005
OMI	38	1.967	0.153	25	0.015	0.017	36	0.011	0.003
EGS	41	2.437	0.173	26	0.011	0.011	28	0.011	0.001

Higher Influence of TFP on NVA Dispersal is in Beverages (IN22), Electricity, Gas and Steam (IN41), RPC (IN31), Food (IN21) and Non-Metallic Mineral Products (IN32) and also Chemicals (IN30). While Beverages, Electricity, Chemicals. RPC, show higher dispersal in HH, Food and NmMP show relatively lesser dispersal than others of this group showing high TFP influence. However, $(b/r)^2$ is higher in Electricity, NmMP, Food, RPC and Chemicals, showing dispersal was influenced by TFPG in these Intermediates, Consumer Non Durable like Food, Capilta Intensive Intermediates like NmMp, Chemicals and RPC and Kgood Indsutry like EGS (IN41).

Thus by the 1980s, Chemicals showed that sunrise industry status has become to get dispersed thereby helping cause of regional and industrial equity in Indian economy. Intermediates have also done well in 1980s and its response to TFPG encourages greater planning for this group of Industries to act as leading industries for grwoth and dispersal.

Food Dispersal shown as getting effected by TFPG can encourage technological, technical innovation in seeds, irrigation, fertiliser and extension programmes to tap this industry's potential to eradicate poverty and rasie surplus for industrialisation.

IMPACT ANALYSIS OF RELEVANT EXPLANATORY VARIABLES ON REGIONAL DISPERSAL MEASURES FOR THE LONG PERIOD OF 40 YEARS, 1956-95

This Section deals with Regression results of HH and CV Measures of NVA and Employment of each of the 2-digit Industries for the period 1959-95 along with the Regional dispersal measures cited in the columns (3) and (4) to make an effective influence assessment through recourse to Grassacks instrument of $(b/r)^2$ for the long term movements of dispersion in Indian Industries .

Table 7.32. Regional Dispersal(HH & CV) of Industries' output(NVA) in response to TFP by Solow (at current prices) 1956-1995

Specification: HH nva = $a + b$(TFP-S); CV nva = $a + b$(TFP-S)

Ind. Name	IN Code	Dispersal Measures		CV nva	CV nva	CV nva	HH nva	HH nva	HH nva
		HHNVA	CVNVA	Industry	$\hat{\beta}$	$(b/r)^2$	Industry	$\hat{\beta}$	$(b/r)^2$
1	2	3	4	5	6	7	8	9	10
Food	21	0.266	3.638	33	0.433	3.989	41	0.867	3.977
Bev'	22	0.197	2.623	34	0.405	2.563	36	0.673	0.754
Textiles	25	0.241	3.020	41	0.38	4.376	34	0.388	2.552
Tex Prd	26	0.173	2.691	32	0.351	1.325	32	0.36	3.703
Wood	27	0.111	1.553	29	0.299	2.794	28	0.32	3.657
Paper	28	0.360	3.193	37	0.279	1.179	37	0.282	1.205
Leather	29	0.187	5.085	25	0.268	1.436	25	0.264	1.621
Chemical	30	0.221	2.377	22	0.225	4.602	22	0.21	0.437
R-P-C	31	0.193	2.714	28	0.189	2.101	30	0.187	0.426
Nm MPrd	32	0.152	2.021	36	0.167	1.743	29	0.185	1.901
BM&A	33	0.188	2.423	21	0.146	0.454	27	0.122	1.063
Met. Prd	34	0.106	1.538	30	0.146	4.278	26	0.096	0.838
MotTr	36	0.238	2.963	31	0.09	0.579	31	0.093	0.166
Tr.Eq.	37	0.102	2.827	26	0.065	0.083	21	0.026	0.005
OMI	38	0.296	3.488	38	0.045	0.018	33	0.019	0.026
EGS	41	0.216	3.101	27	0.034	0.046	38	0.012	0.048

Metal Products (IN34), Transport Equipment and Parts (IN37), Electricity, Gas and Steam (IN41) and Basic Metals and Alloys (IN33) show higher effect of TFP on NVA. A higher $(b/r)^2$ is given by Electricity, Gas and Steam (IN 41) and dispersal of NVA in EGS is noticed to be influenced by high TFP Growth in the the long run. In Basic Metals and Alloys (IN33) and Metal Products (IN34), these being Intermediate Capital Intensive Industries, TFPG influence as a cause for dispersal is not definitive. This is a cause for concern.

The least influence of TFP on NVA of industries is seen in Other Manufacturing Industries (IN38), Wood (IN27), Food (IN21), Chemicals (IN30), Textile Products (IN26) and Rubber-Petroleum-Coal (IN31), Basic Metals and Alloys (IN33). High NVA dispersal and high $(b/r)^2$ in Chemicals (IN30) means that low TFPG influence as revealed in b , itself is a factor for dispersal in this industry.

Table 7.33. Regional Dispersal (CV&HH)of Industries' employment in response to TFP by Solow (at current prices) 1956-95 Specification:

CV emp = *a* + *b* (TFP-S) HH emp = *a* + *b* (TFP-S)

	Measures of Industrial Dispersal			CV emp	CV emp	CV emp	HH emp	HH emp	HH emp
In. Nm	IN Code	HH emp	CV emp	Industry	$\hat{\beta}$	$(b/r)^2$	Industry	$\hat{\beta}$	$(b/r)^2$
1	2	3	4	5	6	7	8	9	10
Food	21	0.112	1.593	33	3.874	108.753	36	1.23	11.913
Bev'	22	0.414	4.684	34	3.189	77.631	30	0.539	2.665
Textiles	25	0.148	2.087	25	2.888	38.259	21	0.395	1.279
Tex Prd	26	0.162	2.265	38	1.717	268.008	33	0.383	1.063
Wood	27	0.123	1.954	21	1.306	15.793	29	0.373	1.150
Paper	28	0.129	1.809	26	1.292	3.241	25	0.346	0.973
Leather	29	0.340	4.996	29	1.098	5.219	37	0.338	1.109
Chemical	30	0.232	3.316	31	0.722	2.348	34	0.332	0.854
R-P-C	31	0.144	2.144	27	0.703	4.619	38	0.199	0.660
Nm MPrd	32	0.113	1.482	30	0.552	2.326	22	0.192	0.297
BM&A	33	0.154	2.205	36	0.48	14.400	41	0.139	1.486
Met. Prd	34	0.174	2.399	32	0.31	0.874	27	0.118	0.065
MotTr	36	0.134	1.942	22	0.187	0.324	32	0.095	0.053
Tr.Eq.	37	0.166	2.347	37	0.162	0.772	26	0.076	0.008
OMI	38	0.185	2.599	41	0.117	0.913	31	0.056	0.030
EGS	41	0.116	2.143	28	0.056	0.052	28	0.016	0.001

Basic Metals and Alloys (IN33), Metal products (IN34), Textiles (IN25), Leather (IN29) show high influence of Total Factor Productivity (TFP) on dispersal of employment.

With higher employment dispersal, especially by CV, higher $(b/r)^2$ implies that TFPG is a cause for employment dispersal in both Labour intensive and Capital Intensive Intermediates.

Paper (IN28), Electricity (IN41), Non-Metallic Mineral Products (IN32), Beverages (IN22) show little influence of TFP on employment dispersal. (b/r) being generally low with concentration in these industries, proves that raising TFPG will cause for dispersal in the long run.

Table 7.34. Regional Dispersal(CV) of Industries' output(NVA) in response to Capital intensity (at current prices) 1956-95

Specification: CV nva = $a + b$(K/L); HH nva = $a + b$(K/L)

In. Nm	Dispersal Measures			CV NVA	HHNVA	HHNVA	CVNVA	CVNVA	CVNVA
	IN Code	CVNVA	HHNVA	Industry	$\hat{\beta}$	$(b/r)^2$	Industry	$\hat{\beta}$	$(b/r)^2$
1	2	3	4	5	6	7	8	9	10
Food	21	1.538	0.010	30	0.118	0.111	21	0.076	0.109
Bev'	22	2.714	0.193	37	0.093	0.079	29	0.065	0.092
Textiles	25	2.377	0.221	32	0.089	0.220	26	0.061	0.029
Tex Prd	26	2.827	0.102	41	0.086	1.849	32	0.059	0.139
Wood	27	3.101	0.216	21	0.07	0.092	27	0.047	0.023
Paper	28	2.021	0.152	29	0.062	0.087	33	0.043	0.058
Leather	29	3.193	0.360	28	0.049	0.021	30	0.034	0.193
Chemical	30	3.638	0.266	26	0.045	0.010	28	0.029	0.008
R-P-C	31	2.963	0.238	33	0.043	0.056	36	0.029	0.005
Nm MPrd	32	1.553	0.111	38	0.038	0.041	41	0.019	0.004
BM&A	33	2.623	0.197	22	0.037	0.009	25	0.016	0.028
Met. Prd	34	3.020	0.241	31	0.032	0.024	38	0.015	0.002
MotTr	36	2.423	0.188	27	0.018	0.007	37	0.014	0.020
Tr.Eq.	37	5.085	0.187	34	0.018	0.009	34	0.013	0.004
OMI	38	3.488	0.296	25	0.015	0.075	31	0.013	0.012
EGS	41	2.691	0.173	36	0.014	0.002	22	0.002	0.002

Higher influences of K/L on NVA dispersal in the long period was in Food (IN21), Leather (IN29), Chemicals (IN30), Non-Metallic Mineral Products (IN32), Paper (IN28), Textile Products (IN26), Basic Metals and Alloys (IN33). But less dispersal and lower $(b/r)^2$ implied that capital intensity (K/L) influence though high, has not been a factor for bringing about high dispersal of NVA in the long run in Indian Industry.

Table 7.35. Influence of K/L on employment dispersal of Indian Industry. (at current prices) 1956-95 Specification HH emp = *a* + *b* (K/L) CV emp = *a* + *b*(K/L)

CV emp Ind.Nm.	CV emp I.N.	CV emp $\hat{\beta}$	CV emp $(b/r)^2$	HHemp Industry	HHemp $\hat{\beta}$	HHemp $(b/r)^2$	Dispersal Measures IN	HH emp	HH emp
1	2	3	4	5	6	7	8	9	10
Wood	27	0.529	0.400	21	0.347	0.808	21	0.112	1.593
EGC	41	0.327	0.835	29	0.266	0.201	22	0.414	4.684
Metal P	34	0.278	0.468	38	0.178	0.311	25	0.148	2.087
OMI	38	0.269	0.652	41	0.089	0.256	26	0.162	2.265
MotTr	36	0.167	0.063	28	0.065	0.019	27	0.123	1.954
Leather	29	0.078	0.029	22	0.054	0.108	28	0.129	1.809
NmMP	32	0.075	0.018	32	0.038	0.045	29	0.340	4.996
Paper	28	0.073	0.024	25	0.035	0.061	30	0.232	3.316
Food	21	0.058	0.025	26	0.031	0.004	31	0.144	2.144
Tex.Prd	26	0.044	0.009	34	0.021	0.025	32	0.113	1.482
Chem	30	0.042	0.014	33	0.017	0.016	33	0.154	2.205
BM&A	33	0.024	0.041	37	0.015	0.014	34	0.174	2.399
Textiles	25	0.024	0.006	27	0.015	0.010	36	0.134	1.942
Ru-Pe-C	31	0.018	0.015	30	0.014	0.001	37	0.166	2.347
Bever'g	22	0.016	0.001	36	0.012	0.000	38	0.185	2.599
Tr.Eq.	37	0.013	0.011	31	0.011	0.006	41	0.116	2.143

Electricity (IN41), Other Manufacturing Industries (IN38), Leather (IN29), Non Metallic Mineral Products (32) show high K/L influence on employment dispersal. While NmMP (IN32) is moderately dispersed, other three show higher dispersal. EGS (IN41) and OMI (IN38) shower higher $(b/r)^2$ implying K/L is cause for dispersal in these capital goods industries. Leather (IN29) and Nonmetallic mineral products (IN32) showed lower $(b/r)^2$ meaning that K/L growth has caused to bring about dispersal in these Intermediates.

The least influence of K/L on employment dispersal of industries was seen in case of Transport (IN37), Beverages (IN22), Rubber-Petroleum-Coal (IN31), Textiles (IN25), Chemicals (IN30). But low $(b/r)^2$ means moderate dispersal in these has not come about through K/L influence.

Table 7.36. Regional Dispersal(HH) of Industries' output(NVA) in response to Capital productivity (at current prices)1956-1995 Specification HH nva = *a* + *b*(K-productivity)

CV nva= *a* + *b*(K-productivity)

Ind. Name	IN	Dispersal Measures		HH nva	HH nva	HH nva	CV nva	CV nva	CV nva
		CVNVA	HHNVA	Industry	$\hat{\beta}$	$(b/r)^2$	Industry	$\hat{\beta}$	$(b/r)^2$
1	2	3	4	5	6	7	8	9	10
Food	21	1.538	0.010	29	0.197	0.120	22	2.12	25.830
Bev'	22	2.714	0.193	37	0.113	0.079	29	0.906	2.996
Textiles	25	2.377	0.221	22	0.108	0.137	28	0.547	33.245
Tex Prd	26	2.827	0.102	30	0.097	0.094	27	0.445	2.750
Wood	27	3.101	0.216	28	0.062	0.107	36	0.365	0.469
Paper	28	2.021	0.152	26	0.053	0.936	33	0.277	0.364
Leather	29	3.193	0.360	32	0.039	0.007	38	0.242	0.373
Chemical	30	3.638	0.266	25	0.033	0.272	37	0.198	0.186
R-P-C	31	2.963	0.238	38	0.03	0.007	31	0.173	0.265
Nm MPrd	32	1.553	0.111	36	0.028	0.003	26	0.114	2.166
BM&A	33	2.623	0.197	21	0.028	0.098	41	0.131	0.078
Met. Prd	34	3.020	0.241	33	0.025	0.003	34	0.063	0.020
MotTr	36	2.423	0.188	34	0.021	0.002	25	0.062	0.349
Tr.Eq.	37	5.085	0.187	31	0.015	0.002	32	0.054	0.014
OMI	38	3.488	0.296	27	0.013	0.001	30	0.053	0.702
EGS	41	2.691	0.173	41	0.011	0.001	21	0.044	0.242

Influence of Capital Productivity on NVA dispersal is more in Leather (IN29), Beverages (IN22), Paper (IN28), Manufacturing other than Transport (IN36) and Other Manufacturing Industries (IN38). Dispersal being relatively high, $(b/r)^2$ in terms of HH does not show to be capital productivity influence to be a determining factor in bringing about dispersal in NVA in these industries in the long run.

Table 7.37. Regional Dispersal(CV&HH) of Industries' employment in response to Capital productivity (at current prices) 1956-95

Specification CV emp = a + b(K-productivity); HH emp = a + b(K- productivity)

Ind. Nm	Industrial Dispersal			CV emp Industry	CV emp $\hat{\beta}$	CV emp $(b/r)^2$	HH emp Industry	HH emp $\hat{\beta}$	HH emp $(b/r)^2$
	IN Code	HH emp	CV emp						
1	2	3	4	5	6	7	8	9	10
Food Pro	21	0.112	1.593	22	1.72	21.753	22	0.232	0.168
Beverages	22	0.414	4.684	29	1.466	6.229	32	0.093	0.022
Textiles	25	0.148	2.087	32	0.861	1.065	29	0.066	0.013
Textile Prd	26	0.162	2.265	27	0.476	0.478	33	0.064	0.022
Wood	27	0.123	1.954	26	0.433	0.747	30	0.062	0.133
Paper	28	0.129	1.809	38	0.289	5.568	34	0.047	0.041
Leather	29	0.340	4.996	25	0.082	0.032	37	0.041	0.016
Chemical	30	0.232	3.316	36	0.061	0.050	26	0.041	0.005
Ru-Pet-Co	31	0.144	2.144	30	0.053	0.003	38	0.038	0.111
Nm MPrd	32	0.113	1.482	34	0.037	0.004	41	0.036	0.013
BM&A	33	0.154	2.205	33	0.032	0.005	36	0.031	0.087
Metal Prd	34	0.174	2.399	28	0.017	0.001	21	0.029	0.004
MotTr	36	0.134	1.942	41	0.017	0.007	27	0.021	0.002
Tr.Eq.	37	0.166	2.347	31	0.015	0.004	28	0.017	0.001
OMI	38	0.185	2.599	21	0.012	0.005	25	0.016	0.013
EGS	41	0.116	2.143	37	0.07	0.046	31	0.012	0.002

In the long term, influence of capital productivity is higher in Beverages (IN22), Leather (IN29), Non-Metallic Mineral product (IN32) in both measures. Leather (IN29) and Beverages (IN22) show dispersal largely due to influence of higher influence of capital productivity on employment dispersal in both measures.

Low influence of capital productivity on employment dispersal in the long run is seen in Rubber-Petroleum and Coal (IN31), Transport (IN37), Food (IN21), Electricity (IN41) manifest in dispersal except Food that showed more concentration and capital productivity was not the cause of dispersal or concentration in the long run.

Table 7.38. Regional Dispersal(CV) of Industries' output(NVA) in response to Labour productivity (at current prices) 1956-95 Specification: CV nva = a +b(L-productivity) HH nva = a +b(L-productivity)

In. Nm	Measures of Industrial Dispersal			CV nva	CV nva	CV nva	HH nva	HH nva	HH nva
	IN Code	CV nva	CV nva	HH Code	$\hat{\beta}$	$(b/r)^2$	IN Code	$\hat{\beta}$	$(b/r)^2$
1	2	3	4	5	6	7	8	9	10
Food Pro	21	1.538	0.010	29	0.725	5.906	41	0.2	0.171
Beverages	22	2.714	0.193	34	0.421	0.269	22	0.198	0.109
Textiles	25	2.377	0.221	41	0.343	0.566	29	0.193	0.122
Textile Prd	26	2.827	0.102	31	0.325	0.461	38	0.19	0.144
Wood	27	3.101	0.216	38	0.246	0.393	25	0.135	1.302
Paper	28	2.021	0.152	22	0.245	0.406	27	0.114	0.054
Leather	29	3.193	0.360	33	0.238	0.320	36	0.079	0.018
Chemical	30	3.638	0.266	30	0.224	0.865	37	0.054	0.194
Ru-P-Co	31	2.963	0.238	26	0.126	0.338	32	0.048	0.010
Nm MPrd	32	1.553	0.111	36	0.12	0.039	34	0.043	0.003
BM&A	33	2.623	0.197	28	0.108	0.041	21	0.038	0.072
Metal Prd	34	3.020	0.241	27	0.107	0.049	30	0.035	0.038
MotTr	36	2.423	0.188	25	0.082	0.240	31	0.028	0.003
Tr.Eq.	37	5.085	0.187	32	0.064	0.012	33	0.015	0.001
OMI	38	3.488	0.296	21	0.063	0.173	26	0.013	0.002
EGS	41	2.691	0.173	37	0.011	0.001	28	0.011	0.002

A 40-year regression of NVA dispersal on L productivity shows maximum Labour productivity influence on Leather (IN29), Electricity (IN41), Other Manufacturing Industries (IN38) and Beverages (IN22). High dispersal with higher $(b/r)^2$ shows Net Value Added (NVA) dispersal has been due to the influence of Labour Productivity. This is an interesting result since contrary to common understanding, capital goods industries like OMI and EGS show that dispersal can occur due to influence of Labour productivity growth.

Labor Productivity showed least influence on NVA dispersal in industries such as Transport Equipment (IN37), Food Products (IN21), Non metallic Mineral Products (IN33), Paper (IN28), Textile Products (In26) and Manufacturing other than Transport (IN36). $(b/r)^2$ being low in L-intensive industries like Food, Textile Products and Paper means low Labour productivity influence did not impact dispersal/concentration in the long run.

Table 7.39. Regional Dispersal(HH&CV)of Industries' employment in response to Labour-productivity (at current prices) 1956-95

Specification: HH emp = a + b (L-productivity); CV emp = a + b(L- productivity)

In. Nm	Measures of Industrial Dispersal			HH emp	HH emp	HH emp	CV emp	CV emp	CV emp
	IN Code	HH emp	CV emp	Industry	$\hat{\beta}$	$(b/r)^2$	Industry	$\hat{\beta}$	$(b/r)^2$
1	2	3	4	5	6	7	8	9	10
Food Pro	21	0.112	1.593	38	0.321	0.873	38	0.308	0.747
Beverage	22	0.414	4.684	21	0.095	0.028	33	0.108	0.164
Textiles	25	0.148	2.087	33	0.086	0.284	30	0.099	0.071
TextilePrd	26	0.162	2.265	28	0.071	0.229	41	0.088	0.066
Wood	27	0.123	1.954	41	0.069	0.038	22	0.076	0.038
Paper	28	0.129	1.809	36	0.065	0.008	26	0.047	0.009
Leather	29	0.340	4.996	26	0.059	0.016	21	0.042	0.016
Chemical	30	0.232	3.316	25	0.058	0.029	36	0.041	0.029
Ru-P-Co	31	0.144	2.144	32	0.04	0.050	32	0.038	0.007
Nm MPrd	32	0.113	1.482	30	0.034	0.007	34	0.035	0.010
BM&A	33	0.154	2.205	27	0.033	0.039	27	0.027	0.043
Metal Prd	34	0.174	2.399	34	0.031	0.019	25	0.024	0.006
MotTr	36	0.134	1.942	31	0.03	0.011	31	0.023	0.003
Tr.Eq.	37	0.166	2.347	29	0.02	0.001	28	0.019	0.002
OMI	38	0.185	2.599	22	0.018	0.003	37	0.016	0.017
EGS	41	0.116	2.143	37	0.017	0.018	29	0.014	0.001

Labour productivity shows maximum influence on employment dispersal in Other Manufacturing Industries (IN38), Food Products (IN21), Basic Metals and Alloys (IN33), Electricity (IN41), Textile Products (IN26). Low $(b/r)^2$ and concentration in Food, EGS and Textile Products means high influence of Labour productivity on employment dispersal did not cause to bring about dispersal. However, OMI (IN38) and Basic Metals and Alloys (IN33) has shown dispersal with higher $(b/r)^2$ implying high influence of Labour Productivity on employment dispersal did cause to bring about employment dispersal in this capital goods (IN38) and the Intermediate (IN33) industry.

Summary and Major Findings

Wood (IN27) comes out as an industry needing attention at least for purposes of employment planning and to boost employment in this wood industry. This will boost rural entrepreneurship and rural employment and being L-intensive and can be used massively for poverty alleviation programme. Adequate marketing can boost tourism in service, housing and improve infrastructure and provide a base for industrial growth and trade.

In 1966-75, the decadal period of recession, Non-Metallic Mineral Products (IN32), Basic Metals and Alloys (IN33), Metal Products (IN34), Machinery other than Transport (IN36) showed $(b/r)^2$ higher implying even in capital goods industry and intermediates with higher capital intensive-ness, recession was a cause for low TFPG influence and not so high Employment dispersal. Food was more concentrated and so high K/L influence could not bring about NVA dispersal of Food Industry. Thus recession not only affected the machine oriented goods industry, it also affected the main agro-industry in India too. K/L growth did not influence NVA dispersal in Textiles (IN25) and Machinery other than Transport (IN36) but it did influence employment dispersal in these industries despite recession. NVA of Intermediates like Leather (IN29) Chemicals (IN30) and Rubber (IN31) dispersed due to capital productivity influence. While $(b/r)^2$ is relatively high, influence of Labour productivity in this period of 1966-75, did not bring about dispersal in Food Industry, a point that reinforces the inference presented in this paragraph before. Similarly, $(b/r)^2$ in HH is relatively high in Rubber-petroleum and Coal (IN31) and despite low influence of Labour productivity on employment dispersal in terms of b^, policy recommendation is in terms of raising Labour Productivity, as dispersal is due to influence of Labour productivity. Labour productivity influence did not bring about employment dispersal in this Food (IN21), a fact that can be again attributed to recession.

Textile Products (IN26), Chemicals (IN30), Rubber-Petroleum-Coal (IN31) and Machinery other than Transport (IN36) with high b/r did not bring about high employment dispersal in this period of 1976-85.

In Rubber, Chemicals and Basic Metals, that are traditional highly capital intensive did show higher dispersal in this period of 1976-85 but it was again not due to influence of K/L.

In 1986-95, Food Industry still showed concentration. Dispersal being higher in Chemicals, high $(b/r)^2$ showed influence of Labour Productivity on NVA dispersal in this decade. In Basic Metals, high b/r could not bring about much NVA dispersal in this decade. Thus Intermediates have not shown dispersal despite its potential. Leather showed dispersal in last decade both in NVA and in employment due to influence of capital productivity.

The long run analysis of 40 years from 1956-95 revealed certain interesting results. High NVA dispersal and high$(b/r)^2$ in Chemicals (IN30) means that low TFPG influence as revealed in b^, itself is a factor for dispersal in this industry. Chemicals Industry (IN30) to sustain itself as a leading industry for balanced industrial development will have to find ways to improve its TFPG.

Basic Metals and Alloys (IN33) and Metal products (IN34), both being capital intensive Intermediates showed high TFPG influencing dispersal, while NmMP (IN32) being of similar nature as IN33 and IN34 showed concentration or non-dispersal with little TFPG influencc on employment dispersal. Thus employment dispersal in these intermediates having shown themselves amenable to higher TFPG, it is necessary that a more detailed input-output planning exercises involving Intermediates is called for. The Economic Reforms of 1990s has not taken Intermediates Planning into account that would have a factor for regional equity and growth in Indian economy.

Chapter 8

Major Findings and Policy Guidelines

Industrialisation is a "process in which changes in a series of strategical production functions are taking place"[1] involving mechanisation of an enterprise, building up of a new industry, opening up of a new market and/or exploitation of a new territory involving a process of deepening and widening of capital. Towards this, an integrated approach to Industrial Development in India over 1956-95 was sought for, making use of the estimated parameters, viz. Partial Productivity of Labour and of Capital, Capital Intensity, Output Elasticities of Factors of Production and Returns to Scale, to trace Causal Linkage Relationships among these measurements. This helped to assess the economic mechanisms for growth in industries' output caused by TFP Growth or otherwise, in either case, due to other factors; and to what extent. Further, analysis of Regional Dispersal of each industry group in terms of size variables and structural relationships among Small States and UT and Large States for comparative knowledge of the effects of size of regions on specificity of industries' was undertaken. The extent of Industrial Dispersal was traced across States and Union Territories over different time periods of each successive decade and of a total of 40 years, 1956-95. This provided to understand causal effects over time as to test Self-perpetuation vis-a-vis Williamson Hypothesis. The influence of Total Factor Productivity (TFP), Capital Intensity (K/L), Capital Productivity and Labour Productivity, each on Regional Dispersal Measures of Net Value Added (NVA) and Employment (NW) of each industry group was analysed to establish Causal Relationships. This was cross- checked by tools of Grossack's[2] study framework to substantiate the extent of contributions by each of the explanatory variables to Regional Dispersal of NVA and Employment in each of the 2-digit industries under study. All those analytical tools of study provided the extent of contributions of the common set of explanatory variables to growth and to regional dispersal of each Industry Group in India.

The Study was benefitted by Review of International Studies versus Indian Industry covering the issues of Returns to Scale, Capital Intensity, Total Factor Productivity (TFP), Partial Productivities, Output Growth and Employment Growth as to assess the importance of factors that contributed to industrial growth.

An analysis of Growth Rates of Factories made clear that Food Industry (IN21) grew at a maximum of 33.1 per cent p.a. to meet the consumption of a densely populated nation indicating growth and spread of food industries. Then followed the Intermediate Input Based Industries succeeded by Capital Goods Industries.

Food Products (IN21) Industry provides vital linkages and synergisation with agriculture and industry. This has been identified as a thrust area and is covered as priority area. Most food processing industries have been exempted from industrial licensing except beer-alcohol and those reserved under SSI. For many processed food items automatic approval for even 100 per cent equity in form of FDI is available. Some of the structural problems that stymie growth are low value addition to raw produce, High wastage, low level of processing, highly fragmented processing capacities, limited access to technology, poor marketing network, unusually long supply chain, multiplicity of regulations, lack of infrastructures. However this industry provides an opportunity for fostering public private partnership. All these can increase returns to scale and act as base for meeting consumption needs of industrial workers and bring about higher returns.

Chapter 4 analysis of Growth Rates of Factories revealed Food Products Industry (IN21) growing at a maximum growth rate of 33.1 per cent, followed by User and intermediates Industries. The Comparative Study of Industries' growth rates of Factories brought out possible weak forward and backward linkages and lack of implementation in terms of numbers corresponding to planning goals.

Net Value Added (NVA) growth rate was the highest in Electricity, Gas and Steam (EGS) at 18.1 per cent followed by growth rate on Textile Products (IN26), with lowest growth rate being recorded by Textiles (IN25), indicating lack of appropriate production planning and weak linkages.

Low growth rates in employment in number of workers in most of the industries except Food Products Industry (IN21) confirmed that most industries in India are low labour intensive ones. Low employment growth rate figures in Beverages (2.2%), Textiles (2.3%) and OMI (1.8%) pointed to lacunae in employment planning and thereby hinted at greater employment absorption capacity.

NVA Growth being the highest for EGS at 18.1 per cent, followed by Textile Products (IN26) at 17.2 per cent, Food (IN21) at 12.6 per cent and Textiles (IN25) at 10.1 per cent indicated priority to non-durable consumption. Employment growth rates revealed lower magnitudes in most industries except Food (IN21) due to low Labour Intensive-ness in large, medium and small industries. NW/FACT was the lowest in Textile Products (IN26). FC growth rate was the highest in EGS (IN41) at 14.4 per cent contributing to high NVA growth rate in EGS. FC growth rate was high also in Metal and Mineral Industries that led to their high NVA and GVA growth rates. Growth rates in FC/Fact however showed low growth rates as Factory growth rates was better than FC growth rates since FC was facing shackles due to increasing prices and uncertain license–permit regime. Capital Intensity (KI2=FC/NW) growth rates were higher in Textile (IN25), followed by Basic Metals (IN33) and Chemicals (IN30), all being Intermediates, which indicate high linkages, both backward and forward, that reveals potential to act as leading industries for overall growth and development of the industries in the economy. However, Other Manufacturing Industries (IN38) had low growth of KI2 that could be due to clustering, assembly line production and further decentralisation and low Labour Intensity, if globalisation is to lead to broad based industrial growth in the country.

In analysing growth rates of GVA/FACT (O1F) and NVA/FACT (O2F), the ordering of industries are similar. In both measures, EGS (IN41) led followed by Textile Products (IN26) at 9.8 per cent and in O1F OMI (IN38) showed 9.1 per cent growth. The lowest growth rate in these measures were in Beverages (IN22), Non-Metallic Mineral Products (IN32), Wood (IN27) and Textiles (IN25). But growth rates in factories being higher and O2F and O1F being lower reveals fragmentation of industries like Beverages (IN22), Textiles (IN25), Wood (IN27) in the long term and even if dispersed, commensurate outputs would be low. Thus there is need for strengthening surveillance mechanism and follow-up of credit delivery off-take by FIs to these industries.

Growth Rate in Fixed Capital (FC) was the highest in Electricity, Gas and Steam (IN41) that is also inferred to be the cause of recording highest NVA growth rate in EGS (IN41). But Intermediates showed low FC growth rate and bolstering FC in these with proper Regional Input Output Planning can alter the overall investment climate.

The highest growth in Capital Intensity was shown in Textiles (IN25) and Capital productivity Growth Rate in Textile Products (IN26) influenced positively its NVA and GVA growth rates. Higher Labour Productivity growth rates in many industries (OMI recorded the highest) contributed to work force growth and in turn to labour intensity, hinting at scale operation leading to both factor intensification and factor productivities and that in turn to NVA and GVA growth. All these results envisaged greater role for Total Factor Productivity (TFP).

Partial Productivity measures of Capital like K1P (GVA/FC) and K2P (NVA/FC) gave similar results in respect of growth rate and ordering of industries, though differing marginally. In case of all industries, Capital Productivity influenced positively its NVA and GVA growth rates. This finding signifies role of FC, K-productivity, Capital Intensity, in all registered large, medium and small-scale industries. However, increasing the scale of operation might influence positively each other's capital intensity, Labour productivity and capital productivity.

The analysis of TFP was undertaken in the framework of Hicksian neutral technological progress. Neutrality implies neither of the Factors' Partial Productivities have influence to raise technical progress to indicate that no single factor of production is responsible to cause Technical Progress (TP). Hence, the measure of Total Factor Productivity (TFP) is a residual over and above those factors' contribution to NVA or GVA Growth or TFP as a ratio measure of TFP to be more than unity. Whether capital intensity (K/L) is reflected in higher growth of output and employment or Partial Productivities of Labour and Capital or TFPG in individual industries caused for higher growth was discussed.

Analysis of Total Factor Productivity of individual industries by Kendrick, Domar and Solow showed that Wood (IN27) Industry had Maximum TFP due to Kendrick ratio and Domar Residual methods. The lowest TFP was noticed in Chemicals (IN30) and Textiles (IN25). Chemicals was a sunrise industry in 1970s and 1980s to which further Technical Progress and Capital were needed to be injected to take advantage of it. Textiles also needed further injection of capital, modernisation, upgradation to the latest technologies to get a boost in efficiency. This being a Labour Intensive industry showed capital intensity growth rate sharply.

In Solow, Labour intensive industries like Paper (IN28), Beverages (IN22), Food (IN21) showed little TFP growth, with low index. TFP growth in Wood (IN27) was high.

TFPG was the maximum in Wood Industry (IN27) and with Chemicals (IN30), Textiles (IN25) and Basic Metals (IN33) also showing higher growth rates, meant Smaller States can grow faster.

Ranking revealed that Food and EGS ranked high in Factories and NW growth rates. Textiles showed remarkable consistency in both Labour Productivity and Employment growth rates. Leather and Beverage, though Labour Intensive, had high FC growth rate that contributed to high output growth.

Food (IN21) topped with respect to Factories' growth rate vis-a-vis All India Industries but 12th in ranking with respect to FC growth rate and 14th in NVA and GVA growth rates. EGS (IN41) tops in FC, NVA and GVA growth rates but 13th in Factories' and 12th in Employment growth rates.

The lower ranks in some Intermediates and Consumer Goods Industries than All India growth rates were due to Low factor productivities and Low TFPG. There is need for both Capital, skilled and unskilled Labour intensification in all industries of all states and UT to minimise unemployment, underemployment and regional disparities in industrial development and growth.

The highest TFPG due to K/L was in Wood (IN27), Beverages (IN22) and Textile Products (IN26). Lower influence of K/L on TFPG was found in Basic Metals (IN33), EGS (IN41), Transport (IN37), Paper (IN28) and Electrical and Non-Electrical Machinery other than Transport (IN36) which were contrary to the usual notion that higher K/L causally influences higher TFPG in Capital Intensive Industry. OMI (IN38) showed higher influences of K/L growth on TFPG than in many Capital Goods and Intermediate Goods Industries.

EGS showed maximum influence of TFPG on NVA growth followed by Textiles (IN25), Machinery other than Transport (IN36), Basic Metals (IN33) and Rubber, Petroleum and Coal (IN31). However, lower influences of TFPG on NVA were found in Textile Products (IN26), Wood (IN27) and Leather (IN29). Influence of TFPG on GVA was similar, though highest influence was in Metal Products (IN34), a Capital Intensive Intermediate, followed by Beverage, OMI and Leather.

Employment Growth showed the highest influence of TFPG as noted in Metal Products (IN34), followed by Machinery other than Transport (IN36) and Beverages (IN22). Employment growth in Basic Metals (IN33), Textiles (IN25), Paper (IN28) showed inperviousness to TFPG growth. However, TFPG influence to raise employment growth is imperative to employment growth both in Capital intensive and Labour-intensive Industries.

Influence of K-Productivity on output measures show higher influence in Beverages, Food, Leather and Paper. NmMP and RPC also show same influence of Capital Productivity on either GVA or in NVA. On Employment growth, K-productivity is strongest in Leather, followed by Beverages, RPC and Food. These results show the need to have policy to increase Capital Productivity in L-productivity industries. Lower influences in EGS (IN41) and Transport (IN37) show that probably K/L and/ or TFPG in these K-Intensive Industries needs to be increased, L-Productivity influence on NVA in them being already higher.

Regression of Labour Productivity on output measures, especially on NVA show higher influence in Textile Products (IN26), Beverages (IN22) and OMI (IN38). Lowest influence is seen in Chemicals (IN30). L-productivity influence on GVA was higher in OMI (IN38), EGS (IN41) and Transport (IN37), all Capital Intensive Industries. Labour productivity influence was least in Food (IN21) whose SSIs do not employ highly skilled Labour as productivity is not a major concern for units selling in the local market. Rubber, Petroleum and Coal (IN31) showed the least influence. Similarly, influence of Labour productivity on employment growth, show maximum influence in Textile Products (IN26), Rubber, Petroleum and Coal (IN31) and Textile Products (IN26) but lowest in Textiles (IN25). Though Labour productivity growth was the highest in Textiles (IN25) both in L1P and L2P, it did not influence Employment growth. In Rubber Petroleum and Coal (IN31) while Labour Productivity showed low influence on output growth, its contribution to employment growth was high.

Analysing Returns to scale, the maximum returns is noticed in Textiles (IN25) followed by Chemicals (IN30), Non-Mineral Mineral Products (IN32) and Electrical and Non Electrical Machinery other than Transport (IN36).

Temporal Shifts is noticed in Textiles (IN25) and recession did not dampen scale economies. In 1966-75, most industries showed IRS but Transport showed CRS. But in last decade, all industries showed CRS except Beverages (IRS).

Some Industries show perennially low returns such as Basic Metals and Alloys (IN33), Rubber Petroleum and Coal (IN31), Beverages (IN22) and OMI (IN38). While onslaught of economic reforms left Basic Metals, an Intermediate high and dry, OMI needs special attention as it is capable of quick decentralisation and act as catalyst for raising Capital Intensiveness and machine efficiency in many Capital Goods and Consumption goods Industries. OMI is amenable to SSI production and requires medium scale investment needs where Commercial Banks can play a large role as lender to potentially efficient entrepreneurs. The problems facing this industry is fragmentation of the market, low awareness of demand potential, design marketing and lack of liaisoning with international producers in East Asia. It can quickly reach out to rural areas and create demand there.

A Causal Analysis showed highest TFPG due to K/L was in Beverages, but lowest in Basic Metals, contrary to common understanding. Influence of TFPG on NVA showed maximum influence in EGS (IN41), followed by Textiles (IN25) and Machinery other than Transport (IN36). On GVA growth, maximum influence of TFPG was in Metal Products (IN34), followed by Beverages (IN22) and OMI (IN38). Similarly, TFP influence on Employment growth rate showed maximum effect on Metal Products (IN34), followed by Machinery other than Transport (IN36) and Beverages (IN22). Thus TFPG influence was seen in both Labour Intensive and Capital Intensive Industries. Lowest TFPG influence in Output (GVA) and employment growth rates was noticed in Wood (IN27).

Influence of Capital Productivity on GVA was the highest in NmMP (IN32), followed by Paper (IN28), Beverages (IN22) and Leather (IN29). Influence of Capital Productivity on NVA was the maximum in Beverages (IN22), followed by Leather and RPC (IN31). Influence of Capital Productivity on employment was highest n Leather (IN29), followed by Beverages (IN22) and RPC (IN31). So improvement in Capital Productivity may be the key to raising the Labour Intensive-ness of Industries.

Labor Productivity is high in generally those industries were Capital Productivity was low. But highest Labour Productivity influence on NVA was in Transport Equipment (IN37) followed by RPC (IN31). Highest Labour productivity influence on GVA growth was in OMI (IN38) followed by Transport Equipment (IN37) and then by EGS (IN41). On Employment, highest influence of Labour Productivity was in Leather (IN29), though Textile Products (IN26) and RPC (IN31) also ranked higher, though it recorded lower figures.

Thus despite high growth in Units, to reap scale economies, a proper agricultural environment and high expectations need to be maintained and nurtured which slackened during the decade of New Economic reforms period. Transport is another industry that showed inconsistent scale economies largely due to inadequate planning. Also, higher growth rate in units does not necessarily bring about scale economies. To improve scale economies, an enabling environment, innovative marketing techniques, development of support infrastructure are necessary. These are conspicuous by their absence in a developing economy due to inadequacy of resources for balanced development of industries and of regions/states/districts; rural vs urban diversity and forward vs backward states/regions. Hence, the following Chapters address to regional dispersal of industries, measures and causal factors for regional dispersal vs. growth, TFPG, Capital Intensity, Factor Productivities, Returns to Scale of Industries, etc. Increasing returns to scale in many industries was noted independent of TFPG. This could be due to higher factor productivities, accrued in turn from output elasticities to those factors/inputs, which was again independent of factor intensities and growth rates of Industries concerned. It may be further concluded that TFPG and output growth and factor productivities caused for increasing returns to scale in many and constant returns to scale in a few.; but the converse necessarily hold good in the sense that returns to scale may remain independent of TFPG of disembodied (Neutral TP) and embodied type.

In the *next Chapter 5,* results of Dispersal Analysis of Indian Industries over Smaller Sized States, Larger Sized States and all States and Union Territories taken together was presented. Small States and UT can show how industrial progress can be size cum location specific. Large States and UT provide greater scope for large-scale highly capital intensive industries to develop. All States and UT taken together can provide a more comprehensive view of industrial dispersal irrespective of size of regions.

As regards the Small States Category, in 1959-65, Food (IN21), Textiles (IN25),Metal Products (IN34) and Transport (IN37) provided consistent and continuous data to yield results for analytic interpretation. Food (IN21) is highly dispersed. This industry, being a User-Based, Consumption Goods Industry with characteristics of non-durability of commodity, Capital Malleability, L-intensiveness and output growth being a possible outcome of low investment. All these characteristics suit Small States Category at initial stages of Industrialisation.

The later decades saw some changes and improvement. In 1966-75, Food (IN21) maintained high dispersal, though Machinery other than Transport (IN37) an Other Manufacturing Industries (IN38) did not lag behind. This was a good sign for building up bases for future industrial and economic development in smaller States and union territories that are predominantly agricultural, feudalistic social structure and lesser accessibility to capital. However, other User-Based Industries did not do well and recession further reduced incentives for expansion and dispersal.

The decade 1976-85 saw Food (IN21) still maintaining high dispersal trend. But other L-intensive and Capital Goods industries also showed dispersal like Leather (IN29) and EGS (IN41). Capital Goods and Intermediate Industries like Transport (IN37), Rubber, Petroleum and Coal (IN31) and Basic Metals and Alloys (IN33) also showed dispersal. So Indian Economy and Industries were showing signs of maturing after having withstood recession, inflation, war, etc. But lack of forward and backward linkage planning could not provide sound infrastructure base as revealed by relative lower dispersal in Transport (IN37), that was a cause of lower growth in 1980s, 1990s and 2000s.

The last decade of our analysis 1986-95 saw user based and Intermediate Industries like Textile Products (IN26) showing high dispersal. This was a sign of great vitality for Indian Industry and Economy. Indian Industry not only showed sense of great cost effectiveness as Labour was relatively cheaper, this industry showed high market sense being aware of the need to be location specific, nearer to areas of market demand. EGS (IN41) did well showing relevance of proposal for greater decentralisation of power reforms. But Industries showing mean values nearer to lowest CV and HH values imply that goal of balanced regional development is till distant.

In case of Large States and UT category, data availability in the initial years was a distinct advantage over Smaller States and UT and it also showed the viability of larger regions to provide supportive infrastructure for industries to flourish.

The first decade 1959-65 saw Wood (IN27), Metal Products (IN34), Transport (IN37) showing higher dispersal. This is different from results in case of Smaller States where apart from the less number of industries, Food (IN21) being a User Based Industry showed maximum dispersal. Thus Large States Category has more economic space to develop for Intermediate Goods Industries to develop to provide a basis for deeper linkage and more integrated planning for more balanced industrial and economic development than small regions.

The next decade 1966-75, despite being recession stricken, showed dispersal in more User Based and Intermediate Industries, a feature that got manifested in 1976-85 in case of Smaller States and UT category. But capital Intensive Industries like Other Manufacturing Industry (IN38), EGS (IN41), Chemicals (IN31), Rubber Petroleum and Coal (IN31), Non- Metallic Mineral Products (IN32) showed mean dispersal values nearer to lowest values. Thus Capital Intensive Goods Industries did not disperse well in the recession hit second decade.

In the third decade of 1976-85, Capital Intensive Industries renewed well to disperse more. Yet while Textiles (IN25) dispersed well, Textile Products (IN26) got concentrated. This revealed how lack of proper Input Output sector specific planning can retard the goal of Balanced Regional Development.

The last decade of 1986-95 showed industries getting dispersed in some variable and not in others. This phase of experimentation showed that planning was not in tune with market sentiments. For Example in Metal Products (IN34) employment (NW) showed mean values nearer highest values but in other dispersal variables of this industry, mean value was nearer the lowest value. So while entrepreneurial initiative went on to create more employment dispersal, PK, NVA, Units showed concentration. This was a policy lacunae as PK injection could have brought about more growth and helped this Intermediate Industry to develop as a 'leading' Industry in the liberalised, globalised era.

In the third category, All States and UT are taken together and dispersal results found out for both the long term of 40 years and 4 decadal periods of 1959-65, 1966-75, 1976-85 and 1986-95.

In the long-term 40-year period, in Food (IN21), dispersal in Productive capital was high but not so in other variables. This showed that though capital injection has been forthcoming, much of it was eaten away by conspicuous consumption. This backwardness of agriculture and high population growth may have the other causes of lower than expected dispersal of employment, units, NVA, K/L in this Industry.

In Beverages (IN22) though employment dispersal was high, it pointed to disguised employment. In Intermediates and Capital Goods Industry showed relatively less dispersal in long term when All States and UT were taken together. In Paper (IN28) employment was concentrated but other variables showed dispersal. Industries that needed big push are Non Metallic Mineral Products (IN32), EGS (IN41), Basic Metals and Alloys (IN33), Paper (IN28), Machinery other than Transport (IN36) and OMI (IN38) for decentralisation.

In the Period Wise analysis, the first decade of 1959-65 recorded highest dispersal in Beverages (IN22), Leather (IN29), Chemicals (IN31) and Basic Metals and Alloys (IN33). NVA in Metal Products (IN34) was more concentrated. So also in Transport (IN37) where all dispersal values were nearer the mean values. In the second decade of 1966-75, Beverages (IN22), Leather (IN29), OMI (IN38) showed high dispersal. In the third decade in 1976-85, EGS (IN41), Beverages (IN22) along with Chemicals (IN30) and RPC (IN31) showed higher dispersal. In the fourth decade of 1986-95,Leather (IN29) EGS (IN41) showed higher dispersal. But employment dispersal in Food (IN21) in this decade of liberalisation measures showed lowest dispersal. Wood (IN27) revealed high concentration. K/L measure of dispersal revealed concentration in most industries. Thus liberalisation is less oriented towards rural areas, consumption User Based Industries and less capital injection through planning mechanism is taking place. Low K/L dispersal is seen in Machinery other than Transport (IN36), Metal Products (IN34) and Transport (IN37).

Conclusion and Policy Inferences—Period Wise

1959-65

Metal Products (IN34) showed more relative concentration in case of Small States Group and All States in India. But this industry did disperse well in 1986-95.

1966-75

In both large states and small states separately in each group, capital intensive industries did not show dispersal. But in case of All States and UT being taken together, Except for three Industry groups, viz; Electricity Gas and Steam (IN41), Basic Metals and Alloys (IN33) and Machinery other than Transport (IN36), most other Capital Intensive industries like Chemicals (IN30), Transport Equipment (IN37), Rubber-Petroleum-Coal (IN31), Other Manufacturing Industries (IN38) showed mean values nearer to the lowest dispersal values.

While Leather, Paper, Wood, Beverages showed high dispersal, Textile, Textile Products, Food showed mean dispersal values nearer to lowest values of the variables.

1976-85

Transport (IN37), Textile Products (IN26) in both Small and Large States and Chemicals (IN30) in Small States showed less dispersal. Textiles showed greater dispersal in both Small States and Large States but Textiles Products showed less dispersal.

1986-95

Metal Products (IN34) showed regional dispersal in All States and Union Territories (UT).

Smaller States and UT failed in many fronts except in Textile Products, Machinery other than Transport and Transport Equipment where high dispersal is noted. But in Large States, NVA in Beverages (IN22), but Non Metallic Mineral Products (IN32) and CV of OMI (IN38) showed more concentration. In All States, Food, Wood emp, showed less dispersal. Food employment may be temporary once a long term planning of this industry comes into operation. But K/L dispersal being low in capital goods industry like Electrical and Non electrical machinery (IN36) and Transport (IN37) show employment dispersal in these industries as not spreading out.

INDUSTRY SPECIFIC POLICY RECOMMENDATION

In the recent two decades of policy initiatives of increasing trade, macro economic stabilisation and industrial liberalisation, Food and Wood are the two are exceptions being directly land based.

In All States and long term 40-year case, Beverages Industry showed higher dispersal in employment but less so in the other four variables. Improvement of labour productivity and greater marketing innovation need to be devised to help in Beverages Industry dispersal.

For the 40 years All States and Union Territories, Wood (IN27), Paper (IN28), Non-Metallic Mineral Products (IN32), Basic Metals and Alloys (IN33), Machinery other than Transport, Electricity, Gas and Steam (IN41) having mean values of variables and Structural ratios nearer the lowest values, implied that these industries were relatively less dispersed over the long term.

So policy directions should enable capital goods and intermediates industries to be more decentralised/ regionally dispersed. Intermediate goods Industries must be dispersed after a careful study of linkages, both backward and forward, and institutional set up and behaviour of the Indian economy. Paper and Wood Industries, being L intensive industries, have greater potential for employment absorption. Employment planning in these industries should be based on regional resource linkages.

Wood (IN27) also did well in Small States category in the first and third decades but showed more concentration in second 'recession' decade. But Wood (IN27) showed more concentration in each of the five variables in the All States-40year long- term category and in 1986-95 period in All States Category. This Intermediate provides inputs to Paper, Ship-Building, Housing, Transport (Trucks' body), Sports Goods, etc. and so market demand surveys, developing marketing channels for its products, intensive agroforestry programmes, reduction of illegal felling of trees with a greater role for decentralised political authority, etc. will help make this industry getting more dispersed and raising its value addition potential and make greater contribution to national income.

Food Products (IN21), a key industry linking agriculture and industry, showed less dispersal in most variables (except PK in 1959-95 in All States category) in the long term. This was supported by Food Industry (IN21) getting concentrated in 1959-95 for Large States Category. More regional Planning in an Input-Output Frame outlining its Intermediate Input Coefficient for regional skill based Industries will cause for greater dispersal in Food Industry.

Non-Metallic Mineral Products, EGS, Basic Metals and Alloys, Machinery other than Transport, being the industries that showed more relative concentration over long term in All States and UT Category implied that Greater Regional Planning in these in an Input-Output frame will bring out their growth potential that will cause for dispersal. EGS can revitalise and enhance power availability and provide much needed lateral boost to industrialisation, Machinery other than Transport (IN36) must be made amenable to decentralisation, this being a key capital goods industry. Probably greater R&D will enable MotTr (IN36) industry to be more dispersed over the regions in the future.

The *next Chapter 6* saw a diagrammatic representation of results of dispersal of all variables of each of the industries over the long term of 40 years period. Long-term analysis has the advantage of revealing the nature and perspectival background of industrial dispersal in India. Long term trends subsume short term ones.

Food (IN21) showed spurt in public Investment in 1974 and mid 60s recession affected this industry's dispersal of NVA. Low dispersal since 1977 was the real cause of poverty and high food prices in 1980s and later. But the year 1994 saw spurt in PK dispersal due to liberalisation and capital flows.

Beverages (IN22) did not expand due to political and economic vicissitudes. But PK dispersal increased during recession of 1965-66. However, employment showed consistent dispersal even though the pre-1963 rise could not be sustained since this is a Labour-intensive industry and requires constant nurturing. But K/L got progressively concentrated implying any further boost to growth could come from higher K injection or increase in Labour productivity, capital productivity and TFP.

Textiles (IN25) showed progressive concentration due to lack of adequate government efforts to disperse this industry. This is reinforced by lack of employment dispersal along with PK concentration. But CV NVA stability around 2 may be due to innate resilience of this industry to do well despite opposition. So strong policy recommendation top boost employment and NVA in this crucial Labour intensive industry is needed.

Textile Products (IN26) showed high dispersal in Units, PK, employment. But Textiles (IN25) was concentrated showing lack of input-output planing region specific demand surveys in this industry. Perhaps lack of planning for technological obsolescence and innovation was cause of disorientation in output trends.

Wood (IN27) showed concentration. But PK dispersal was higher showing much optimism for growth in Wood Industry as this is a User and Intermediate Industry for infrastructure sector. But employment in this industry got concentrated and this was a cause for concern though NVA was dispersing. K/L is low, revealing high corruption and high unaccounted for commission culture.

Paper (IN28) showed long term concentration in all its variables and structural ratios. But being a Labour-intensive industry, great potential exists for growth. Leather (IN29) is more dispersed but there is scope for further employment dispersal along with need for greater capital infusion.

Chemicals (IN30) is more concentrated and needs more of institutional cum technological decentralisation along with big push for this potentially leading industry due to scope for expansion in pharmaceuticals, fertilisers, etc.

RPC (IN31) is more concentrated though dispersal in NVA is high. NmMP (IN32) is concentrated but needs employment planning and more capital infusion. In Basic Metals (IN33) liberalisation overlooked the industry's potential. Metal Products (IN34), Machinery other than transport (IN36), Transport (IN37) are concentrated in long run.

In OMI (IN38) NVA is dispersed but other variables show concentration. Same results in EGS (IN41).

Finally, whether industrial growth leads to Perpetuation or Williamson and in which periods and in which industries therein, is brought out tentatively. Perpetuation is one where industrial growth leads to concentration in those periods, but later dispersal. Here growth leads to concentration and does not imply causation or growth causing dispersal. Williamson hypothesis implies initial growth with disparity but later concentration.

Thus study of long run dispersal of Indian Industries justified Perpetuation Hypothesis in case of inputs dispersal/concentration and since there is more concentration in Intermediate and Capital Goods Industries. This seemed inevitable because Indian economy is a capital scarce economy and K-allocation followed Heavy Industry model. But regional disparities manifested in 1970s, efforts to tackle this meant capital investment had to suffer.

Thus, while Consumer and User and Intermediates show greater dispersal, Capital Goods and Capital goods Intermediate are more concentrated in long term Indian Industrialisation.

Beverages, Leather, Metal Products and EGS in each of the respective Groups show a contrary trend vis a vis trends in variables and structural ratios of their respective groups.

More clear-cut policy formulations await Chemicals, Electrical and Non electrical Machinery, Textile Products for each of these to act as leading sectors of growth.

Williamson hypothesis of Growth leading to concnetration in long-run is proved in Food Products (IN21), Textiles (IN25), Metal Products (IN34).

Wood (IN27), Textile Products (IN26), Transport Equipment (IN37) and Electrical and electronic machinery (IN36) prove Self-Perpetuation hypothesis. However, concentration comes about due to low growth and industry-specific and region specific policy packages to boost their key factor use to raise efficiency will help in greater dispersal of Indian Industry.

In *Chapter 7*, the effect of various factors like TFP by Solow, K/L, K-productivity, L- productivity on each of the measures of dispersal, HH and CV, for each of the industries was studies and results inferred. Grossack's $(b/r)^2$ was computed to cross check influence of explanatory variables on each of the regional dispersal measures for each of the 2-digit industries.

Regression of TFP on regional dispersal measures of NVA for the short decadal period of 1959-65 yielded results that showed Textile Products (IN26), Textiles (IN25), Non-Metallic Mineral Products (IN32) bearing higher influence of TFP on NVA dipersal. When TFP was regressed on each of measures of regional dispersal of employment (HHNW and CVNW), greater influence was recorded in Textiles (IN25), Textile Products (IN26), Basic Metals and Alloys (IN33), Beverages (IN22), Rubber, Petroleum and Coal (IN31). But Food (IN21), OMI (IN38) and EGS (IN41), in this first decade, did not show TFP influence on employment dispersal. When K/L was regressed on employment (NW), Textiles (IN25), OMI (IN38) etc. showed larger influence of K/L on employment dispersal. But Leather (IN29) showed low K/L influence on Employment dispersal. Higher K/L influence was seen in Textiles (IN25), NmMP (IN32) and Metal Products (IN34). This is a useful result that showed K/L influences Intermediate Industries more to bring about dispersal. When K-productivity was regressed on employment measures of dispersal, its influence was seen to be high in Textiles (IN25), Chemicals (IN30), Beverages (IN22) and Paper (IN28).

Labour Productivity was regressed on employment dispersal measure (HHNW and CVNW), it showed high influence on Paper (IN28), NmMP (IN32), Machinery other than Transport (IN36), EGS (IN41). It showed weak influence on Wood (IN27) and RPC (IN30). But when L-productivity was regressed on NVA dispersal, higher influence was noticed in NmMP (IN32), RPC (IN30), Textiles (IN25), OMI (IN38) and Metal Products (IN34).

In 1966-75, TFP regressed on NVA dispersal measures showed higher influence in Textiles (IN25), EGS (IN41), RPC (IN31) and Chemicals (IN30) dispersal. TFP influence on employment dispersal was maximum in Food (IN21), Textiles (IN25), Chemicals (IN30), RPC (IN31) and EGS (IN41). When K/L was regressed on NVA in this recession period, higher influence was seen in Food (IN21), Textile Products (IN26), Beverages (IN22), Metal Products (IN34) and Basic Metals and Alloys (IN33). When K/L was regressed on employment, higher K/L influence was seen in Textiles (IN25), Machinery other than Transport (IN36) and EGS (IN41).

In 1966-75, the decadal period of recession, Non-metallic Mineral Products (IN32), Basic Metals and Alloys (IN33), Metal Prodcuts (IN34) and Machinery other than Transport (IN36) showed higher $(b/r)^2$ implying that in Capital Goods Industry and Intermediates with higher capital intensiveness, recession was a cause for low TFPG influence and not so high Employment Dispersal. Food was more concentrated and so high K/L influence could not bring about NVA dispersal in Food Industry. Thus recession affected not only the machine goods indsutry but also the main agro-industry in India. K/L growth did not influence NVA dispersal in Textiles (IN25) and Machinery other than Transport (IN36) but it did influecne employment dispersal in these indsutries despite recession. NVA of Intermedaites like Leather (IN29), Chemicals (IN30) and Rubber (IN31) dispersed due to Capital Productivity influence. While $(b/r)^2$ was relatively high, influence of Labour Productivity in this period of 1966-75, did not bring about disperal in Food Industry. Similarly, $(b/r)^2$ in Hhemp is relatively high in RPC (IN31) and despite low influence of Labour Prodcutivity on employment dispersal in terms of b^, L-productivity should be increased, as dispersal is due to influence of L-productivity, as revealed by high b/r.

When K-productivity was regressed on NVA, higher influence was seen in RPC, Leather, Beverages. Its influence on Employment dispersal was higher in RPC (IN31), Leather (IN29), EGS (IN41) and larger size could retain its share of employment. When L-productivity was regressed on NVA, high influence industries were EGS, Wood. L- productivity influence on employment saw high influence on Food and EGS. So influence of partial productivity of factors was high in User Based industries. EGS showing high influence of partial productivity of factor on growth variables showed this industry despite being K-intensive still showed characteristics of clay as much as putty and therefore amenable to greater decentralisation. But as seen above, K/L influence on growth variables in EGS remains negligible.

In 1976-85, TFP influence on NVA dispersal was higher in Beverages (IN22), RPC (IN31), BM &A (IN33) and large regions retaining their hold. Similar dispersal occurred in employment in RPC (IN31), MotTr (IN36), Chemicals (IN30) and Textile Products (IN26). K/L showed higher influence on NVA dispersal in RPC (IN31), Food (IN21), Metal Products (IN34), Paper (IN28) Wood (IN27) and BM & A (IN33) but dispersal occurred. Influence of K/L on employment dispersal was higher in Textiles (IN25), Leather (IN29), Food (IN21), EGS (IN41) and BM & A (IN33). But least influence of K/L on NVA was in EGS (IN41).

K-Productivity's influence on NVA is higher in OMI (IN38), RPC (IN31), BM &A (IN33) and Textile Products (IN26) showed concentration. Transport (IN37) showed least influence but showed the way to infrastructure development. On Employment dispersal, K-productivity showed high influence on Employment (NW) dispersal measures in Food (IN21), EGS (IN41), Paper (IN28) though Paper (IN28) showed more concentration in this period. Food (IN21) and Paper (IN28) benefitted irrespective of regions. High influence of L-productivity on Employment (NW) dispersal noticed in Leather (IN29), and EGS (IN41).

In the final decade of our analysis i.e. in 1986-95, TFP showed higher influence on NVA dispersal of Metal Products (IN34), Transport (IN37), EGS (IN41) and Non Metallic Mineral Products (IN32) retaining their spread of NVA. TFP influence on Employment dispersal was higher in Non Metallic Mineral Products (IN33), Mot Tr (IN36), Food (IN21) and Leather (IN29). K/L influence on NVA dispersal in NmMP was high. Similar was the case in OMI (IN38) and RPC (IN31). Higher influence of K/L on employment was also seen in NmMP (IN32) and also in Food, Beverages, Wood and Textile Products (IN26). Wood showed concentration.

K-Productivity showed higher influences on NVA dispersal in EGS (IN41), OMI (IN38), Leather (IN29) and Chemicals (IN30). It was also encouraging that Leather (IN29), a L-intensive industry showed higher Capital Productivity influence on dispersal of output growth in this period of liberalisation. K-Productivity's Influence on Employment was higher in EGS (IN41), Chemicals (IN30) and Transport (IN37).

L-Productivity's influence on dispersal of NVA is higher in EGS, MotTR, Chemical (IN30) and RPC (IN31). L-Productivity influence on employment was higher in EGS (IN41), Wood (IN27), BM&A (IN33), Transport (IN37). High influence on EGS showed feasibility of decentralised power reforms. But high $(b/r)^2$ could not bring about much NVA dispersal in this last decade of analysis in Basci Metals and Alloys (IN33).

In the long-term period of 40 years, TFP influence on employment dispersal and NVA dispersal was higher in NmMP, Metal Products, Textiles (IN25) and Leather (IN29), though mean values were nearer the lowest values in IN32 and IN34, though relatively, across industries, IN32 and IN34 gained better dispersal. Thus relatively, Intermediates did well but its values being nearer to lower dispersal values meant cause of lower dispersal is to be found in its growth and productivity figures as well as in lower influence in L-productivity, K-productivity, K/L, TFP on disperal measures. K/L influence is higher in Food (IN21), Leather (IN29), NmmP (IN32), BM &A (IN33), Paper (IN28) and Textile Products (IN26).

In Chemicals (IN30), smaller regions benefitted. K/L influence on employment dispersal was high on EGS (IN41), OMI (IN38), Leather (IN29), NmMP (IN32).

Capital Productivity influenced dispersal of NVA in Leather (IN29), EGS (IN41), OMI (IN38) and Beverages (IN22). Labour Productivity influence on NVA was higher in Leather (IN29), EGS (IN41), OMI (IN38) and Beverages (IN22).

Food, Wood, Paper, Textile Products and EGS need greater attention for more balanced regional dispersal of Indian Industries and economic growth. EGS showing great amenability to L-productivity influence, despite being a K-intensive industry and the rest being more L-intensive, it augurs well for Indian Industry and Economy if labor gets more disciplined, there is less of labour turnover and greater political trust along with incentives like productivity linked wage reforms and higher R&D output and productivity with highly dispersed institutional cum technological development.

Policy recommendations will be that if K/L or PK or FC importance is more and more in decades or long term, then more skill will be needed. So investment and focus must be towards more investment in R&D in industries, education, knowledge economy must be quickly brought to focus, with Electronics, software, hardware ICT and its spread to rural areas. Primary education especially in rural areas or for people below certain income level rather than reservations, must be an essential component of policy orientation change and implementation.

Wood (IN27) comes out as an industry needing attention at least for purposes of employment planning and to boost employment in this wood industry. This will boost rural entrepreneurship and rural employment and being L-intensive and can be used massively for poverty alleviation programme. Adequate marketing can boost tourism in service, housing and improve infrastructure and provide a base for industrial growth and trade.

In 1966-75, the decadal period of recession, Non-Metallic Mineral Products (IN32), Basic Metals and Alloys (IN33), Metal Products (IN34), Machinery other than Transport (IN36) showed $(b/r)^2$ higher implying even in capital goods industry and intermediates with higher capital intensiveness, recession was a cause for low TFPG influence and not so high Employment dispersal. Food was more concentrated and so high K/L influence could not bring about NVA dispersal of Food Industry. Thus recession not only affected the machine oriented goods industry, it also affected the main agro-industry in India too. K/L growth did not influence NVA dispersal in Textiles (IN25) and Machinery other than Transport (IN36) but it did influence employment dispersal in these industries despite recession. NVA of Intermediates like Leather (IN29) Chemicals (IN30) and Rubber (IN31) dispersed due to capital productivity influence. While $(b/r)^2$ is relatively high, influence of Labour productivity in this period of 1966-75, did not bring about dispersal in Food Industry, a point that reinforces the inference presented in this paragraph before. Similarly, $(b/r)^2$ in HH is relatively high in Rubber-petroleum and Coal (IN31) and despite low influence of Labour productivity on employment dispersal in terms of b^, policy recommendation is in terms of raising Labour Productivity, as dispersal is due to influence of Labour productivity. Labour productivity influence did not bring about employment dispersal in this Food (IN21), a fact that can be again attributed to recession.

Textile Products (26), Chemicals (IN30), Rubber-Petroleum-Coal (IN31) and Machinery other than Transport (IN36) with high b/r did not bring about high employment dispersal in this period of 1976-85.

In Rubber, Chemicals and Basic Metals, that are traditional highly capital intensive did show higher dispersal in this period of 1976-85 but it was again not due to influence of K/L.

In 1986-95, Food Industry still showed concentration. Dispersal being higher in Chemicals, high $(b/r)^2$ showed influence of Labour Productivity on NVA dispersal in this decade. In Basic Metals, high *b/r* could not bring about much NVA dispersal in this decade. Thus Intermediates have not shown dispersal despite its potential. Leather showed dispersal in last decade both in NVA and in employment due to influence of capital productivity.

The long run analysis of 40years from 1956-95 revealed certain interesting results. High NVA dispersal and high $(b/r)^2$ in Chemicals (IN30) means that low TFPG influence as revealed in b^, itself is a factor for dispersal in this industry. Chemicals Industry (IN30) to sustain itself as a leading industry for balanced industrial development will have to find ways to improve its TFPG.

Basic Metals and Alloys (IN33) and Metal products (IN34), both being capital intensive Intermediates showed high TFPG influencing dispersal, while NmMP (IN32) being of similar nature as IN33 and IN34 showed concentration or non-dispersal with little TFPG influence on employment dispersal. Thus employment dispersal in these intermediates having shown themselves amenable to higher TFPG, it is necessary that a more detailed input-output planning exercises involving Intermediates is called for. The Economic Reforms of 1990s has not taken Intermediates Planning into account that would have a factor for regional equity and growth in Indian economy.

The Salient Points to Conclude

In Chapter 4, an Analysis of Returns to Scale over a long period of 40years, saw Increasing Returns to scale (IRS) in many industries like IN25, IN21, IN27, IN28, IN30, IN32, IN34, IN36, IN37. But scale economies did not necessarily reflect growth in NVA, GVA or Employment. Scale Economies does get reflected in Factories Growth Rate and therefore are a cause of entry and exit of firms to industry. Factories showed higher dispersal in IKI group of Industries in Chapter 6, but less dispersal in other variables.

Wood (IN27) showed highest TFP in Domar and also showed higher Capital Productivity in both K1P and K2P (measures of capital productivity) and yet remained problematic with low GVA, NVA, Emp, FC, dispersal and in scale. Thus employment and investment and planning for regional spread of Wood (IN27) is needed.

Capital Productivity needed to be improved generally in IKI indusrties and Kgoods industries as also in Food (IN21).

In Food (IN21), Textiles (IN25) and Wood (IN27), NVA and GVA growth rates are low and to boost these industries, FC growth seems necessary.

Metal Products Industry (IN34) did well to raise its K-Productivity, but FC growth being low, capital injection needed to boost dispersal. Similar prescription is seen in Textiles Products (IN26). Factory growth rate in IN26 being low and also NW/Fact in IN26 being low, employment planning in an inter-regional framework is needed. FC boost needed in Wood (IN27) and Paper (IN28) too.

Capital Intensity is low in Wood (IN27), Beverages (IN22), Leather (IN29), RPC (IN31), Metal Products (IN34) and OMI (IN38). K/L gowth is high in Textile Products (IN26), Food (IN21), Textiles (IN25), EGS (IN41), Chemicals (IN30), NmMP(In32), Basci Metals and Alloys (IN33), Machinery other than Transport (IN36) and Transport Equipment (IN37).

Capital Intensity influenced TFP the most in Beverages (IN22), Textile Products (IN26) and Wood (IN27).

TFPG influenced NVA most in EGS (IN41), Textiles (IN25), MotTr (IN36), BM&A (IN33), Food (IN21). RPC, Metal Prodcuts and Leather, Transport showed high TFP influence on GVA. TFP influence on employment highest in IN34, IN36, IN22, IN30 and IN31.

Capital Productivity showed high influence on GVA in NmMP, Paper, Beverage, Leather, Food, Chemicals, RPC and OMI in that descending order. Kproductivity higher influence on NVA growth in IN22, IN29 and IN31. Kproductivity influence on employment higher in IN29, IN22, IN31 and IN 21.

As regards dispersal as seen in Chapter 5, in long term of 40years, 1956-95, higher dispersal was in Beverages (IN22), Textiles (IN25) and Other Manufacturing Industries (IN38) as mean values are nearer higher dispersal values.

The Capital Intensive Intermediates of Chemicals (IN30), Rubber, Petroleum and Coal (IN31), Non-Metallic Mineral Products (IN32), Basic Metal and Alloys (IN33) and Metal Products (IN34) need greater planning and integration with Capital Goods Industry, especially in OMI (IN38) and Electrical and Non Electrical Machinery other than Transport (IN36), if industrial sector is to contribute more to GDP and enable it to increase its employment absorption capacity that could lead to greater regional equity in Indian Industry and act as a major and sustainable instrument for poverty alleviation to raise standard of living of rural and urban economy.

REFERENCES

1. Pei-Kang Change—*Agriculture and Industrialization,* Cambridge, Massachusetts, Harvard University Press, 1949, pp. 19.
2. Grossack, Irvin, M—The Concept and Measurement of Permanent Industrial Concentration. *Journal of Political Economy,* Vol. 60A-1972, pp. 745-760.

Bibliography

BOOKS

Ahluwalia I.J.- Industrial Growth in India-Stagnation since the Mid-Sixties—*Oxford University Press,* Delhi-1985.

Ahluwalia Isher Judge—Productivity and Growth in Indian Manufacturing—*Oxford University Press*, Delhi-1991.

Allen, Michael Patrick- *Understanding Regression Analysis*—Plenum Press, New York-1997. Balance Robert and Sinclair Stuart—*Collapse and Survival: Industry Strategy in a Changing World*; 1983-George Allen and Unwin-UK. Ch-1, pp. 12.

Brahmananda P.R.—'*Productivity of the Indian Economy—Rising Inputs or Falling Outputs*' (1982).

Burns Tibor—'On Measuring Capital' in the Theory of Capital, ed. By Lutz FA and Hague, pp-85, London, *Macmillan* 1961.

Chizmar J K—1972—'An Econometric Examination of Organisational Change in Production Functions of Major Industries- The Indian Case' Boston College, *Ph.D. Thesis.*

Christensen L. R., Cummings, D. and Jorgenson D.W.—'Economic Growth 1947-73: An International Comparison' in Kendrick J.W and Vaccara B.(ed) '*New Developments in Productivity Measurements*', *Studies in Income and Wealth-Vol-41*—Chicago, University of Chicago Press, 1980.

Christopher Freeman and Luc Soete—"Factor Substitution and Technical Change"—Technical Change and Full Employment—1987 Edited-*Basil Blackwell*, Oxford OX4, UK, pp. 40-41. Goldar in his 'Productivity Growth in Indian Industry' (1986).

Gupta S.C. and V.K. Kapoor—*Fundamentals of Applied Statistics*—Sultan Chand and Sons, New Delhi-110002, 1995-Chapters 2 and 3.

Hanson A H—The process of Planning- *A study of Indian Five Year Plans*—1956-64.

Jones H.G.- *An Introduction to Modern Theories of Economic Growth*, Ch7 and 8-TataMcGraw Hill, pp. 133.

Kaur Kulwinder in "*Structure of Industries in India: Pattern, Framework, Disparities*" also writes that, that level of per capita income has been found to be correlated with degree of industrialisation—Deep and Deep Publications, 1983, Ch. 1, pp. 18.

Kendrick J.W.—Productivity in the USA- *NBER*, Princeton.

K L Krishna's article—'Industrial Growth and Productivity in India' in Professor Brahmananda's book '*The Development Process of the Indian Economy*'-1987.

Krishna K. L. (1992) booklet "What do we learn from productivity studies?" in his *Presidential Address to the Tenth Annual Conference to AP Economic Association in Andhra University*, Waltair, 8-9 February, 1992.

Kulwinder Kaur- *Structure of Industries in India- Pattern- Framework- Disparities* - Deep and Deep Publications, 1983- Ch-1, pp. 18.

Kuznets, S. -*Six Lectures on Economic Growth*-Free Press of Glenocoe, Inc, 1959, pp-122. Kuznets, S. -*Modern Economic Growth-Rate, Structure and Spread*, New Haven: Yale University Press, 1966, pp. 127.

Mehta, S. S., Productivity, Production Function and Technical change—A Survey of Some Indian Industries-*Concept Publishing House*, New Delhi-1980, pp. 10-20.

Jorgenson D.W.-'Econometric Methods for Modelling Producer's Behaviour' in Griliches, Z and Intriligator, M.D. (ed.)- *Handbook of Econometrics, Vol. III*-Amsterdam, North Holland. 1986.

Oulton Nicholas and O' Mahony, Mary—Productivity and Growth- A Study of British Industry-1954-86- *National Institute of Economic and Social Research*-1994.

Panchamukhi V.R- A Survey of Economic Studies in the fields of Production, International Trade, Money and Banking' in *ICSSR*, A Survey of Research in Economics, Vol VII, *Econometrics,* Allied Pub. New Delhi.

Rao C. Radhakrishna- *Linear Statistical Inference and Its Applications*—Wiley Eastern Private Limited, New Delhi-1974, p. 263-290

Rao C.R.- *Essays on Econometrics and Planning*- edited-Oxford, Pergamon Press.

Smith A.D., Hitchens D.M.W.N. and Davies S.W- International Industrial Productivity: A *Comparison of Britain, America and Germany, Cambridge*, Cambridge University Press-1982.

Somayajulu, V V N. – Industrial Development of Andhra Pradesh-1956-82-University of Hyderabad-*ICSSR Report*-1987.

Spiegel R. Murray- *Schaum's Outline of Theory and Problems of Statistics*—2nd edition in S.I. units- McGraw Hill Book Company-1992 Metric edition.

Surekha- Strategies of Industrialisation: Small Scale and Large Scale Industrial Development in Andhra Pradesh- An Econometric Analysis-University of Hyderabad- *Unpublished M.Phil dissertation*-1993.

Wallis Kenneth- *Topics in Applied Econometrics*-Second Edition- Basil Blackwell-Oxford-1979-Chapter-2.

Wolff E.N. and Dollar D- Capital Intensity and TFP Convergence in Manufacturing-1963-1985 in Baumol WJ, Nelson W.W. and Wolff E.N ed- *Convergence to Productivity-Cross National Studies and Historical Evidence*-New York, Oxford University Press, 1994.

Mahajan O.P.—*Regional Economic Development in India-1950-66*, Ph. D. Dissertation, Kurukhetra University, 1972.

Mehta S.S. - '*Productivity, Production Function and Technical Change*—A Survey of Some Indian Industries'-1974.

Leontief—Estimates of capital stock of American Industries, 1947, Cambridge, mass. 1953.

Harvard Economic Research Project, pp. 21-22.

Panchamukhi V.R- A Survey of Economic Studies in the fields of Production, International Trade, Money and Banking' in *ICSSR*, A Survey of Research in Economics, Vol VII, *Econometrics,* Allied Pub. New Delhi.

Pathak C. R., "Regional Disparities in Industrial Development in India" Chapter-6, pp-113-124; in the book *"Economic Liberalisation and Regional Disparities in India-Special Focus on the North-Eastern region"* edited by A. C. Mohapatro and C.R. Pathak, Star Publishing House, Shillong, 2003.

Sandeep Kumar's published Ph.D. work on 'Regional Disparities in Industrial Development' (*Pub-Classical Publishing Company)*, New Delhi-15, 1999.

Sims C. A -'The Dynamics of Productivity Change—A Theoretical and Empirical Study' (*Unpublished dissertation, Harvard Univ,* Aug 1967),

Somayajulu V V N.- *Industrial Development of Andhra Pradesh-1956-84*- 1994- ICSSR Study- University of Hyderabad.

Surender V. -'*Indian Industries*'- B. R Publishing Corporation in Ch-5- 1986.

Vijay Seth-'Industrialisation in India—A spatial Perspective'—*Commonwealth Publications,* New Delhi-2-1987.

JOURNALS

Abramovitz Moses: Welfare Quandaries and Productivity Concerns—Presidential Address delivered at the Ninety-third meeting of American Economic Association, September 6, 1980, Denver, Colorado-*American Economic Review*-March 1981, Vol.71, No. 1, pp. 1-17.

Agarwal A. L- 'On estimation of Cobb Douglas Production Function in Selected Indian Industries' *in Artha Vijnana*, June 1986, V-28, N-2, 152-170.

Anuradha and AVVSK Rao—'An Analysis of Interstate Industrial Disparities in India 1970-71-1985-86'-*Indian Journal of Regional Science*, Vol. 27, 1995.

Arrow K.J, H. B. Chenery, B. S. Minhas and R. M. Solow- Capital-Labour Substitution and Economic Substitution—*The Review of Economics and Statistics*—Vol. XLIII, No. 3- August 1961, p. 225-249.

Awasthi Dinesh - 'Trends in Regional Dispersal Inequalities in India 1961-1978'- *Anvesak*- Vol-19, Nos:1 and 2.

Balakrishnan and Pushpangadan-'TFP Growth in Manufacturing Industry—A Fresh Look—*Economic and Political Weekly (EPW),* March-1994.

Banerjee A—'Productivity, Growth and Factor Substitution in Indian Manufacturing' *Indian Economic Review,* 1971.

Basu Susanta in *Quaterly Journal of Economics (QJE)*, Vol-111, pp-639-1268, 1996(Pro Cyclical Productivity: Increasing Returns or cyclical utilization?)

Blakemore Arthur E. and Schlagenhauf Don E—Estimation of Trend Rate of Growth of Productivity—*Applied Economics*- 1983- 15- 807-814.

Burns, Arthur Robert—The Process of Industrial Concentration—Summary- *Quaterly Journal of Economics* (*QJE)*- Vol-XLVII-1932-33-Vol-47.

Chatterjee, Anil Kumar—Productivity in Selected Manufacturing, *Economic and Political Weekly (EPW)*, Nov 24, 1973;

Chenery, H.B.- Patterns of Industrial Growth—*American Economic Review*, 50, September 1960, p. 624-654.

Chowdhury M.D.- *Behaviour of Spatial Income Inequality in a Developing Economy: India, 1950-70"* Paper presented at the 9th Conference of the Indian Association for Research in National Income and Wealth-January 1974.

Christensen L R. Jorgenson D.W. and Lau L.J.- Transcendental Logarithmic Production Frontiers, *Review of Economics and Statistics*, Vol. 55, 1973, pp. 28-46.

Dadi M. M. -*Indian Economic Journal*; 1973, Vol-28; Oct-Dec 1980; Vol. 2, pp. 28.

Dadi and Hashim—An adjusted capital Series desired for Indian Manufacturing 1946-64 *Anvesak*, December-1971. (Dadi M. M. and Hashim S. R. - *Capital-Output Relations in Indian Manufacturing*, Dept of Economics, Faculty of Arts, M. S. University of Baroda- Baroda).

Datta, S and Mukhopadhyaya, F. (1999)—in 'Industrial Disparity in India: A test of Convergence' in *Indian journal of Regional Science* (*IJRS)*, Vol-31, No-1, 1999-p-19-30.

Dhar P. N. and D.U Sastry, "Inter-State Variations in Industry, 1951-61*, Economic and Political Weekly*, 4, March-1969, pp. 535-538.

Denison E- why Growth Rates Differ- *The Brookings Institution-Washington DC*-1967.

Desai Padma-'Growth and Structural Change in Indian Manufacturing Sector: 1951-1963 in *Indian Economic Journal* (IEJ)-Vol. XVII, No. 2, Oct-Dec-1969.

Desai Rohit—Changing Pattern of Regional Industrial Diversification—A comparison over time—*Indian Journal of Regional Science (IJRS)*-Vol. 18, N-1, 1986.

Dhananjaya R.S., Sasikala Devi N and Madhavan M—Patterns of growth and structural change: A Study of Indian Factory Sector Industries in 1973-74 to 1989-90, *Economic Growth and Change*, Vol. VI, Sept-Oct-1996.

Domar Evsey-On total productivity and All That—*Journal of Political Economy*, 1962-1970- December.

DN—Low Employment Growth—*Economic and Political Weekly (EPW)*-May 25-2004, p. 2192-4.

Dougherty C. and Jorgenson D.W.- International Comparison of Sources of Growth, *American Economic Review (AER)*-Vol. 86-May 1996, pp. 25-29.

Dutta M. M.—'Production Function for Indian Manufacturing'—*Sankhya* -1955.

Dutta Majumdar—'Productivity of Labour and Capital in Indian Manufacturing 1951-61'— *Arthaniti* (1966).

Findlay Ronald—Modeling Global Interdependence: Centers, Peripheries and Frontiers' *American Economic Review (AER)*-86, -1996 No. 2, pp. 47-51.

Hasan Rana (2002)— 'The impact of imported and domestic technologies on the productivity of firms: panel data evidence from Indian manufacturing firms'—*Journal of Development Economics*- 69-2002, pp. 23-49.

Hiau Looi Kee-Policy Research Working Paper 2702—'Productivity versus Endowments—A Study of Singapore's Sectoral Growth—1974-92'—*World Bank Development Research Group Trade—Nov-2001.*

Hollis B. Chenery and Lance Taylor in "Development Patterns: Among Countries and Over Time"—*The Review of Economics and Statistics*—Vol-L, No. 4, 1968, p. 391-416:

Lakhwinder Singh and K C Singhal—'Economies of Scale and Technical Change' in *Productivity*—1986 XXVII, 1, 55-60.

Lucas—'On the Mechanics of Economic Development'- *Journal of Monetary Economics*, Vol. 22z, 1988, pp. 3-42.

Gordon R. J.-1969-$45 Billion of US Private Investment has been Mislaid—*American Economic Review (AER)*—June 1969, 59 (3), pp. 221-38.

Grossack Irvin- The concept and measure of permanent industrial concentration—*Journal of Political Economy*, Vol. 60-(4)- 1972, pp. 745-760.

Hall and Jones –Levels of Economic Activity Across Countries—*American Economic Review (AER)*-Vol. 87-1996-7, pp. 173-4.

Hicks John—The Assumption of Constant Returns to Scale—*Cambridge Journal of Economics*, 1989 March, No. 1, Vol. 13, p. 9-17.

Ishaq Nadiri M—'Some approaches to the Theory and Measurement of TFP'—A Survey-*Journal of Economic Literature*, Vol. VIII—*American Economic Association*, Pennyslyvania-1970, pp. 1137-1177.

Islam Nazrul—'International Comparisons of TFP—A Review'—*Review of Income and Wealth*, Series 45, December 1999-N-4.

Jaume Ventura- Growth and Interdependence- *The Quarterly Journal of Economics (QJE)*—Vol. 112, No. 1, 1997, pp. 57-84.

Jayadevan C. M. of National Labour Institute, Noida –*Indian Journal of Regional Science (IJRS)*, p. 41-56, Vol. XXVII, Number-1&2-1995.

Jeemol Unni, N Lalitha and Uma Rani in a Special Article—'Economic Reforms and Productivity Trends in Indian Manufacturing', *Economic and Political Weekly*, Oct-13, 2001.

Jeffrey William—"Regional Inequality and the Process of National Development", *Economic Development of Cultural Change*, Vol. XIII, No. 4, Part-II, pp. 3-84, July-1965.

J. Mohan Rao—in 'Manufacturing Productivity Growth—Method and Measurement. *Economic and Political Weekly (EPW)*, Vol.-XXXI- No-44, Nov-2, 1996.

Kaplinsky, R-'India's Industrial Development: An Interpretative Survey' *World Development*, Vol. 25, No. 5, 1997, pp. 681-694.

Kelkar V. L. and Kumar R—Industrial growth in 1980s—Emerging policy issues—*Economic and Political Weekly (EPW)* January 27, pp. 209-222-1974.

Krishna Kumar P. (2000) (Ch-16-pp-264-271 titled 'Returns to Scale and Technical Progress in Indian Manufacturing' in book by *VVN Somayajulu's "Econometric Studies of Economic Reforms in India"* published by Academic Foundation-2000.

Kuznets S- "Quantitative Aspects of the Economic Growth of Nations—Vol.-II- Industrial distribution of National Product and Labour Force"-*Economic Development and Cultural Change*- July 1957- Supplement to Vol. 5, No. 4, pp. 17, pp. 391.

K. Rana in '*Industrialisation of Hill States in India*' Deep and Deep Pub. in Chapter-VIII—(1988).

Krishna Raj and Mehta S. S.—Productivity Trends In Large Scale Industries, *Economic and Political Weekly (EPW)*, Oct 26, 1968.

Lahiri R.K.—"Some aspects of Interstate Disparity in Industrialisation in India", *Sankhya*, 31, Series B, Dec. 1969.

Mahadevan Renuka—'Trade Liberalisation and Productivity growth in Australian Manufacturing Industries'—*Australian Economic Journal*—Vol. 30, No. 2, June 2002-pp. 170-18.

Majumdar Sumit—'Fall and Rise of Productivity in Indian Industry—Has Economic Liberalisation Had an Impact?' in *Economic and Political Weekly (EPW)*-1988-89 (p-M-46- M-53).

Mathur Ashok, "Regional Development and Income Disparities in India: A Sectoral Analysis-*Economic Development and Cultural Change*, Vol. 31, No. 3, April 1983, pp. 475-505.

Mehta S. S and Krishna Raj—Productivity Trends In Large Scale Industries, *Economic and Political Weekly (EPW)*, Oct 26, 1968.

Mohan Rao—for 1973-93—*Economic and Political Weekly* (*EPW*)-Nov-2 1996.

Moses L and Williamson H.W., *American Economic Review (AER)*, Vol. LVI 1967, pp-211-22 'Location of Economic Activities in Cities'.

Murti V.N. and Sastry V.K.—Production Functions for Indian Industry—*Econometrica*—Vol. 25, Number 2, April 1957, p. 205-221.

Nadiri Ishaq M—Some Approaches to the Measurement of TFP—A Survey—*Journal of Economic Literature*-1970.

Nagaraj R (1994) 'Employment and Wages in Manufacturing Industries—Trends, Hypothesis and Evidence' in Special Article in *Economic and Political Weekly* (*EPW*)-Jan 22-1994, p. 177-186.

Nair, K. R. G., " A Note on Inter-State Income Differentials in India-1950-51 to 1960-61", *Journal of Development Studies*, 7 July 1973, pp. 441-447.

Nath V- 'Regional Development Policies', *Economic and Political Weekly (EPW)*- Special Number July 1971, pp. 1601-1608.

Pandit M. L.- 'Industrial Income in the States-1960-69'—*Indian Journal of Regional Science*, Vol. VI, No. 2-1974, p. 124-136. "*Spatial Variations in Rates of Industrial Development in India" for M. Phil degree* at Centre for Studies in Regional Development, Jawaharlal Nehru University.

Paul Krugman- 'The Myth of Asian Miracle'—*Foreign Affairs*, Vol. 73, No. 6, 1994, pp. 62-78.

Power Laura (1998) in 'Missing Link: Technology, Investment and Productivity' in *Review of Economics and Statistics*, Vol. 80, 1998, p. 1300-312.

Pravin Krishna and Devashish Mitra (1998)'Trade Liberalisation, market discipline and Productivity Growth: New Evidence from India' in *Journal of Development Economics*, Vol. 56, pp. 447-462.

Quandt's (1960)—Tests of hypothesis that a linear regression obeys two separate regimes, *Journal of American Statistical Association*, 55, 324-30.

Rao Hemlata, "Identification of Backward regions and the Study of Trends in Regional Disparities in India", Paper presented at the Regional Imbalances Seminar, *Indian Institute of Public Administration (IIPA)*, New Delhi, 1972.

Romer P. –'Increasing returns and long run growth'—*Journal of Political Economy*, Vol. 94, 1986, pp.1002-37.

Sandesara J.C.—Industrial Growth in Indian Economy (1982) in *Indian Economic Journal* Oct-Dec-1982.

Sengupta D. N.-'Indian Manufacturing Industry—Growth Episode of the Eighties' in *Economic and Political Weekly (EPW)*, May 29, 1999, pp. M-54-M62.

Schamensas Richard—Using H Index of Concentration with published data: *Review of Economics and Statistics*, Vol. LIX-1977, pp. 186-193.

Singh R. R.—Productivity Trends and Wages—*Eastern Economist*, April 29, 1966.

Somayajulu VVN—Structural Changes and Growth in Indian Industries -1946-1970, *Asian Economic Review*, December-1974, Vol. 17, No. 1, 2,3.

Somayajulu V.V.N.- Measurement of Structural Changes in Small versus Large Industries, 1965-1975, *Economic and Political Weekly (EPW)*, 1976.

Somayajulu V.V.N. –Industrial Development in India 1878-1978—A Resume' *Productivity*, Vol. XXI, No. 1, April-June 1980, p. 9-66—p. 39-66.

Somayajulu VVN and George Jacob in 'Production Function Studies of Indian Industries: A Survey' in *Artha Vijnana*, V-25, N-4, Dec 1983, pp. 402-418.

Somayajulu V.V.N.—Industrial Stagnation and growth in Indian Industries of Andhra Pradesh, 1956-1985-Re-Examining Mid Sixties Explanations for India's Industrial retrogression, *Artha Vijnana*, Vol. 13, pp. 127-140.

Solow R. M.—Technical Change and Aggregate Production Function—*Review of Economics and Statistics*—Vol. 39-1957, pp. 312-20.

Sunil Kumar-'Inter-state Variations in Productivity in Indian Manufacturing Sector: A Translog Approach'—*Indian Journal of Regional Science (IJRS)*, Vol.-XXXI, No. 2, 1999- pp. 82-94.

Uday Sekhar—Trends in Interstate disparities in Industrial development in India 1961-1975-*Indian Economic Journal*- Oct-Dec-1982 Vol. 30, No. 2.

Upender M-'Elasticity of L—productivity in Indian Manufacturing' in *Economic and Political Weekly (EPW),* 25 May 1996.

Venkataramiah P—*"Inter-State Variations in Industry, 1951-1961: A comment"*—*Economic and Political Weekly,* 4- August, 1969, pp. 1280-1.

Vijay Bhasin and Vijay Seth (1980)'Estimation of Production Functions for Indian manufacturing Industries'-Jan 1980, *Indian Journal of Industrial Relations*, No. 3, Vol.15. Wolff Edward-'Capital Formation and Productivity Convergence Over the Long Term' in *American Economic Review* (*AER)*-Vol-81, June-Dec-1991, p. 565-579.

Yeong Yeh –'Economies of Scale for Indian Manufacturing Industries'—*The Econometric Annual of Indian Economic Journa*l-1966.

Young Alwyn—'A tale of Two Cities: Factor Accumulation and Technical Change in Hong Kong and Singapore' *NBER Macroeconomics Annual*-1992, pp. 13-53.

Young A.—'The Tyranny of Numbers—Confronting the Statistical Realities of East Asian Growth Experience'-*Quaterly Journal of Economics*, Vol. 110, No. 3, 1995, p. 641-668.

A Database on Industrial Sector in India—*Economic and Political Weekly Research Foundation*-2002.

GOVERNMENT REPORTS

Annual Survey of Industries—*Reports of the Results of the Factory Sector* 1959-71, 1973-98 Published by the *Central Statistical Organisation* (CSO), Government of India (GOI), Kolkata.

CMI- GoI, Directorate of Indian Statistics, CMI, 1946-58, Manager of publications. Report of Working Group on Identification of Backward Area- *GOI*, New Delhi-1969.

Annual Survey of Industries Classification (ASIC) 1959 (onwards), as followed in ASI (Census Part) and NSS (Sample Part of ASI) Reports, Published by Central Statistical Organisation (CSO), NSS Organisation (NSSO), *Government of India*, New Delhi, Statistical Abstracts.

Index